All the Hometown Boys

.

ALL THE
HOMETOWN
BOYS

Wisconsin's 150th Machine Gun
Battalion in World War I

BRAD LARSON

The University of Wisconsin Press

The University of Wisconsin Press
1930 Monroe Street, 3rd Floor
Madison, Wisconsin 53711-2059
uwpress.wisc.edu

Gray's Inn House, 127 Clerkenwell Road
London EC1R 5DB, United Kingdom
eurospanbookstore.com

Printed in the United States of America

This book may be available in a digital edition.

Library of Congress Cataloging-in-Publication Data

Names: Larson, Bradley G., author.
Title: All the hometown boys: Wisconsin's 150th Machine Gun
Battalion in World War I / Brad Larson.
Description: Madison, Wisconsin: The University of Wisconsin Press, [2019]
| Includes bibliographical references and index.
Identifiers: LCCN 2018045758 | ISBN 9780299322205 (cloth: alk. paper)
Subjects: LCSH: United States. Army. Machine Gun Battalion, 150th.
| World War, 1914–1918—Regimental histories—United States.
| World War, 1914–1918—Personal narratives, American.
| Soldiers—Wisconsin—Biography.
Classification: LCC D570.34 150th .L37 2019 | DDC 940.4/1273—dc23
LC record available at https://lccn.loc.gov/2018045758

Contents

Illustrations

Preface

My interest in World War I began when I was a boy. My grandfather fought in that war, surviving the sinking of the USS *Tuscania* and the killing fields of the Meuse-Argonne. I heard snippets of his stories and held a well-worn shell splinter that hit his chest after it was spent. But he was a man I never fully knew, his life torn by divorce and the abandonment of his two sons and, perhaps, of a young life torn by war.

When I met my wife, her family was full of tales of a great-aunt named Lola, an odd character who grew a roomful of violets and wore old-fashioned clothes. Back then she was called an "old maid." When Lola died, she left behind photograph albums full of images of a very fashionable, pretty, bright-eyed young woman, always by the side of a handsome lad known only as "Ray." Later, Ray appeared dressed in the uniform of a doughboy but in 1918 he disappeared from the albums forever. My wife always treasured a tiny, faceted perfume bottle left behind by Lola. It was French perfume, and the label said, "Violet, Paris."

Throughout my museum career in Oshkosh, I heard stories about a company of men in the 150th Machine Gun Battalion, part of the famous 42nd "Rainbow" Division. The tales were vague and, as I later came to understand, largely incorrect. As I uncovered pieces of that story, at some point I realized that I wanted to pull it all together, to resurrect their memories. However, I quickly learned the Oshkosh story was tied to other communities.

There were already excellent books on the Rainbow Division that fully explained shifts in command, strategy and tactics, and overall operations. What seemed lacking, at least to me, was the voice of the doughboy. As the research evolved, the idea of using the men's words to carry their experiences emerged.

Letters were lifelines for both those in France and in America. There are some, but not many, original soldier letters from the 150th Machine Gun Battalion held in various archives. Newspapers were a voice for the community they served. I discovered that local newspapers printed letters the men sent home to family and friends as a way to convey to residents what the "hometown boys" were doing.

While I was unable to determine exactly how letters made their way to the local newspapers, it seems likely that family members and friends simply brought them to the editor. Editors were eager to receive letters, for they represented the voices of the local lads in uniform. Some letters were quite graphic, and others helped reinforce why the nation was at war. I think it is unlikely the newspaper edited them. I was assisted greatly in this task by two devoted and enthusiastic researchers, both dedicated to preserving the stories and the memory. Wayne King went through the Fond du Lac newspapers day by day, meticulously scanning and citing hundreds of letters and associated articles. In Appleton, Joe Gaerthofner gave me access to his personal scrapbook of newspaper letters, made contacts within the community on my behalf, and provided other material on Company A. Although the Appleton company was a star of the 150th, their letters are few compared to those from Fond du Lac and Oshkosh. Letters from the men of Berks County, Pennsylvania, are lacking. However, the postwar book *The Reading Militia in the Great War* (1919) often quotes letters sent home. The whereabouts of those original letters are unknown.

Letters convey a great deal about the Guardsmen's experiences. Although I acknowledge that letters were censored by company officers to exclude sensitive military information or to eliminate pessimism, they remain a valuable tool for learning what the common man went through. The Guardsmen did not necessarily want to cause unnecessary worry back home, but at the same time, they were young soldiers full of spirit and bravado. Occasionally someone bragged, especially during their first few months in France, and I suspect they exaggerated. Nonetheless, letters conveyed heroics and danger and a dedication to why they were in France. National Guard companies included older men, and their letters deliver a different message, one more of assurance and also to minimize the level of danger and risk they were exposed to. Since the writer's personality is unknown, I tried to find a level of context and interpretation by looking at who he was writing to and then comparing his content and style to his previous letters or to the letters of his comrades. In all cases, I retained the original spelling and sentence structure. I came to appreciate these men through their words, and when someone wrote to a sister or friend in an attempt to assuage grief, it was heartfelt. Carefully analyzing dozens of photographs, held in museums and family albums willingly shared, put faces to the voices of the 150th Machine Gun Battalion.

There are periods when few letters were published. These coincide with times when the battalion was on the move or in combat, especially in the autumn of 1918. The men knew each other well and keenly felt the loss of comrades. In postwar letters written while on occupation duty in Germany, men wrote home to explain situations, deaths, and incidents that happened during combat. While letters sometimes leave the reader wondering if an unpleasant incident hadn't been changed to help the family cope, various details were helpful in revealing the broader story.

Diaries reveal not only what the writer was doing but now and again what he thought. I cite entries from four diaries, plus two narratives that could rightly be considered diaries, *A Brief History of Old Company "F"* (anonymous) and *A Brief History of Appleton's "Old Company G"* (Allan B. Ellis). By far the best diary is that of Lieutenant Arthur Bahr in the Oshkosh Company, held by Andrew DeCusati. This gem was freely shared with me, along with Bahr's photographs and personal materials, and I am profoundly thankful for his generosity. The diary of Herbert Ralph Granger in Company B is a close second, and I suspect that Granger was quite a character. Those pocket diaries could be brought out when a man lay in a shell hole or dugout. A terse entry, like those of Robert Holterman in Company B, done in a quick hand while under stress, says much. The Pennsylvania Company uses diary entries from a Sergeant Smith, cited in the published history of the unit, *Reading Militia*. Although the author, J. Bennett Nolan, does not identify the diary writer other than "Smith," it was probably William J. Smith. The whereabouts of the original Smith diary is unknown. I was unable to uncover a diary for any man in Company A, but I remain hopeful that one exists, perhaps tucked away in an attic someplace.

After the war, typically on anniversaries of major events, newspapers sought out veterans for interviews. The *Appleton Post-Crescent* was especially good in this regard. Reporters' questions to the ex-soldiers were helpful in revealing stories, making connections, and offering clues and leads. However, because years had passed between the event and the telling, the recollections do not carry the same passion, sense of authenticity, or tone. The *Post-Crescent* also published historical pieces by Lillian Mackesy in the 1960s in a feature called "Historically Speaking." She knew the stories and perhaps some of the men, and her articles provided invaluable clues.

My goal was to give voice to the men of the 150th. In the process, I hope the reader gains an appreciation for the achievements of these stalwart American soldiers so that they will not be forgotten. This book is dedicated to these men and to my grandfather, Martin Larson, to my wife's great aunt, Lola Mueller, and to her Ray. Like the men of the 150th, each left part of their hearts in the wheat fields and forests of France.

All the Hometown Boys

Prologue

The citizens of Oshkosh have every reason to be proud of the manner in which they have chosen to perpetuate the memory of their native sons who made the supreme sacrifice for their country.

Secretary of the Army Wilbur M. Brucker,
quoted in *Oshkosh Daily Northwestern*,
August 5, 1957

The August sun was warm as the group of elderly men and their families gathered to dedicate a new park along the west shore of the Fox River in Oshkosh, Wisconsin. They sat on folding chairs or stood quietly waiting for the 2:00 p.m. start of the ceremony. The community Veterans of Foreign Wars band, directed by Ralph Rothe, played a selection of patriotic music. On the river a few hundred feet away—a river that was becoming increasingly polluted—pleasure boats cruised by that summer day in 1957, the occupants perhaps wondering why a group of people would be formally gathered under the fluttering stars and stripes of Old Glory on a Sunday afternoon instead of enjoying the day. Across the river on the east side stood the old Paine lumber mill, looking dirty and rundown but still in operation. But the factory was a landmark in this community of 46,000 and a physical connection to the city's lumbering heritage. To the south, on the other side of Oshkosh Avenue, was the Pluswood plant, also looking somewhat seedy. Oshkosh's most recent park and boat launch was clearly a benefit to this industrial neighborhood that had seen better days.

The gray-haired men were veterans of World War I. These former warriors had waited forty years for this day, for a community acknowledgment of what

3

they had done when they were young and in the prime of life. As they waited now for the ceremony to begin, they perhaps talked about the *Spirit of the American Doughboy*, the heroic statue by sculptor Ernest M. Viquesney that the people of Appleton, twenty miles to the north, had erected in 1934. Or possibly they reminisced about the small concrete bridge over Weyerhorst Creek south of Oshkosh, named in honor of one of their old comrades, Kurt Graf.[1]

Maybe the men and their families discussed popular culture to keep their minds off the past or to deflect resentment. The 1957 movie *Gunfight at the O.K. Corral* with Burt Lancaster and Kirk Douglas was popular across the nation, but the upcoming release of a World War I film, *Paths of Glory*, starring Kirk Douglas again, had a direct connection to why they were dedicating the new park. But more likely, their thoughts were farther away—much farther.

Memories of certain events and experiences that happen when a person is young often remain clear and sharp in detail, etched forever in the mind. These men were true comrades, their ties forged to one another through something few people understood. They had once learned to totally, utterly depend on each other, to help and comfort one another in all circumstances. They had gladly shared their last piece of bread or cigarette; they often stopped bleeding wounds without a second of reluctance. At times these men had cried on each other's shoulders. They had kept each other warm as they lay side by side in French barns in the dead of winter. Together they shared misery and terror, as well as great joy and euphoria. When the men finally returned home, they visited the still grieving families of the comrades they left buried in French soil and tried to console the brokenhearted.

It's easy to suppose that these men thought about friends who were not sitting beside them: Elmer "Dad" Bullis, Nicholas Mand, young Otto Spaedtke. Possibly they were dismayed that relatives of their comrades had passed away before this day. Did they once again hear the soft rustle of ripe French wheat fields along the Ourcq River or smell the tangy scent of sweat, blood, and cordite? Or did they recall a pleasant memory: a buddy's laugh, a parting word, a shared bottle of French wine? Possibly it was the recollection of a smile, like Kurt Graf waving good-bye. Did they look around at the gathering of comrades and see them not in white shirts and ties but remember them standing in muddy boots, helmets askew? In all likelihood, these veterans had become expert at shutting out the awful scenes that might have robbed them of sleep in the years since 1918. The battle on the Ourcq River was their great dividing line. Before they encountered that small tributary to the Marne River, before they forced their way to the heights on the other side, their experiences as soldiers were far different. But that was another August, and it was in their thoughts now. Perhaps the park dedication had been planned to coincide with the August anniversary of the Ourcq crossing, to celebrate the storming of those fortified heights. Before they advanced toward the Ourcq, the war had been kind to them. After the heights were taken and the Germans cleared out, their war had changed, and they had left more than the bodies of their comrades buried in those fields. Maybe some of the faraway cries of agony still echoed in their minds, came up from the depths out of those secret places where they had been safely anchored for four decades. But this dedication ceremony was not the place for darkness; it was time to publicly honor.

For a community the size of Oshkosh, the ceremony was not well attended. At most, a few hundred people were present, primarily family and friends who came to show their respect. On this Sunday, the men were to some extent satisfied that Oshkosh's newest park would be named for them, but they had to push for it. Because the city's plan didn't include a sculpture or marker, the men decided to raise and donate money so that a historic marker could be erected, their gift to the community. The city, and these same veterans, had honored the men of the Spanish-American War with a beautiful bronze sculpture that stood not a quarter of a mile from where they sat, but nothing like that was proposed to pay tribute to the Great War veterans.[2] There had been talk of honoring the fallen, of course, but nothing happened. It no doubt seemed ironic and perhaps somewhat cruel that the old warriors had to honor themselves. In small, neat handwriting at the bottom of a park dedication program, someone in George Holland's family wrote, "George tried to get the City to help but was turned down.... We paid for this marker and placed [it]," and then underlined "none helped only us."[3] There was a quiet bitterness.

The men were not wealthy in money, at least not by the standards that some judge prosperity. Yet many of these men had already given the public something they cherished deeply: their richest memories of youth. In the decades after the World War, many of the veterans or their families had given treasured photos, letters, and mementoes to their community museum so their story would live on.

The aged veterans were carpenters, teachers, mill hands, farmers, and laborers, some already retired. They wore the hats of the American Legion or Veterans of Foreign Wars but aside from that, nothing about them revealed their past. They were all that remained of the comrades who had left for France forty years before. The men were all veterans of the 150th Machine Gun Battalion, 42nd Division, the illustrious "Rainbow" Division of World War I. As their lives were drawing to a close, they had come together one last time to give their division's name to this new park. In so doing, they hoped future generations would recall their sacrifices, their role, and their courage. Forever after, this former lumber yard would be called "Rainbow Memorial Park." The speeches were appropriate and fitting. The spindly young trees waved in the breeze alongside a grand American flag. At the close of the hour-long ceremony, it was solemnly proclaimed that the park and its marker would serve as an "everlasting inspiration for all generations to come."

The word "Memorial" was dropped at some point and it was just Rainbow Park until 2018, when "Memorial" was returned to the name. The trees have matured and grass grows on what was once bare, hard-packed soil. The river is cleaner than it was in 1957. The old Paine mill was demolished in the early 1980s and, in its place, a modern restaurant and microbrewery was built. Customers enjoy the view up and down the river, sitting where the mill's great bull slide once pulled massive logs into the saws. They look west across the river at the park and notice it is a busy place on a fine summer day. Indeed, the park is a well-liked spot to launch boats; almost three thousand craft are put in every year. In their anticipation of enjoying a day on the water, few boaters or fishermen stop to read the 1957 marker that dedicates the park to a group of soldiers who left Oshkosh, Wisconsin, in the summer of 1917.

1

The War to End All Wars

The Great War came to signify lives wasted to no purpose; in that, it
had no rivals.

Ann Wroe,
"The Great War," *The Economist*,
November 18, 2013

The gently rolling French agricultural land has absorbed the scars and debris
and waste of 1914–18. Cathedrals, farms, and homes once rocked by explosions
have been rebuilt. French battlefield crews still clear away untold numbers of
unexploded artillery shells.[1] Special reverence is observed as the teams lay to
rest the seemingly endless bone fragments unearthed every year from the con-
tested ground where so much blood was once shed. The American Battle Monuments Commission superbly maintains the final resting places of the 30,922
Americans from 1917–18 who sleep beneath French soil. The white crosses in
long, impeccably kept rows all face west, back to the United States of America.
The first chairman of the Commission, General John J. Pershing, promised that
"Time will not dim the glory of their deeds." The French people remember the
Americans who came to help them in their hour of need.

In the heat and humidity of a Washington, DC, summer, or the bone-chilling
dampness of a DC winter, America's finest soldiers guard the Tomb of the Unknown Soldier at Arlington National Cemetery. With dignity and precision,

these stoic sentinels maintain an atmosphere of reverence at this hallowed place of remembrance. Within two years of the armistice ending the war, the decorated veteran Edward F. Younger had selected the exhumed remains of one U.S. soldier whose identity had been lost as representative of the entire nation's nameless war dead. President Warren Harding dedicated the imposing marble sarcophagus on November 11, 1921. The tomb reads: "Here rests in honored glory an American soldier known but to God." The disillusionment of the postwar era was yet to come, and in 1921 Americans believed it was right and fitting to honor the fallen. Every state sent a veteran delegate. Wisconsin was represented by a disabled Appleton man named John Hantschel.

The conflict was so appalling that it has almost been erased from collective memory. Acts of remembrance for this war are troublesome. It was not atypical that Oshkosh dropped the word "memorial" from the park's name. Few people think of those soldiers today, and the men who fought and suffered are largely forgotten. What's more, few *want* to know anything about it, except a handful around Memorial Day. It is perceived as unimportant, even though four empires fell and the conflict literally changed the world. From 1915 to 1918, the Allies suffered a staggering 22,062,427 military casualties; the Central Powers 15,404,477—more than thirty-seven million military casualties.[2] The costly struggle killed an entire generation and destroyed Europe's complex social order that had evolved for generations.

Between 1918 and 1939, the war came to be called "The War to End All Wars," "The European War," "The Great War," or most commonly, "The World War." Only after Nazi Germany invaded Poland in 1939 did it come to be called the "First World War." Unlike the GIs of World War II, the men of 1917–18 were not immortalized in popular movies, newsreels, special radio broadcasts, television shows, magazines, and countless books. Most people today recognize the Big Band music of 1941–45; they have little idea of what the young men of 1917–18 listened to.

When America's heroic soldiers came home in 1919 from the nation's first major overseas war and were welcomed by flag-waving parades, no one dreamed the nation would ever forget the gruesome price of warfare and what it took to free Europe from its seemingly eternal struggle. America itself suffered 323,018 casualties—116,516 dead—in the nineteen months it was at war.[3] In the euphoria of the November 11 Armistice, those who had lost so much believed that generation after generation would stand in silent respect and reverence when the names were read, or the hard-fought victories at Château-Thierry and the Argonne Forest were recalled. School children would forever after learn about the sacrifice American men gave to world freedom. It truly would be the war to end all wars, the sacrifices justified.

After the war, though, things were never the same. The United States realized what the war failed to achieve as well as its gruesome realities. Few wanted to hear the soldiers' stories or help carry the pain that burdened veterans emotionally and physically. The soldiers' senses had been shocked through sheer overload, but they blocked it out and kept going. The knowledge of Post Traumatic Stress Disorder (PTSD) was generations away. The ex-soldiers of the Great War were forced to bear their suffering and fight their ghosts on their own.

War in Europe broke out in late summer 1914. It is probably fair to say the common people of Europe had no real idea of why or how it happened. Although more educated as a whole than many Europeans, the same could be said for most ordinary Americans. Only a handful of people in Oshkosh, Fond du Lac, or Appleton, Wisconsin, or in Reading, Pennsylvania, might have known the reason for the war. It was far too complex and few Americans really cared one way or another if European nations again went at one another. America was a nation of promise and prosperity, and it looked to the future.

The trigger was an event on June 28, 1914, when a young Serbian named Gavrilo Princip murdered the Austrian-Hungarian archduke Franz Ferdinand and his wife, Sophie.[4] Serbia was a little country nestled next to the ancient Austrian-Hungarian Empire. And at the time, resentment toward Austrian rule was strong and deep. The *Appleton Evening Crescent* reported the details of the murder and explained that it was yet another tragedy to strike Franz Ferdinand's uncle, the eighty-four-year-old Emperor Franz Joseph of Austria. There was no mention that it might cause war. Nonetheless, the assassinations were not taken lightly in Vienna. Convinced that the Serbian government was responsible for planning the strike, Austria wanted to declare war on Serbia and bring it under their total domination, but the problem was that Austria could not do that alone.

Despite good weaponry, Austria's military was outmoded. Serbia was Slavic, and anything Slavic was protected by Russia, a nation that could field millions of soldiers. Austria-Hungary needed its ally Germany and its modern and professional army. "[T]here is reason to believe that Austria," said the editor of the *Oshkosh Daily Northwestern* on July 29, 1914, "with titanic and stern-visage Germany giving it aid and countenance, anticipates that the conflict can be localized . . . that Austria and Serbia will be permitted to fight out their differences and that other nations will merely form a ring around them."[5] A few days later, the *Appleton Evening Crescent* reprinted an article from the *Milwaukee Journal* that quoted Edward T. Heyn, a respected foreign correspondent, who warned readers that should hostilities break out, "It will be the worst war in the history of the world" because of Germany's and France's perfected military machine. Heyn expressed the view that a confrontation, reduced to the simplest and most straightforward explanation, would be "a war for domination by the Slavic against the Germanic races."[6]

Germany's last emperor (Kaiser) and king of Prussia was Wilhelm II, and military matters dominated his thinking. The organization and supply of the Imperial Army, tightly linked to the incredibly efficient German rail system, enabled exceptionally rapid mobilization and transportation of reservists. France was rightly concerned that this meant a quick overwhelming concentration of force on its eastern border. The German martial machine was superbly equipped, trained, disciplined, and exceedingly well-supplied.

Germany, strong and prosperous, believed their nation was surrounded by opponents. That country did indeed face formidable enemies on both their eastern and western borders. That was the perception of at least some German Americans in Wisconsin's Fox River Valley. The editor of the *Oshkosh Daily Northwestern* expressed the view on August 14, 1914, that Germany was "Ringed round, on land and on sea, by hostile peoples and nations" and believed that Germany was in "a spectacular and thrilling fight for life." Germans fervently believed their war would be in defense of the Fatherland. Kaiser Wilhelm II supposed that Austria would bluff, but he did not think they would provoke the wrath of Russia.

Assured that Germany was behind them, Austria declared war on Serbia, its small neighbor. The Serbians fought tenaciously, and Austria was thoroughly trounced. Although Russia was backward and poorly governed, its leaders were astute enough to realize that Austria would not have risked war unless it was fully backed by German military might.

Russia's generals were suspicious that Germany was up to no good, and Russia honored its pledge to protect Serbia. Germany came to Austria's aid, and France was bound to help Russia.[7] France declared war with confidence that its colorfully clad army would give the kaiser's army a sound battlefield thrashing. Britain, however, was not directly allied to anyone. The profound question was whether England would involve itself in a continental war. Although its army was small, the Royal Navy became a major player in the war. Although the government vacillated, the tired British cabinet finally decided the British Empire and its resources should enter the conflict because helping France was the right and honorable thing to do. The stage was now set for a global conflict.

By August, the alliance of the Central Powers of Germany (Germany, Austria-Hungary, the Ottoman Empire, and Bulgaria) were pitted against the Triple Entente of Russia, France, and Britain. Everyone believed the battle would be over in three or four months; anyone who thought otherwise was deemed a pessimist and realized that intense battle by industrialized nations was too costly to support longer than a few months.

The declaration of war ended decades of uncertainty against heredity enemies. War would rebuild French pride and establish who would economically and politically dominate the Continent. For Russian leaders, war was viewed as the way to reassert the power of the largest country in Europe and erase the disgrace of their humiliating defeat by Japan in the Russo-Japanese war of 1904/5.

The kaiser's armies then had to deal with two formidable adversaries. They attacked France first because it was the strongest and most imminent threat, while Russian armies were held at bay. German armies surprised everyone with the speed by which they mobilized and advanced across neutral Belgium. The small but proficient Belgian Army delayed enemy infantry columns for days. The setbacks were minor, but they worked against Germany.

Atrocities were committed when German armies advanced through neutral Belgium. When civilians took up arms, reactions were swift and brutal. German commanders rounded up civilian hostages—men, women, and children— from the areas where attacks occurred. To the horror of the world, captives were executed, and British and French propaganda made the most of Belgium's suffering. The murder of Belgians soon symbolized the menace that Germany posed to the world. In contrast to only reporting German atrocities in the opening months, at least one Fox Valley newspaper, the *Oshkosh Daily Northwestern*, revealed terrible cruelties to Germans by Belgians, stating "excesses against German citizens have taken place which should be expected only from savages. . . . German women have been stripped, dragged through the streets by the hair, when naked, and shamelessly abused."[8]

Second-guessing their decisions at a critical time, the German High Command deviated from their precise invasion plan and speedily sent part of their army against Russia. Then, a second costly mistake: German commanders exposed the open flank of their own army. With the help of Britain's small but competent Expeditionary Force, French forces crashed into the flank of the kaiser's tired, straggling army. The chance of a short war died on what was called the Miracle of the Marne. Shocked by the magnitude of the death and carnage they had unleashed, the stunned nations sank back in sheer exhaustion. It was simply not supposed to happen like this; there were no plans for a long war. What now? The opposing armies dug in.

Other nations joined the struggle. The Japanese government declared war on Germany in August because the conflict was an ideal opportunity to acquire Germany's Chinese possessions and Pacific colonies. Turkey—the old Ottoman Empire—had signed a secret alliance with Germany in August 1914. The Ottoman Empire had lost territory during the Russo-Turkish War of 1877–78 and wanted to recover those territories. With German and Austrian advisors and supplies, the Ottoman Empire came into the war on the side of the Central

Powers. In so doing, they created a threat to the Suez Canal, via the great arteries through which the wealth and manpower of the empire flowed.

After war erupted and even though many influential old-line families and industrialists in the United States supported Britain, President Woodrow Wilson sought to keep the United States neutral and isolated from this most terrible war. It was soon apparent that his heart was with Britain. To most Americans, including those in Wisconsin's Fox River Valley, the European conflict was not all that important. Certainly no one thought of sending American boys to fight in Europe's war, and that feeling was especially strong in Wisconsin. Loyalties were mixed for some German American families, and neutrality seemed the wisest course. A high percentage of the state's citizens were of German ancestry, and many retained cultural and family ties with their homeland. In fact, Oshkosh was the epitome of a German city in America. On July 4, 1914, the city had dedicated a new bronze sculpture on a marble base to the German American journalist Carl Schurz. Members of Oshkosh's two National Guard companies participated in the ceremony, as did the Oshkosh *Kriegerverein* (veterans' association) and *Maennerchor* (men's chorus), the latter singing a song in German. With strong ties to Germany, the outbreak of war was front-page news in state newspapers. But in a matter of months, the battles became items of only passing interest.

The *Appleton Evening Crescent* reported that fifteen local citizens from Germany made the decision to return to the Fatherland. For example, Michael Volti and Max Zagleur decided that they would return to their homeland and serve in the kaiser's army. The German families living in Appleton promised that they would look after the Volti and Zagleur families and their property, along with anyone else who decided to return to Germany.[9] Family ties to Europe meant that local people would also experience the grief of war. Under the title "Substitute Was Killed," the *Daily Northwestern* reported that a Fond du Lac farmhand, William Alvers, who had recently emigrated from Germany, had received a letter from his mother living near Hamburg, Germany. "All your schoolmates and young friends are either killed or wounded," his mother wrote. "Most of the young fellows you knew here are dead. Your brother is badly wounded, and your brother-in-law is at the point of death in a field hospital."[10]

About the time the war broke out, the celebrated showman Colonel William F. Cody, better known as "Buffalo Bill," was in Oshkosh in August 1914 with the Sells-Floto Circus. Cody was well-acquainted with several of Europe's leaders from his many engagements abroad, and he knew and respected Kaiser Wilhelm. When a reporter from the *Daily Northwestern* interviewed Cody in his special train car, he asked the former Indian fighter his opinion of the war. Cody replied, "And there can be no doubt that our attitude of strict neutrality in the European matter is the proper one for this great nation of ours. We do not want war." He then went on to frankly observe that "America is bound to benefit from it. Those people in Europe will have to be fed, and when they run out of supplies they are bound to go where they can buy provisions."[11]

Others believed that the war would indeed help America. Because sources of German fabric dye would be cut off, the Paris fashion world would be impacted. "One effect of this, naturally, will be to popularize American fabrics and measurably increase their consumption, which will be a good thing."[12] War would also help with the servant problem as Europeans fled the war and came to America. In a tongue-in-cheek look at the implications of a European war, the Appleton paper noted that talcum powder would be in short supply. "Many of the young ladies would have to seek a life of retirement, fearing an exposé of their secrets."[13]

In France, the opposing forces were already deadlocked in a depressing kind of warfare. To get below the rain of bullets and explosives, soldiers dug holes and then interconnected trenches. Before long, a vast and complex arrangement of hastily dug trenches ran from the North Sea to Switzerland. The desolate strip of churned earth between the opposing trenches was given the forbidding name of "No Man's Land." This strip of land was dominated by machine guns, barbed wire, and artillery.

No one was prepared for a horrifying type of modern killing and the innovative new weapons that traumatized infantrymen. All the warring nations used machine guns, but it was the German army which openly embraced that marvelous weapon. They had more machine guns than any other army and sent their best soldiers to special schools. They knew about interlocking fields of fire, long-range fire, plunging fire, and everything in between. Their standard machine gun, the Maxim's rhythmic pup-pup-pup, made sure that nothing moved in No Man's Land.

By the second year, the conflict escalated when Bulgaria joined the Central Powers and Italy joined the Allies.[14] It now became apparent that this would be a long war. When the enemy trench was taken and a breakthrough occurred, neither side could exploit it. After battling through No Man's Land and the first line of defense, the surviving assault troops were utterly exhausted—and then they faced fortified reserve trenches, fresh enemy divisions rushed in to fill the void. Attacking units had no effective way to communicate their situation or needs, and bringing up artillery and replacements took so long that the enemy had time to recover and create new defenses.

A turning point occurred in May 1915, when the German submarine U-20 sank the British ocean liner RMS *Lusitania* with the loss of 1,193 lives, including 128 Americans. Many women and children drowned, and the world turned against Germany. Every newspaper in the Fox River Valley carried the story, and there was no sympathy for Germany, stating that the ship carried only innocent civilians and was not carrying anything of war value.[15] Of note, Appleton's newspaper ran an editorial from Milwaukee's *Germania-Abendpost*, expressing, "[W]e are under pressure of the most cruel situation which an American citizen of German extraction may have to face . . . the most heinous crime that could be committed against civilization has apparently at least become a possibility— a war between the two countries dearest and nearest to our hearts. . . . We are American citizens, who, under all considerations, have to conserve their loyalty to the great country of their adoption."[16]

Germany realized that sinking the *Lusitania* was a serious mistake. The British excelled at mobilizing public opinion, and images of dead women and children dominated the media. The *Lusitania* incident reinforced the growing belief that all the appalling actions the German forces were accused of were, in fact, true. President Wilson would not let the incident fade away until Germany finally agreed to restrain the U-boats.

Propaganda assumed great importance because it was essential that the populace in each nation support the war. But it has been said that truth is often the first casualty in war. Britain and France successfully painted Germany as a ruthless Teutonic monster that killed women and children and destroyed cultural treasures.[17] Germany was depicted as an all-powerful, domineering brute that wanted to control the world and destroy liberty. When the Germans executed a British nurse, Edith Cavell, for helping prisoners of war escape, and then later executed a British merchant captain, Charles Fryatt, for heroically defending his ship, their case was doomed. British misinformation effort reached far and wide and included every state. Painting Germans as cruel, inhuman beasts fit British needs perfectly. President Woodrow Wilson was greatly influenced by the flow of British and French propaganda. With scant information coming from Germany, the British and French gave the distinct impression that they were winning.

Offensive after offensive failed. French casualties averaged a staggering forty thousand men every month. It became a terrible contest to see which nation would be the first to become exhausted. The Germans could simply not contemplate further offensive action and had reinforced their defenses in depth; time was against Germany. In addition, the European winter of 1916– 17 was brutal. The Royal Navy's blockade of the North Sea from Norway to Scotland resulted in severe shortages of food, medicine, and other materials. Because the usual potato harvest that year was extremely poor, Germans referred to those desperate months as the "Turnip Winter." The level of suffering in

Germany grew with each passing month. While the hard-fighting soldiers might hold their enemies at bay, if the civilian population collapsed, so would the armies.

Germans proved to be formidable soldiers. Yet there was only so much the army could do. They turned to the U-boat (undersea boat) to change the course of the war. Submarines were, at this juncture, strange and sinister craft. The world wanted them to operate by the long-held rules of prize warfare, the "Cruiser Rule," which stated that merchant ships must be stopped by a *surfaced* U-boat. A ship from a neutral nation was to be searched for war material. If found, crews were to be put in lifeboats before the ship was sunk. But U-boats were silent hunters with small crews. They were most effective—and terrifying— when striking without warning, but their thin hulls were vulnerable to even a small-caliber shell fired by a merchant vessel. Prize rules favored England and France, not Germany.

Germans realized that American neutrality and the second of Wilson's Fourteen Points—freedom of the seas—was a sham. President Wilson did not object to the British blockade of Germany, only Germany's blockade of Britain.[18] German merchant ships and passenger liners that were in American ports at the outbreak of war were interned as ships of a belligerent nation. British ships were allowed to come and go as they pleased. It was not difficult for German leaders to see that without American munitions, the war would be very different. The U-boat attacks continued. In the autumn of 1916, U-boats sank 487,000 tons of shipping.[19] Germany's top commanders convinced Kaiser Wilhelm to unleash submarines in unrestricted warfare in 1917. This meant that merchant vessels could be torpedoed without warning within a declared war zone around France and England. Without control of the sea, Britain's Expeditionary Army could not be sustained with materials from the United States. British Admiral Sir John Jellico warned his government that at the present loss rate from U-boats, the supply system would collapse and Britain would be out of the war by summer.[20]

Encouraged by U-boat successes, in January 1917 Germany announced it would resume unrestricted submarine warfare against merchant shipping in the declared war zone. The German high command clearly understood this decision would doubtless bring America into the war. Their goal was to quickly break England by depriving her of vital goods from overseas and force her from the war and into a separate peace or truce. The German high command was more concerned about America's tremendous industrial might and capacity than it was about the little American army. They calculated that it would take two years for the United States to raise, train, equip, and transport to France an army of several million men. Their aim was to force England into a separate truce *before* the United States could impact land battles. By February, one out of every four ships leaving a British port was being sunk.

Deeply worried that Germany's strategy was sound, and concerned that the United States would be unable to contribute before Britain was forced to capitulate, in April the British and the French launched large-scale offensives; casualties exceeded three hundred thousand, and both nations faced severe manpower shortages. The two nations needed a miracle—they needed America if they were to see victory.

Gloom lay over France and England. In Russia, Czar Nicholas II had abdicated and a provisional government directed the nation. In Petrograd [Saint Petersburg], "soviets," or worker councils, governed the capital. Germany, seeing opportunity, sent Vladimir Lenin back to Russia from his exile in Germany to help the growing power of the Bolsheviks take Russia out of the war. If Russia dropped out of the war, which seemed apparent, Germany would shift battle-experienced troops, weapons, and munitions to France. With these reserves, Germany would concentrate its military might. U-boats proved deadly, effective, and were growing in numbers.

2

Men of the Guard

The structure is designed to meet every known need. . . . Nothing
has been slighted to make it modern, safe and convenient in every
detail.

"New Armory Plans Are Announced,"
Daily Commonwealth,
January 16, 1911

The massive stone and brick armories are gone. Citizen and soldier alike
cherished the appearance and permanence of these great structures. The very
design and its embellishments marked the armory as a community focal point.
Inside the spacious drill hall, historic flags and paintings of heroic men and
their deeds lined the walls and paid homage to the uniformed dead so that
their memory lived on. Above everything was the Stars and Stripes, a symbol
of freedom and promise. Then, gigantic steel balls swung at the ends of cables
flattened what was once so lovingly admired. Planners called it "urban re-
newal." Parking lots and nondescript postwar buildings replaced the fortress-
like armories. The impressive carved stone symbols that recalled an age of glory
passed into memory.

A strong "preparedness" movement emerged in the United States in 1915,
focused around the uneasy realization that America's military was entirely inadequate for modern warfare. When compared to the armies of England,
France, and Germany, the United States Army was almost an embarrassment.

President Wilson opposed the concept of military preparedness. However, attacks by bandits along the Mexican border and then the sinking of the *Lusitania* eventually led to the passage of the National Defense Act in June 1916, which increased the size of the U.S. Army and the National Guard. The Guard itself had evolved from the concept of militia, and most communities of any size had a company. The Wisconsin cities of Appleton, Fond du Lac, and Oshkosh were united by many factors, not just National Guard companies.

Much of eastern and central Wisconsin was scoured flat thousands of years ago by massive glaciers. When the ice sheets receded, an immense watershed had been created. The defining feature of that watershed is the Fox River, a two-hundred-mile-long north-flowing river that empties into Lake Michigan at Green Bay. About midway on its journey, the slow-moving Fox River broadens into a series of lakes, until finally emptying into a huge, shallow lake twenty-eight-miles long and ten miles wide. The Algonquin-speaking natives of the region named this lake *Wenepekow*, later Anglicized to "Winnebago." Wisconsin's big lake was a feature that linked the three cities.

At the southern end of Lake Winnebago is the city of Fond du Lac. At the northern end, the river discharges and flows north. Appleton lies just above where the river leaves the lake. And right in the middle of the lake, where the broad river empties, is Oshkosh. It is about fifty miles from Fond du Lac to Appleton, not even an hour's drive today on Highway 41. The biggest tributary of the Fox River system, the Wolf River, flows south as it drains a huge area of northern Wisconsin, emptying into the shallow lakes. This vital artery brought the natural resources of the vast northern forests down to Oshkosh. In the nineteenth century, seemingly endless stands of white pine were cut, then floated down the Wolf River to sawmills in Oshkosh and Fond du Lac, the latter focusing on lath and shingles. Fond du Lac was also home to Soo Line repair depots and the Ruepling Tannery, one of the largest tanneries in Wisconsin. Similar wood industries linked Oshkosh and Fond du Lac, but the northern forests also yielded an endless supply of pulp trees, perfect for making paper. After the Fox River leaves Lake Winnebago on its northward journey, it falls 164 feet over a short distance. This water power provided the energy for turning the pulp trees into paper products, and Appleton's economy prospered as its mills met the growing demand for paper. And each of the three cities in turn served the smaller communities and farms clustered throughout the broad, rich Fox River Valley. By the end of the nineteenth century, the region was a vital part of the state's economic diversity and strength, and some of Wisconsin's wealthiest families lived there. On the eve of war, Oshkosh was clearly the most powerful city, but Appleton's influence was growing. Fond du Lac, the smallest of the three cities, had clout, too.

Another feature that set the three cities apart from others is that all had institutions of higher learning. Lawrence College was in Appleton, a state Normal School was located in Oshkosh, and Fond du Lac had Grafton Hall, a prep school and Junior College for young ladies. Fond du Lac also had a vocational school, a recent addition to the state's educational system. The years before the war were a time of change, and that included education. The vocational school system provided education and training for boys and girls aged fourteen to sixteen who had quit high school and were learning a trade, or for adults who wanted more education. Higher education was beyond the grasp of the working-class men who later became soldiers in the 150th. Most boys did not graduate from high school, eighth grade being a typical cut-off point. Instead, males were expected to enter the world of work in their teenage years as laborers, tradesmen, or apprentices. Industry needed skilled and semiskilled labor, and immigrant families needed money, so children started work early in life, finding work as delivery boys, clerks, or mill hands. Hard manual work was a fact of life.

It would not have been unusual to hear German spoken in any of the three cities. German immigration to the region had started before the Civil War and had accelerated in the last quarter of the nineteenth century. Most of these new Americans did not think of themselves as German but identified themselves by the Germanic regions they came from: they were Prussian, Pomeranian, Saxon, or Hessian. All three cities were Germanic, but Oshkosh probably had the highest percentage of Germans, followed closely by Appleton. The immigrants were proud of their heritage and maintained strong cultural links to the land of their ancestors. This revealed itself in German singing clubs and German-language newspapers, church services in German, shooting clubs called *Schuetzen-verien*, and ethnic food and drink.

On the eve of war, the three cities were physically connected by a transportation system, their Germanic heritage, and to some extent even their economies. It was the military facet that seemed the strongest bond during this disquieting period. Wisconsin's National Guard was close to forty years old in 1917 and consisted of the 1st, 2nd, and 3rd Infantry Regiments. Each of the communities had Guard companies that were part of the 2nd Wisconsin Infantry Regiment. Fond du Lac had the newest armory, a magnificent three-story brick-and-stone building on East Second Street, constructed in 1911 at the astonishing cost of $45,000. The 70-foot by 110-foot building was modern in every way, "designed to meet every known need." It was anchored by towers with battlements on the front corners, and over the arched doorway was a carved stone eagle set in a niche.[1]

Appleton's armory stood on its main street, College Avenue, across from the Masonic Temple. It was constructed of beautiful red-brown brick with contrasting limestone accents and medieval-like battlements along the top, reminiscent of a twelfth-century Norman castle. A round turret crowned with battlements anchored the building's east side. Over the center double doors was an American eagle carved in stone, a striking icon. Armories were more than just the meeting place of companies: they were beautiful symbols of permanence and America's tradition and commitment to the idea of citizen-soldiers.

While Appleton and Fond du Lac each had one Guard company, Oshkosh was unique in that it had two, both headquartered in its own armory. One armory was south of the Fox River, the other located on the north side. The north armory, built in 1890, was constructed of cut limestone block and brick as a *Turnverein* hall, a place for athletics. The Romanesque-style building was beautiful, imposing, and roomy, a point of pride and the headquarters of Company B.

The other armory was a distinct contrast. Like the north armory, the Queen Anne–style structure was also built in 1887 as a *Turnverein* hall, and it was generally referred to simply as "Turner Hall." When the Turnverein ended in 1901, it became the Badger Club, a spot for dancing, parties, and social gatherings. But unlike the north armory, there were no grand public structures nearby. Rather, it was in a working-class neighborhood across the street from the sprawling wooden Buckstaff furniture factory. While the drill hall itself was large and roomy at 60 by 120 feet, it was constructed of wood and was not grand or impressive by the standards of the day. If anything, it was just the opposite. Nonetheless, it was the headquarters of Company F and home to the National Guardsmen who would serve in the 150th Machine Gun Battalion.

Most of the Company F men were from Oshkosh neighborhoods south of the Fox River. That part of the working-class community was the most heavily Germanic part of the city, the majority of those families having emigrated from southern Germany, Austria, and the Czech Republic (then known as Bohemia). Both Appleton and Fond du Lac were also largely Germanic. In contrast to the wealthy men and their families in the Valley, the enlisted men who served in the three companies were all working class. They labored in places like Oshkosh's Diamond Match Company and the Paine Lumber Mill, Appleton's paper mills, and the Ruepling Tannery in Fond du Lac, primarily doing manual or semiskilled labor. They were the backbone of local industry, and they joined the Guard for many reasons. Certainly patriotism was a factor, an especially attractive motivation during times of need or national emergency. Other reasons were personal. Men joined the Guard for excitement and for social and economic reasons. The pay was minimal, but the small amount helped make ends meet. Then as now, having friends or family in the National Guard was a powerful motivator.

On the eve of the United States' entry into the European war, America was still more rural than urban. America had a tremendous abundance of natural resources and was the world's leader in industry and the production of coal and steel. American agriculture was incredibly productive, and food was abundant. The nation had benefitted throughout the nineteenth and early twentieth centuries by wave after wave of European immigrants seeking the freedom and promise of the New World. Their labor helped fuel the growth of industry and the economy. Unionization was gaining strength, too. Immigrants wanted to be Americans. Regardless of national identity or how they felt about the nation of their birth, they did not want their sons and daughters to be viewed as hyphenated citizens.

The population as a whole was hard working, energetic, and confident, and people saw opportunity everywhere. Public school and church lessons taught children not to feel sorry for themselves but instead to work hard, save, and look ahead. Whether an old-line Yankee family or first-generation immigrant, people were proud of what the nation was and what it stood for, and they embraced the American ethos. Young and old believed in self-reliance and independence, and there was a strong desire for self-improvement.

Christianity was the backbone of the nation. For most Americans, material compensation for labor was viewed as God's reward for virtue and hard work. All three communities were building beautiful churches, grand structures of stone and brick with magnificent stained-glass windows. Membership in a church was almost universal, and a school often adjoined the more modern brick-and-stone houses of worship. Those who wore Uncle Sam's uniform believed they were fighting for everything that was right and good and American, and all had a deep, firm conviction that God was on their side. As if to underscore this relationship, Appleton's armory was next door to a handsome brick Presbyterian Church. Religion played a role in motivating men to fight and served as a justification for war. Once in France, letters reveal that strong faith often helped the men make sense of the suffering they witnessed.

Fox Valley residents had good reason to be optimistic. Education was viewed positively; education and hard work went hand in hand. The number of students attending high school continued to increase each year. The standard of living was increasing at a rapid pace, especially for the middle class. There was a tremendous and growing variety of consumer goods, an abundance of food, and people had more time and money for recreation. Citizens in Oshkosh, Fond du Lac, and Appleton had access to new and well-stocked public libraries, giving opportunity to read and better themselves. Electrical service, telephones, and indoor plumbing reached more and more homes and businesses, and phonographs brought music into middle-class homes. Those homes also had coal-fired central heating for the winter months. But for others, especially those on farms and the working class, the family still gathered around a single central stove during the winter. They made music, sang together, and played cards. During the heat of the summer they could escape the smells of the city and the stress of work by fleeing to a cottage on a nearby lake or heading to northern Wisconsin on the train. The heat of summer was mitigated by swimming or relaxing in the shade at waterside parks. The only vacations for most workers were holidays like Christmas or plant shutdowns. Women were finding employment outside the home in positions other than teachers and clerks; fully one-third of all clerical workers in business and industry were female.

The Guardsmen who would soon man Hotchkiss machine guns were all born in the last quarter of the nineteenth century and were products of a Victorian upbringing. The first decade of the twentieth century, however, was marked by many changes. The workplace and education evolved as Progressive ideas slowly impacted society, and yet life still revolved around a fairly strict social and moral code of conduct for both men and women. Both sexes had fixed roles in society, and most people knew what their place was. Men tried hard to live up to the model of masculinity. Service in a National Guard uniform seamlessly fit that model. In a time when the era of rugged individualism was ending, replaced by a more standardized and mechanized society, males were still expected to embrace athletics and outdoor adventure.

Regardless of social class, people behaved according to the standards society established for them. For example, men were expected to respect, protect, and reinforce feminine virtue and the ideal of womanhood, a standard that had tremendous appeal to American men. Failure to show respect to females, to openly flirt or speak plainly in public about subjects such as pregnancy or vices, was simply not done. When war did come, posters and other media created by the Committee on Public Information reinforced the idea that American men were fighting not only for the essence of liberty and justice but also to save from harm everything Americans held dear.

Working men and immigrants, especially, were required to show polite deference to employers, teachers, clergy, and other superiors. Public swearing, drunkenness, and many other infractions were serious breaches of accepted societal conduct. To violate those rules brought humiliation, loss of employment, or in some cases loss of memberships in clubs and organizations. To be rejected in one's community was a profound and serious thing.

Men were clearly dominant; women could not even vote. But beginning in the 1890s, opportunities for women broadened dramatically. Women were entering higher education in increasing numbers, and economic, political, and social opportunities were emerging for married women. There were "radical" women called "feminists" who were pushing for reforms of all types, including the right to vote. Oshkosh seemed to be at the center of these changes, with prominent women of the community like Jessie Jack Hooper, a suffragist, peace activist, the first president of the Wisconsin League of Women Voters, and a vocal advocate for Progressive change in Wisconsin and beyond. The changing role of females was a frequent topic of newspapers and magazine articles. Without a doubt, the Guardsmen were familiar with the figure of the "independent woman" as depicted in mass media. As young men, they saw the pen-and-ink sketches of the Gibson Girl in magazines like *Life* and *Colliers*; they saw women portrayed in film and nickelodeon shorts either as self-reliant or as helpless, dependent females. Societal change that started in the Progressive Era would be greatly accelerated by the World War. The Jazz Age of the 1920s completed the transformation.

The men had grown up and reached maturity during an exciting time in America, a time of promise, optimism, and change. As boys, they grew up hearing about the excitement of the Alaskan gold rush and the victory over Spain in 1898; they learned about American inventions and were awed by the opening of the Panama Canal and the thrill of moving-picture shows. Advances in medicine were nothing short of amazing. While the men grew up with horses, mechanical things like automobiles and engines were increasingly common, and for the most part, modern machinery and the associated technology appealed to young men. By 1912, the United States produced 32 percent of the world's manufacturing output and was a leading exporter of farm products. Other changes, however, were viewed as not so positive. Some parts of the country experienced labor unrest, and with the change to the U.S. Constitution in 1913, the Sixteenth Amendment allowed the federal government to tax a person's income. Most men who would serve in the 150th Machine Gun Battalion had no hand in reelecting Woodrow Wilson as president of the United States simply because they had not reached the age of twenty-one in 1916.

The soldiers who would soon wear the small rainbow patch sewn onto the shoulder of their tunics knew little about the situation in France other than what their local newspaper reported. Shortly after the war started in 1914, the British had cut the cable from Germany to America. All news from Europe was supplied either through Allied sources or sent back by reporters and diplomats assigned to cover French and British efforts and opinion, not that from Germany. Anything from Germany, including dispatches sent by American reporters, was stopped or severely edited. War news was carefully controlled and gave citizens the impression that Germany was in the wrong . . . and losing.

All the National Guard units across the entire country that would come together in 1917 to form the famous 42nd Division had one thing in common:

they had all been mobilized in 1916 for action on the Mexican border. In June 1916, the Militia Division of the U.S. War Department issued a nationwide order that National Guard units might be called into service on the Mexican border. The border had been troubled since 1910, and regular U.S. Army troops were already stationed there. That year, the Mexican president Porfirio Díaz was overthrown by Francisco Madero, the leader of the constitutionalist party. When Madero was assassinated by General Victoriano Huerta in 1913, the situation went from bad to worse. A Robin Hood–like bandit by the name of "Pancho" Villa took action against Huerta; he was eventually forced out and replaced by Venustiano Carranza. But Villa continued a rampage, moving against United States citizens and their properties along the border. National Guard units had been on the border alongside army units since 1914 but not in any organized or carefully planned campaign. When Pancho Villa increased his assaults on American soil, the National Guard was mobilized.

National Guard units across the United States were called into active service. The stated objective was to protect the southern border, but another purpose was to improve the training of existing Guard units and test the leadership of officers.[2]

At first, service along the Mexican border was exciting to the Wisconsin soldiers, men who had scarcely been out of their own counties, let alone having traveled to other parts of the nation. For one thing, the Badger boys were introduced to a new type of "automobile truck" being built in Clintonville, not too far from their home cities.[3] However, border duty was not easy. As summer wore on, service on the border lost whatever appeal it might have had when the troops were called into active service. If the men had romanticized dreams of heroic action against Mexican bandits, the reality of military life quickly quelled those visions. Instead, it was the regular army units that pursued the Mexicans, trying to capture or kill Villa. Moreover, food was poor, and there were long and taxing hikes in the desert. All of that, combined with lack of action, general boredom, and longing for home, played a part in making the time on the border less than idyllic.

But the border duty toughened the Guardsmen. Amid the desert setting and the sand, cactus, yucca, and mesquite, the purple mountains looming in the distance, the Guardsmen learned how large bodies of soldiers could move in unison, and how to communicate and achieve a common objective. They discovered how to effectively organize and move the essential supporting units. The U.S. Army itself had a great deal to learn about how to keep fighting men in the field. Long columns of trucks and horse-drawn supply wagons brought combat units food, clean water, ammunition, and forage for horses and mules. Sanitary arrangements had to be determined, tested, and refined, for sickness as a result of poor hygiene would rob a unit of men just as surely as enemy bullets. The border mission made it apparent that on a battlefield it was crucial that every unit be well-supplied, fed, and serviced. Among the complaints were worms in the corned beef and in the corn, and, even worse, receiving a mere two dozen pickles for one hundred men. While outwardly this seemed minor in the larger challenge of updating a complex military organization, food was of utmost important to soldiers and ultimately to the combat effectiveness of units in the field.[4]

As fighting infantrymen, the Wisconsin boys practiced with small arms; the Badger soldiers shot their Model 1903 Springfield rifles and Colt Model 1911 .45 pistols—and they were very good marksmen. Once on the rifle range, it was obvious that there were some real rifleman in the Fox Valley companies, and their scores were among the highest in the Wisconsin units; these men even earned coveted shooting medals.[5] As well, they trained with the British Lewis light machine gun. The National Guardsmen were under the control of the U.S. Army and, because it was apparent based on reports coming from France, there was no escaping the ruthless reality that twentieth-century combat included close hand-to-hand fighting. The men trained for hours in bayonet drill. Knowing how to place and move feet, to use body weight, to jab and twist, to keep the opponent on the defensive, all took time. The only way to achieve proficiency and confidence with the bayonet was by hours of correct parrying and thrusting. From the French Army came specific information on current defensive tactics and how to blunt an enemy offensive. The U.S. Army instructors had the Guardsmen lay out and dig trenches complete with shooting steps and dugouts. From these accurate and faithful replications of fortifications on the Western Front, the men were sent out on realistic patrols and ambushes. Everything possible was done to mimic what Allied soldiers were currently experiencing in France. After war was declared and the men were in training, a Pennsylvania company joined the battalion. One of the Bucktail soldiers wrote that their training in France merely duplicated what they had already learned in the desert. The leadership qualities of the men were also coming to the forefront. In Oshkosh's Company F, for example, soldiers agreed that Sergeant Arthur Bahr was in line to be an officer, a change that the men thought appropriate.

With each passing week, their strength and skills improved. By the time the War Department called for the withdrawal of the Guardsmen from the Mexican border in January 1917, the Wisconsin men were far more experienced and confident in their role as soldiers. They returned to Wisconsin in the late winter of 1917. All men were awarded special medals by the state and, in some cases, by their community. Despite the boredom and challenges of border service, they wore these emblems with great pride. In that short time, the national mood was quite different from when they left for Texas ten months before. Germany had resumed unrestricted submarine warfare, and on February 13, 1917, President Wilson had broken off diplomatic relations with Germany.

As the European war continued, Allied propaganda increasingly painted the kaiser's soldiers as barbaric, murderous beasts. The news of the invasion, occupation, and continued brutality of life in Belgium was never allowed to die. In one way or another, this sort of news regularly made the papers or was transferred into effective misinformation that built anger and hatred toward Germany. Official reports by American diplomats to President Wilson and other world leaders became war news. As Germany deported Belgian workers to supply badly needed labor in the fall of 1916, the U.S. Belgian minister, Brand Whitlock, reported, "I am constantly in receipt of reports from all over Belgium," he wrote, "that tend to bear out the stories one constantly hears of brutality and cruelty . . . a deed so cruel that German soldiers are said to have wept in its execution and so monstrous that even German officers are now said to be ashamed."[6] The sufferings of the Belgian people were real, as were instances of brutality, but there were also many fabricated stories of German cruelty. Most of these tales centered on rape, mutilations, and bestial behavior because they had the ability to shock, inflame, and incite.

Due to the continuous flow of misinformation, Americans had little sympathy toward Germany, yet few were convinced that this alone merited war. Many larger newspapers had invested in new technology that enabled them to provide readers with clear, detailed images of the war. The new "rotogravure" pictorial sections of newspapers showed the war to America. Images graphically depicted the battles at sea, the destruction of French cathedrals and villages, and the steadfast stance of British and French soldiers holding the German menace at bay. But the suffering of the German people that winter was not depicted. In the summer of 1916, Oshkosh's Grand Opera House showed the nine-reel film *On the Firing Line with the Germans*, showing the German side of the war.[7] For ten cents, viewers could watch the stark reality and brutality of war. Despite the film, local sentiment was still not in favor of Germany. The nation's industry and workers prospered as England and France spent vast sums to buy American munitions and materials. By 1917, the Allies owed billions of dollars to U.S. firms.

The abdication of Russia's Nicholas II worked in President Wilson's favor; a Russian provisional government was then in charge. If Russia's absolute monarchy had remained in power, war meant that the democratic United States would be fighting alongside an absolute autocracy, one that prevented Russian peasants from having political power. The new government stated that it wanted land reforms and a parliamentary form of government. That change meant that the United States could support Russia because it would give more freedom to its people.

Submarines were again the topic of the day. The U-boat offensive bolstered the growing sense in Wisconsin and across the nation that America should prepare itself for war because Germany was against America. The *Oshkosh Daily Northwestern* ran a United Press piece stating as much; it also claimed that U-boat sinkings were "not sufficient to give real hope of victory to the German government."[8]

3

War Comes to America

It is hard for Germans to fight the land of their birth, but to do
otherwise would be disloyal to the land of their adoption and traitorous to their country.

> Appleton postmaster **Gustave Keller,**
> April 9, 1917

The infamous Zimmerman Telegram was the straw that broke the camel's
back. The telegram was a secret coded message from Arthur Zimmermann, the
German foreign minister, to Germany's foreign ambassador to Mexico, stating
Germany's pledge to help Mexico regain American territory if she declared
war on the United States. President Wilson had addressed a joint session of
Congress on April 2, 1917, and asked for a declaration of war. Two days later,
the Senate voted 82 to 6, with eight abstentions, for hostilities. On Good Friday, April 6, the House voted 353 to 50 to support Wilson's request. The reso-
lution was rushed to the president on April 6, and he signed it with a gold
fountain pen. The United States was at war with the most powerful military the
world had ever known, and the message was immediately telegraphed to ships
at sea.

Under the heading "The Supreme Test of Patriotism," the editor of the
Oshkosh Daily Northwestern expressed the opinion shared by many: "It has become plainly evident that Germany and her allies had arrayed themselves against
the entire world." In a distinct change from the editorial in August 1914, the
newspaper stated that Germany had become a "menace to civilization" and "the

28

primary blame for this whole unhappy state of affairs rests plainly at the doors of Germany. The injuries, assaults and affronts borne by the nation at last became unendurable."[1] Wilson successfully labeled the war as a way to "make the world safe for democracy," an expression crafted by the British. The phrase had incredible appeal to Americans as a reason for war and would be cited time and again in letters home. In April 1917, U-boats sank 516,394 tons of shipping,[2] underscoring the urgency of the situation.

Three days after war was declared, the city of Appleton held a "Loyalty Day" parade, as well as war meetings in public buildings and churches around the city. The parade was full of people dressed in their finest clothing and waving small American flags. Loyalty Day went beyond showing that citizens supported President Wilson and his Declaration of War. Demonstrating Appleton's commitment to the European war was critical: no one wanted the city's allegiance questioned because of a large German population and its German-language newspaper. In the editorial on April 10, 1917, the *Crescent* stated, "Significant in the extreme was the fact that all the German societies were represented in full," that even though there were German veterans of the Franco-Prussian War present in the parade, they all showed "a new allegiance to freedom and humanity."[3]

On April 9, the Appleton postmaster, Gustave Keller, addressed 1,200 people gathered at the Appleton Theater. "It is hard for Germans to fight the land of their birth," he told the crowd, "but to do otherwise would be disloyal to the land of their adoption and traitorous to their country. . . . In many instances, Germans will be called upon to fight their own flesh and blood, but they will not be found wanting! . . . men of German descent will fight against the Kaiser if need be, for we are now Americans." Frank J. Harwood presided over the meeting at the theater. "History has been made today in Appleton," he told the crowd. He closed the public gathering with a powerful declaration: "Our community has demonstrated . . . loyalty to flag and country."[4]

Despite the preparedness movement, the United States had a third-rate army of fewer than 150,000 active-duty soldiers and no large pool of reservists. Shortly after the declaration of war, England and France sent a delegation of high-ranking officers to Washington, DC. They appealed emotionally for men, asking that a half-million American soldiers be sent to France by the end of 1917. Shortly thereafter, Wilson received honest reports from American officers sent to France to appraise the situation; he was shocked to learn that Germany was winning.

Achieving the necessary number of soldiers required a totally new way of thinking and organizing the nation's military assets. Among the most basic and undeniable facts was that reaching numbers of men in that time frame required not just the draft but also the mobilizing of the National Guard. The National Defense Act of 1916 had allowed the National Guard to expand to 450,000 men, so there was a pool of citizen-soldiers who had at least a basic level of military training. Many Guard units were fairly well-equipped and supplied, although some of their materials were outmoded by modern army standards of the time. Outdated or not, things were serviceable until the supply system could ensure that all divisions were correctly and uniformly equipped. The units that had served on the Mexican border, however, had already modernized much of their equipment.

All companies immediately began recruiting up to war strength. By May 1, local newspapers reported that Appleton was in the lead with 181 men, Fond du Lac was fourth with 133 troops, but the strength of Oshkosh's company was unknown because it failed to turn in a report.[5] To spur recruiting efforts in Fond du Lac, a local veterinary doctor, J. W. Tooley, donated a fine Morgan horse to the captain of the company. "The mare is standard bred and registered," the *Daily Reporter* explained. The handsome black "horse will be used for recruiting purposes, and in the event it becomes necessary to dispose of the animal the money will go to the company treasury."[6] Men joined the Fond du Lac Company from rural areas and the surrounding villages; four men from nearby Campbellsport enlisted that spring.[7] The *Appleton Evening Crescent* noted with pride that the company was almost full, and that young Harvey Pierre had just enlisted, no doubt encouraged by his brother, John, who had been in Company G for some time.[8]

Equipment and supply concerns aside, there were regular army officers who opposed sending the National Guard overseas. These officers claimed that the Guard was essentially "a social organization," which was largely true.[9] They quickly pointed out that there was a lack of strict army discipline and that enforcement of military regulations was lax, both of which were correct. Finally, they argued, Guard officers were too well-liked by their men to lead effectively. When Oshkosh's captain was wounded in an accident and sent home, Lieutenant Arthur Bahr wrote with emotion, "We all miss our dear old captain very much . . . he seemed like a father to all."[10] Guard officers could indeed be popular. Officers and enlisted men lived and worked in the same community, went to the same churches and taverns, and had mutual friends. When Appleton's company returned home from the Mexican border, the local newspaper declared in a front-page article that "Captain Graef was probably the most popular man with the rank and file. . . . He personally looked after the welfare of his men, saw that they had proper medical attention, and 'stuck up' for them when they were in trouble, without letting down on discipline in the least. It is safe to say that if Graef again takes charge here, and there is need for active services, he will find many volunteers to the colors."[11]

A Fond du Lac officer provided an example of the relationship that existed between officers and enlisted men. Adelbert R. Brunet enlisted in Company E on May 17, 1897, as a private and a year later was promoted to sergeant. In 1903, he was commissioned as a second lieutenant, and five years later he advanced to first lieutenant. On the eve of departure for war, Brunet was promoted to captain, a move the local newspaper supported because he was a "mainstay" of the company. "He is equally as popular among the men. He will be a willing leader and can be depended upon to bring home a good record of himself and his company."[12] Whether men like Adelbert Brunet could effectively lead their men—their friends—through the realities of brutal modern combat remained to be seen.

When the discussion about the use of the National Guard in France began, one officer embraced the Guard and encouraged its use in combat. A flamboyant, well-spoken colonel named Douglas MacArthur eloquently urged the full use of the Guard in France. He made a compelling case that it represented the people in a democratic state, and therefore people back home would take a far deeper interest in the war and be more inclined to support it. "The National Guard were the 'home soldiers,'" wrote Raymond Tompkins in his short 1919 history of the Rainbow Division. "Somebody in every little town belonged to the State organization. The girls all went to their dances and they always marched in the Decoration Day [Memorial Day] and Forth [*sic*] of July parades and the armories were the scenes of every community's biggest 'affairs.'"[13] Indeed, newspaper would regularly refer to the men in France as the "hometown boys." Colonel MacArthur also made it a point to emphasize that the Guard was well-organized, already equipped, experienced from its recent time spent on the Mexican border, and could be mobilized without delay—all concerns weighing heavily on the minds of military planners. And time truly was of the essence. As if to emphasize the race against time that faced both sides, U-boats sent 549,987 tons of Allied shipping to the bottom in May.[14] At that point, a decision was made to create divisions from state units.[15]

In the army's divisional numbering system, National Guard units were formed into divisions based on the geographic location of the state units. Divisional numbers 26 through 41 were reserved for Guard regiments. Secretary of War Newton D. Baker ordered Major General William Mann, the chief of the Militia Bureau, to bring together a new National Guard division composed of all units that had experience and training on the Mexican border. Since this new division was to be a merger of National Guard units from twenty-five states and the District of Columbia, rather than from a single or group of states, it was given the next number: 42.

MacArthur was named a colonel in the division's 84th Brigade, and during a press conference, he said the new 42nd Division had the structure of a rainbow, covering the country from one end of the sky to the other. The name stuck. The divisional patch was a half circle with three colored bands representing a rainbow.[16] "America's sons from the north and the south, the east and the west, were at last going to fight side by side to make the world safe for democracy. America was sending a 'Rainbow' of hope to Europe. So of course it thrilled the nation."[17] By war's end, the Rainbow Division was a household name.

The army planned to establish twenty-eight-thousand-man divisions, each fully supported and supplied. This was an incredible challenge to the existing military structure, in part because American divisions would be much larger than the divisions of other nations. Each division was to have four four-thousand-man infantry regiments, three machine gun battalions, three artillery regiments, a trench mortar battery, an engineer, and signal, supply, sanitary, ambulance, hospital, police, transport, and headquarters units.

Wisconsin's National Guard officially went on active service in July. Only recently returned from the Mexican border, the men now faced another parting from their families. Since the declaration of war, everyone had assumed that activation was imminent, and all local newspapers made it clear that their National Guard company would soon leave. In Oshkosh, a "patriotic picnic" was held at Menominee Park on August 3. The newspaper reported, "While it is on the eve of the departure for Camp Douglas—they go Monday—it is intended . . . [as] a testimonial of esteem rather than a farewell . . . it is planned to make a jolly good time with a 'big feed' for the boys."[18]

A similar event was held in Fond du Lac, but it was combined with a "Mess Fund Dance" at the armory to raise money to purchase food to augment field rations. More than twelve hundred Wisconsinites crowded into the building to listen to a ten-piece band and enjoy the "garrison ration" supper. The Guardsmen were in full-dress uniform; the armory was superbly decorated with flags and bunting, including a giant Liberty Bell illuminated by electric lights hanging from the center dome. The newspaper declared it a "delightful" evening and proudly declared that the event raised $700 for the troops.[19]

The size of the public turnout for the departure was utterly amazing and thoroughly covered in the *Daily Commonwealth*. The depot platforms could hold not more people, so the tracks were lined on both sides with well-wishers. The more physically fit and daring scampered to the tops of nearby rooftops to get a look at the uniformed men marching to their trains. Anticipation and excitement were high as the Guardsmen said their good-byes on August 6, 1917,

Surrounded by tremendous crowds, the Oshkosh company departed for Camp Douglas in July 1917. Oshkosh Public Museum.

and boarded special trains to return them to active service at Wisconsin's Camp Douglas in Juneau County. The *Oshkosh Daily Northwestern* reported that "An immense crowd of Oshkosh people said goodbye to Oshkosh's two infantry companies. . . . Tears were plentifully shed . . . the sight of that line of soldiers leaning out of their car windows and waving as long as the station and its crowd remained in view, was one long to be remembered."[20]

There was also a tremendous outpouring of support in Fond du Lac. Mayor J. F. Hohensee asked that all stores be closed until 9:30 a.m. to allow everyone the opportunity of seeing the company depart. Before the company started on their route to the station, Bernard Iddings Bell, a well-known Episcopal priest and author and the dean of St. Paul's Cathedral in Fond du Lac, offered a prayer. He asked the Lord to "Protect them insofar as may be possible during the days that are to come from the violence of the enemy." The troops, wearing red carnations, marched from their armory to the train through a "valley of humanity." Men took off their hats and stood in silence. "The realization of the seriousness of the present struggle seemed to dawn on many people for the first time," the newspaper reported. The somber mood was appropriate because it was a "time for thought and not exterior manifestations," the *Commonwealth* declared. But when the band played the national anthem as the engine engaged its gears and the cars started moving, there was a tremendous release of tension and emotion as the crown burst into a spontaneous and rousing cheer, with more than a few tears.[21]

Before the hometown boys left, they gathered for a group photograph on the steps of the courthouse. The Fond du Lac Guardsmen looked proud, fit, and confident. The photograph was published in the *Daily Commonwealth* under the title "The Pride of Fond du Lac," and the paper published the names of all the men on the day they left for Camp Douglas. In Appleton, twenty miles north of Oshkosh, the soldiers of Company G lined up in front of their armory for a last photograph and then said good-bye to family and friends before they too received a rousing send-off. The scene was repeated across the state as men in other Wisconsin communities joined the mobilization of Guard units answering the call to duty. By early August, more than fifteen thousand Wisconsin National Guardsmen were at Camp Douglas, ready to enter the U.S. Army. There, the citizen-soldiers were formally and honorably discharged from the Wisconsin National Guard. That done, they were immediately mustered into the regular army and assigned to the 42nd Division. Companies E, F, and G were redesignated as Companies B, C, and A, 150th Machine Gun Battalion.

The army had largely ignored machine guns, in part stemming from the belief that there were few overseas threats to the nation and that the army would not be involved in wars like the one raging in Europe. Instead, the army's role was viewed as far more limited and confined to conflict within the nation's borders. Infantry tactics focused on aimed rifle fire and refining infantry techniques. The army had a few Colt Model 1895 machine guns and the problem-plagued 1909 Benet-Mercie light automatic rifle, and even a few 1904 Maxim guns. Once war was declared in April, though, everyone understood that a speedy transformation of the army was necessary and that the European war required tens of thousands of heavy machine guns and their trained crews.

Despite its inward focus, the U.S. Army had not kept its head in the sand. Key officers realized the devastation caused by modern weapons. They knew that the British had created a special machine gun corps composed of select, highly trained men, and that the corps operated independently from infantry. The secretary of war, Newton Baker, appointed a group of officers to look into the issue and make a recommendation. Much to the disappointment of infantry officers, the group proposed the creation of independent machine gun battalions of three 170-man companies. Battalions were to be commanded by a major and assigned to each infantry brigade. This provisional organization, approved in 1917, created a system that kept the battalions independent from the infantry. The 150th Machine Gun Battalion was commanded by Major William B. Hall of Oconto, with Lieutenant Allan B. Ellis of Appleton as adjutant.

Lieutenant Arthur Bahr, seated, with unidentified officers. The photo was taken in Germany on March 27, 1919. Arthur Bahr Collection.

A captain was in charge of each company. Captain Lothar G. Graef of Appleton commanded Company A, Captain Adelbert R. Brunet led Company B, and Captain Gustave C. Schwandt was in command of Company C. Under the captain were four or five lieutenants assigned to the platoons.

One of the officers in Company C was twenty-eight-year-old Arthur R. Bahr. A solid, common-sense man, he looked suitably dashing with his angular face, gray eyes, hair swept back off his forehead, and a small, well-groomed moustache. He was a clothing salesman at Oshkosh's Baranowski and Stein Company. With his father's permission, he had joined Company F in 1908. Bahr was utterly dependable, performed well along the Mexican border, the men respected him, and he was smart. By 1916 he had risen through the ranks to first sergeant, and in July he was promoted to second lieutenant. The company endorsed the promotion, for on the Mexican border Bahr had shown that he was a fair and talented leader. Bahr kept a diary during his time with the 150th and recorded both the day-to-day details and his thoughts.

It was one thing to establish the organization on paper, quite another to make it a reality and put well-trained soldiers on the battlefield and use them effectively in combat alongside infantry. The army did not have a heavy machine gun, let alone training manuals and programs. In order to have officers and men knowledgeable and skilled enough to use and deploy this formidable weapon, gunners had to be selected and training programs developed. The United States was able to use the knowledge of the French and British military, but it is remarkable that the U.S. Army was able to put well-trained, highly effective machine gun battalions into combat in just six months.

As was finally determined, each company had an authorized strength of 170 men and was commanded by a captain. Each company had a small headquarters section, mess and supply sections, a stable sergeant with men under him to care for the animals and equipment and also act as teamsters, and two buglers. The rest of the troops were runners, ammunition handlers, or medics.

Companies had three platoons of about forty-five men, and each platoon had four machine guns. Platoons were led by a lieutenant, a platoon sergeant, and four corporals. It took twenty-four men to crew the four machine guns, ten serving as runners or mechanics, five drivers, and one person trained to use the optical range-finding unit. The three platoons were intended to remain together to deliver massed fire, but in combat they were often divided, reducing the effectiveness of the guns.

Platoons were divided into two sections, and each section into two squads. This was the group of comrades that the men worked with and consequently bonded closely as a team. A section sergeant was in charge, and in combat he made the decisions as to how and where to place the guns and issued the fire commands. Each gun was to have a sergeant or corporal, a gunner, and a loader, plus three men to run ammunition, and a teamster or driver for their cart.

Because the use of machine guns was physically and intellectually challenging compared to infantry combat, great care was exercised in the selection of men. Soldiers had to understand mathematical formulas to compute firing solutions, have mechanical aptitude to repair their guns, and be physically

strong enough to carry the guns and wooden crates of ammunition. Men with
experience in working with and handling animals were also needed. Men from
the three Fox Valley companies met all these requirements. Many had worked
in lumber or paper mills or factories and knew the operation of machines. In
the case of the Fond du Lac Company, there were also men who had worked in
the repair shops of the Soo Line Railroad. As well, a number of the soldiers had
been raised on farms. Like today's farmers, they understood how to mend and
get equipment working again with minimal tools, and they had handled horses
every day. Quite a few had graduated from high school, a noteworthy accom-
plishment at a time when a typical education stopped at the eighth grade.

The requirements for machine gun officers were demanding, and previous
service in the National Guard was advantageous. Officers "must be intelligent,
resourceful, bold, and must have good judgment . . . the men must have superior physique."[22] Machine gun fire, like that of artillery, was directed by mathematical calculation, and it was essential that officers understood and were skilled
with equations. "Machine gun differs a great deal from that with a rifle," Bahr
wrote, "as it requires a man to use his head much more than with the rifle and
also there is plenty of hard work as the type of gun we have is very heavy and the
gunner must be able to carry it over all kinds of ground in a kneeling and crouch-
ing position. Besides there are forty mules to be looked after and guns and
ammunition carts to be kept in good shape."[23]

As with infantry officers, a machine gun officer had to be able judge ground
area to tactical advantage and know how to effectively command men. The
army preferred officers with at least six months in uniform and those who could
shoot at least at the sharpshooter level with a rifle. National Guard officers had
often been in uniform for years and regularly shot for qualification with their
men. The casualty rate for machine gun crews was high because guns were always
priority targets, but despite the hazards there was an unusually strong, tight-
knit sense of camaraderie among the squads and within the companies, something that National Guardsmen thoroughly understood. Taken as a whole, these
attributes combined to make National Guardsmen a good source of machine
gun officers.

The companies were introduced to what it meant to be in a "Machine Gun
Battalion," a term and form of organization new to them and to the army as a
whole. Although the 150th had no guns, they learned that they would man
what was called a "heavy machine gun," defined as a gun that fired from a stable
platform and usually from a prepared position. The gun was actually aimed,
fired, and loaded by a team of two or three men. Because the guns used an
extraordinary volume of ammunition, each company would have either Ford
trucks or twenty-four mule carts for hauling the heavy wooden boxes of machine

gun cartridges and the guns themselves; the men were, of course, eager for the trucks. In the case of animals, the disagreeable but strong mules were under the supervision of a stable sergeant who had men assigned to him to help handle and care for the animals, keep them shod, and drive the carts as close as practical to the front or area of combat. Once in France, the value of the mules and the men assigned to them would become apparent to the gun crews.

Camp Douglas was exciting and demanding, although there was time for a few baseball games between companies. The men received new uniforms and equipment, but their beloved Model 1903 Springfield rifles were taken away and Colt Model 1911 pistols issued instead. Side arms were important because a machine gun squad was expected to defend their weapon when necessary, as a heavy machine gun was not very mobile. A rifle was cumbersome when hauling heavy boxes of ammunition, and a pistol was deemed more practical. A newspaper correspondent from Fond du Lac noted in somewhat convoluted prose that the change was striking. "[It is] of a totally different character than the old," he observed. "Through the men only it will preserve its identity with Company E." The reporter explained that it was point of pride that the community soldiers were assigned to such a prestigious unit. Not only would the unit soon receive the most modern guns, it also had its own mechanics and wagoners, and even its own hospital unit. As if that were not enough, he wrote, perhaps hopefully, that the battalion "will be equipped with Ford trucks in place of the honored but somewhat antiquated army mule."[24] As a point of distinction, the men of the 150th discarded their army-issued canvas puttees and purchased formed leather leg guards, like the officers wore.[25]

The essential equipment they needed for warfare, such as helmets, gas masks, and hobnailed trench boots, would be issued to them once in France. The U.S. Army did not even have helmets when war was declared, so the War Department adopted the British Mk. I, which the army designated as the M-1917. They did, however, have an infantryman's most important tool: a shovel. The men had the Model 1910 Entrenching Tool, which was carried on top of their haversack. It was referred to as their "etool."

The 42nd Division had two Infantry Brigades, the 83rd and the 84th, and three Machine Gun Battalions that supported the infantry, the 149th (Pennsylvania), the 150th (Wisconsin), and the 151st (Georgia). The 84th Infantry Brigade consisted of the 168th Iowa and the 167th Alabama Infantry Regiments; the 83rd Infantry Brigade, consisted of the 165th New York and 166th Ohio Infantry Regiments. The 150th was assigned to support the 83rd Brigade. It was announced that the Wisconsin men would meet their respective infantry regiments when all the National Guard units in the division came together in the coming weeks. It was also considered a mark of distinction to be part of the new 42nd. "[O]nly those units which had marked ability making them worthy of distinction were chosen. . . . To be among them is an honor."[26]

From Camp Douglas, the Guardsmen entrained on September 3 for the journey to the East Coast. It was an exhilarating trip for the men. Aside from their recent service in Texas, most of the men had never traveled outside their home state. Much of the trip south had been on slow secondary trains that had to pull onto side tracks to let other trains move. As they clambered aboard the five Pullman coaches, a baggage car, and a kitchen car, they learned it was a high-priority military train. Shortly after the war ended, an unidentified Oshkosh man in Company C typed a detailed manuscript recording the history of the company from the declaration of war to the return home. As the troop train slowly pulled out of Camp Douglas and gained momentum, he wrote, "Soon the bands began playing that old familiar hymn, 'God Be With You Till We Meet Again,' and as the last notes died away in the distance we resolved that the people of old Wisconsin would never regret the choices they had made in choosing her troops for the Rainbow Division."[27] Lieutenant Arthur Bahr recorded in his diary, "The last we saw of Camp Douglas was the waving of Hats and Handkerchiefs. . . . I will say this surely was no easy parting for us."[28] A reporter from Fond du Lac who watched the men leave wrote that the men "were a happy, cheery lot."[29] Thoughts of home and family gradually receded as the landscape of their native state was replaced by a panorama of scenery.

It took three trains to move the 150th, and they all pulled in at Mineola, Long Island, on September 5, after traveling twelve hundred miles. The Guardsmen's destination was Camp Mills, which was about two miles from the station. The army had not yet built barracks and mess halls at the training camp sites for the millions of citizens who would be turned into soldiers. Instead of barracks, a great sprawling city of tents greeted the Guardsmen as they joined the rest of the 42nd Division units arriving from points across the entire country. Regiments from other states were already there, and the Badger boys were introduced to their fellow soldiers. Bill Heiss, son of German immigrants and valedictorian of Appleton High School Class of 1916, was not impressed with the Guardsmen from Alabama. "They're country the whole bunch. Got head lice and gray backs. Positively the dirtiest, filthiest gang of supposed to be men I ever saw."[30]

A few men brought small cameras, called "Soldier's Friend" or "Soldier's Camera"; its official name was the "Vest Pocket Kodak." This common, affordable, and effective compact camera folded to a size not much larger than a pack of playing cards. At least two men in Oshkosh's Company C, Arthur Bahr and John Matschi (who might have been the anonymous author of *Brief History of Old Company "F"*), used them to record their grand adventure in France, and John Pierre Jr. and Bill Heiss in Company A carried cameras as did Leo Uelmen and Robert Holterman in the Fond du Lac company.

As soon as the tents were up and the gear stowed, the 150th immediately began training. What they had to learn must have seemed incredibly daunting to citizen-soldiers whose basic level of organization was a state regiment. Officers were expected to learn the art of leading men in modern combat through reading, lectures, and drill. "We were issued 17 books to study from (on modern warfare)," recorded Bahr with evident dismay, "should devote our spare time (can you beat it)."[31]

War excitement was high. It was exhilarating for young men to be part of the magnificent struggle to rid the world of the terrible Kaiser Wilhelm. There was a real sense that they were unique, part of a new division of men from twenty-six states, among the first to march to the aid of the beleaguered French. Smart new uniforms, patriotic music, beautiful September weather, and being near New York City all contributed to a general sense of purpose and cheerfulness. There probably was not much thought of danger or the possibility of death, at least among the younger men. France and the war remained a world away. With almost a sense of disbelief, Sergeant William Heiss told his brother, "If anyone had told me then [while in Texas] that a year later I'd be in New York, I'd said he was crazy." A United Press correspondent visited the unit and sent optimistic dispatches describing the training and the men's attitudes toward war. He profiled the 150th and told a little bit about some of the unit's personalities. It was a front-page article in many hometown newspapers.[32]

Handsome, seventeen-year-old Private Otto Spaedtke, the oldest son in a family of nine children, had left his job in Oshkosh at the Bartola Instrument Company to take part in the crusade. He was excited about the big adventure in which he was a participant. Weekend passes to New York City allowed Spaedtke and his comrades to experience the fabulous city they most likely thought they'd never see. The good-looking teenager teasingly wrote to his friends back home from Camp Mills: "Well how is the old fish trust gang. I suppose still laying on Brays point and watching for game wardens and hell divers [i.e., a grebe, a small diving bird].... I wish you were here to see some of these girls. I was out with Rockefeller's daughter last night tomorrow night I am going out with Aster's daughter."[33] Like most seventeen-year-old boys, the few letters that survive suggest that Spaedtke had a zest for life and seemed to be a happy-go-lucky guy. Spaedtke would go through that sometimes-rocky evolution from adolescent to young adult as a combat soldier.

Visiting New York City was an awe-inspiring experience for Sergeant Heiss and his two buddies, Rex Spencer and Pat Sullivan. They all received passes for Saturday, September 29, and spent the day in the Big Apple, returning to Camp Mills at 3:00 a.m. The huge urban center with its arrogant display of wealth and activity was a bit much for a conservative midwesterner like Heiss. He wrote to younger brother, Tim: "You might imagine Bdway [Broadway] as a big boulevard, but if you do you will be disappointed when you see it. It's a common ordinary street with lots of theaters and cabarets. At night it's all lit up and makes some sight. Fifth Ave. is some street. Here's where you see crowds and crowds. Autos so thick you can't see how they move. And is all packed with swells." He took the elevator to the top of the Woolworth Tower, the world's tallest building at the time, and reported home that "[T]he view . . . was wonderful . . . it's a long ride up + down and you ought to see the elevators go. Whew but they travel. When they started down I thought my insides were going to come out on me." The highlight for the three Company A men was the Statue of Liberty. "[T]hat's some statue," he told Tim. "It's about ten times as big as I imagined it to be. . . . It sure is a wonderful thing."[34] Nicholas Mand, another fellow Guardsman, was a sign painter back in Oshkosh, a skilled job that required considerable artistic talent. During his day in New York City, he evidentially used that talent to sketch and paint well-dressed women.[35]

Walter P. Melchior was a Wausaukee man serving with Appleton's company. In a long letter home telling of daily life at Camp Mills, he related his experience in New York City and wrote that he had no desire to return. The biggest worry for the companies, at least according to Melchior, was whether they would get Ford trucks or be stuck with animals. "[N]early every private is in fear that he shall have to whip the Kaiser with a mule," he wrote.[36]

But the men had far more serious work to do than watch pretty girls in New York or worry about mules. "Being unused to great armies they didn't all know what a 'division' was . . . [they were a] mixed-up mass of men who represented many different American ideals, traditions and temperaments as they represented American commonwealths and communities."[37] It was not an easy task to teach these men from such vastly different geographic areas and cultural backgrounds to work together. All the Guardsmen, including the Wisconsin men in the 150th, tended to see themselves first and foremost as state units, not yet as part of an army division. Despite time on the border, their experience working outside the state structure was limited. Now though, dozens of experienced, tough regular army officers and sergeants went to work. As training progressed, they began to see themselves as a modern division, "a wonderfully smooth machine."[38] One thing the Wisconsin men did have was cohesion. Unlike units made up of drafted men and new volunteers that came from many states, the 150th was homogenous. They all came from the same neighborhood, city, or surrounding area, shared the same Germanic heritage, and had about the same level of education. What is more, they knew the same families, places of work, and often went to the same church. In short, the battalion had a level of unity not found in most army units. They did not know it yet, but a fourth company would join them in France: the former Company I, 4th Pennsylvania Infantry from Reading, would become Company D.

4

Hello France

Well, tell Pa not to worry about us.
Private Ben Golz
to Mr. and Mrs. Louis Golz,
March 1918

The air grew chilly within a few weeks of arrival at Camp Mills. The soft light of early autumn gave the fields and shores of the training area a tranquil look, yet there was a deep, pervasive sense of urgency and importance. The feeling of excitement grew as the units trained, were issued supplies, and packed for the great voyage to war. As departure time closed in, the division had turned in any remaining outdated state-issued equipment and replaced it with regulation army gear. Every division had an identifying shoulder patch. The Rainbow patch for the 42nd Division was a complete half arc and contained thin bands representing three colors in a rainbow: red, gold, and blue. Since there was yet no method for the government to provide the patches, seamstresses in Hempstead, Long Island, sewed Rainbow patches out of strips of felt on squares of brown wool uniform cloth. The soldiers immediately loved the design.[1]

Their collars sported two new bronze collar disks. One identified them as part of a Machine Gun Battalion, and the other disk replaced the old "NG" (for National Guard) disk with "US," meaning they were part of the federal army. They also were issued a different kind of disk. Two 1¼-inch diameter aluminum

43

disks stamped with a name and his unit, and religion if they so chose. They were always to wear them on a cord around their neck. No one had to explain why. One thing they lacked was adequate cold-weather clothing, underwear, and socks. Appleton and Oshkosh troops received knitted sweaters made by women in their hometowns. For those men who weren't so fortunate, the Red Cross supplied extra clothing. Despite these shortages, confidence was high, and the men were eager to get "over there," as they referred to France in deference to the song of that title by George M. Cohan, which was popular that summer. In mid-October, the men were issued long wool overcoats, and many men submitted forms to have $10–$30 withheld from their monthly pay to be "banked and held for their return." Walter Thorne in the Oshkosh company confidently told his mother that he was sending $10 home every month, "so by the time I come back I will have a good starter."[2] When their baggage was marked "A.E.F. [American Expeditionary Forces] France," there was no doubt departure was imminent.[3] Rather than wait for additional supplies, the army ordered the 42nd Division to sail in mid-October. There were not enough transports to send the entire division from one point of embarkation, so several ships were used, and some units crossed the following month.

The three Wisconsin companies of the 150th were assigned to the USS *Covington*, a modern ship built in Germany in 1908 by the Hamburg America Line and originally named the SS *Cincinnati*. The *Cincinnati* was in Boston at the start of the war in 1914 and was therefore interned as the ship of a belligerent nation. It was taken over by the U.S. Navy in the summer of 1917, renamed *Covington*, and quickly converted to carry troops. The Pennsylvania men were sent to the USS *President Grant*, also a former German ship.

The ships weighed anchor promptly at 6:00 p.m. on October 18, 1917. During the trip across, T. Edward Sullivan, one of four brothers from Fond du Lac, sat in a "swell little salon" under a glass skylight and penned a moving description of the ship's departure. "The Statue of Liberty bade us a safe voyage and held on high a bright light to guide the expedition through the darkness on the way over," he wrote, "[the lights of New York] left a lasting impression in the minds of all those who had a parting look at the greatness, of the land of the free and home of the brave." Sullivan reassured his parents that the trip was fine, explaining they had popular magazines to read courtesy of the Red Cross, bands gave concerts, and they often played cards to pass the time.[4]

Enlisted men were packed into the hold, and officers were assigned staterooms. Lieutenant Bahr noted details of the voyage in his diary, explaining that the men were "packed in like cordwood . . . and all Port-holes are closed, and all the lights turned out, and the men don't get any fresh air again till the next day when they are let out for deck leave."[5] The men had grown up around the shores of Lake Winnebago, Wisconsin's largest inland lake, and had no doubt been on steamboats for excursions and local travel, but they were nonetheless landsmen. The ocean was a far cry from Winnebago. Great ships, long journeys, and even the very idea of travel over that immense gray Atlantic must have been intimidating, for under those waves lurked the menace that had occupied everyone's thoughts since the 1915 *Lusitania* tragedy.

For some lucky units, the ocean was smooth during the crossing, nothing more than gentle swells. For others, the voyage was turbulent; it was a rough autumn sea for the 150th. The *Covington*'s constant pitching and rolling was too much for the tender stomachs of some of the Badger boys. Down in the hold with his men, Bahr was in a bad way. "What makes it so much harder is that a man has to stay right down in that old hole, and every time the old ship goes up and down, you think sure you have to die."[6] On March 19, 1918, after being in France for several months, Private Ben Golz wrote home to his mother who was living on Twelfth Street in Oshkosh to tell her about the voyage. "Oh, yes, I like the ride on the boat all right. I was seasick the first three days . . . that is one of the worst things there is. You don't care for anything." He closed his letter on a bright and reassuring note, "Well, tell Pa not to worry about us, for we are all well and happy, and as long as we feel that way, why, I guess the Kaiser won't get us."[7]

The trip was largely uneventful for the Wisconsin men, except when two men on an accompanying battleship were swept overboard and drowned. The American and British navies were gaining in the battle against Germany's formidable undersea raiders. American destroyers had entered the naval battle in May and sinkings by U-boats began to decline, but the threat and fear of submarines remained very real. As the *Covington* entered the danger zone of known U-boat activity near the French coast, "the suspense began to tell on some of the men and they grew anxious . . . some of them imagined the subs would be about as thick as ducks on Lake Poygan."[8] The thought of a torpedo striking the ship, of being trapped below decks while the vessel burned and sank, surely crossed their minds.

The Pennsylvania Bucktails on the *President Grant* were not so lucky. The ship was badly overcrowded and the sanitary conditions "indescribably bad." What was worse, however, was that the ship itself was disorganized. "It seemed more like a lunatic asylum than a transport carrying U.S. troops," wrote one soldier. It was so bad that some of the Pennsylvania soldiers had to serve as stokers and firemen in the boiler rooms. Three days out, the *President Grant* broke down and was forced to return to Hoboken, New Jersey, arriving October 28. The men waited for three long weeks; rainy, gloomy weather contributed to generally downcast spirits.[9]

Despite fearless lines in letters home, Ben Golz's pa did worry, and so did everyone else. Unlike their sons heading in harm's way, families saw the departure of the 150th not so much as a grand adventure but rather more like entering the lion's den. A "grand cause" meant nothing compared to the safety of sons, husbands, and brothers. France was a long way from the gentle fields and forests of Wisconsin.

The *Covington* dropped anchored in St. Nazaire, France, on Wednesday, October 31. "[Y]ou ought to see how the boys danced for joy," wrote Bahr, "like a lot of kids. I was just as happy as any of them, it sure is some relief to know we are almost out of these dangerous waters."[10] For five days they sat aboard the *Covington* waiting to go ashore. St. Nazaire was a small port, and the French had not fully prepared for such a fast influx of Americans with their huge divisions and vast amounts of equipment. After three years of war, labor and transport were unavailable, so the French were not immediately able to handle the arrival of thousands of doughboys and their supplies.[11] During their shipboard confinement, the men were entertained by French children and women who clustered around the ship selling apples and souvenirs, which the men bought by lowering their campaign hats on a string. The officers had more serious tasks. For one thing, they attended a sobering lecture by a major in the Medical Corps. The major's talk must have been quite explicit, for Arthur Bahr confided in this diary that, "our hearts will have to turn to stone to be able to fulfill our duty to our country."[12]

After fourteen days on the ship, the men were anxious to get onto "Mother Earth," as Lloyd Ray of Green Bay told his cousin, Alva Ray, in Fond du Lac. Pearson Brown of Campbellsport was severely seasick the entire voyage. "Dearest Daddy," he began his letter, "When were taken ashore for exercise the first time, I was so weak that I could hardly walk the 1½ miles for exercise and nearly had to learn to walk over again."[13] Finally stepping onto foreign soil, the port seemed exotic, exciting, and intimidating, creating a blend of emotions and perceptions. France needed the manpower of its colonies in this fight for the nation's life, so they brought soldiers and resources from their far-off colonies to help. Colorful Moroccans wearing their trademark red fez, Sudanese soldiers, British Ghurka soldiers from India, Vietnamese truck drivers, and *mademoiselles* competed for the doughboy's attention. Company A's Edward E. Lutz told his mother that, "everything looked terribly strange, just like the old-fashioned pictures I have seen." Commenting on the colonial soldiers, he continued, "There were soldiers from every nation to greet us and some of the oddest uniforms ever imagined."[14]

For men whose worldview was limited, it must have been a heady feeling seeing people from all over the world. They also saw their adversary for the first time in the form of prisoners of war. Shoddy-looking German POWs worked around the dock unloading ships, under the watch of tired French soldiers in their well-worn "horizon blue" uniforms. The sight of such diverse groups of people must have been incredibly stimulating. The POWs impressed the Badger boys, and quite a few soldiers told the folks at home that the Germans worked under minimal guard. "[T]hey seemed to be more enthusiastic than the French people," Walter Melchior penned. "On our way we passed prisoners who even threw kisses at us . . . [one German said he] had no desire to fight again and was strong against the Kaiser." Closing his letter, he advised any soldier coming to France to stock up on tobacco. "It is what the soldiers want most and it is the hardest to get."[15]

The French viewed the enthusiastic, well-fed American soldiers as their saviors, the warriors who would prevent their nation from once again suffering defeat and humiliation at the hands of German armies. Letters reveal over and over the wonderful welcome the men received wherever they went. Soldiers from the United States gave the war-weary French soldiers and civilians a much-needed jolt of confidence and a tremendous boost to sagging spirits. When Frenchmen shouted *Vive les Americains!* they meant it. As children, the doughboys had learned the basics of American history. These citizen-soldiers knew that independence from Great Britain during the Revolutionary War was made possible by the intervention of French General Marquis de Lafayette and French troops, and that story was now told and retold. When the first American soldiers proclaimed, "Lafayette, we are here,"[16] it referenced the debt the United States owed France for helping guarantee independence from Great Britain. The wide-eyed doughboys arriving in France might not have known the whole story of the Revolutionary War, but they knew enough to realize there wouldn't be an America if it hadn't been for the French. Now it was their turn, generations later, to repay that debt.

Britain was just as much a part of the war as was France, and some American divisions trained and fought with them. The letters and diaries show that the Wisconsin doughboys believed they were "over there" to save France from the Germans and made little reference to the British.[17] In command of the American forces was General John J. Pershing, known as "Black Jack" for his previous command of African American troops. The men of the 150th had served under him in 1916 while on the border, but letters seldom if ever mentioned him. Pershing and his staff had arrived in France in June to prepare for the arrival of American troops, but he first had to stand up to France and Britain.[18] Since the United States' entry into the war, the Anglo-French high command had urged that America's soldiers be used as replacements in the British and French armies, but Pershing and his staff were against having America's young

men serve under a foreign flag like mercenaries. Pershing insisted that his soldiers fight as a unified all-American army, led by American officers, and that
the impact and effectiveness of American troops not be diminished by dividing
them between French and British armies. This issue would not be resolved for
many months.

When the Badger boys finally crowded into unheated wooden "40 and 8"
boxcars[19] on November 6, they were surprised and unimpressed at the small
size of the French trains, calling them "a cigar box train with a peanut whistle,"[20]
or similar such phrases. French trains were smaller than American trains, and
after four years of war and minimal maintenance, they were in tough shape.
Even under the best conditions French rail cars were primitive, with simple
wooden floors and often without basic benches. The cars did not have any sanitary arrangements or drinking water, and the closest thing to comfort was dirty
straw on the floor. The trains stopped twice a day to allow the men to exercise
and have coffee. French civilians cheered and waved at the doughboys during
the three-day trip, giving a lift to their spirits during an otherwise uncomfortable journey. It was cold and rainy, and the soldiers huddled together to stay
warm; they talked over the latest war news, some of which was not good.

Russia was in internal turmoil from a group called Bolsheviks who were
trying to consolidate workers groups. The Bolsheviks were in charge and had
taken Russia out of the war. On the Italian front, news came that Italy had suffered a devastating battlefield defeat at Caporetto, severe enough to leave the
Italians ineffective against the Central Powers. It didn't take a West Point officer
to appreciate that those two changes were in Germany's favor. To the men
crowded in the small, icy French boxcars thousands of miles from home, rocking
and rolling south and east toward the combat zone, the war had taken a different
turn. In the anticipation and excitement of that journey, many "renounced ex-
pectations of ever going home again."[21] What the men did not know, however,
was that the last few months of 1917 had cost Germany dearly and had set
things in motion that would make 1918 a fateful year. A massive battle at Cambrai started as a huge British victory but ended up as a loss for both sides. German morale on the home front and in the trenches was poor, and some German
leaders were prepared to strike a do-or-die blow before American troops offset
French and British losses.

The 42nd Division was the second American division in France, and the
logistics of transporting, training, and supplying them had yet to be perfected.
There was no single locale large enough to cope with twenty-eight thousand
soldiers and their equipment and supplies, so regiments and battalions had to
be broken up into smaller units and sent to villages focused around a central

headquarters location. The 150th learned the train was headed for the general area around the southern end of the French defensive line, in the Province of Lorraine near the Vosges Mountains.

About this time, the Pennsylvania soldiers finally got underway on a different ship, a British vessel named the RMS *Cedric*. From New York they headed north to Halifax and joined a convoy, then set a course for Ireland across the winter-tossed North Atlantic. When the convoy finally approached land, a U-boat attacked. The torpedoes missed the vessels, but the attack scattered the convoy. The *Cedric* scooted into Belfast harbor unharmed on December 1. The Bucktails arrived in France on December 12, and the cold, tired, and stiff soldiers finally exited their grubby train cars a few days later.

After two days on the train, the battalion detrained at the city of Vaucouleurs, near Toul. If they knew this was birthplace of Joan of Arc, the famous fifteenth-century warrior who helped drive the English armies from France, no one mentioned it in their letters. Here, they were to be trained in trench warfare techniques from combat-experienced French soldiers and thus learn the basics of modern combat from men who had seen it firsthand. For Machine Gun Battalions, it was more complex. They arrived without arms and had yet to receive their machine guns, and then they had to learn how to service those guns and put them to maximum use in all conditions. This all must have seemed daunting to the officers, who had already been provided extensive instructions to learn and memorize.

That wasn't the only challenge. Upon arrival, the companies were told that the army had decided to break up the division's Machine Gun Battalions to give each infantry battalion a machine gun company. Infantry officers had never supported the idea that Machine Gun Battalions were autonomous units and continued to lobby for their placement under the command of the infantry. This order distressed all companies, for they had trained, worked, and lived together as an independent battalion; the thought of breaking the cohesion of the unit weighed heavily on them. Lieutenant Allan B. Ellis, an Appleton soldier in the Headquarters Company, dryly recalled, "All this time we were more or less under the infantry and it was more or less unpleasant."[22] The companies were dispersed to various training locations according to where their respective infantry regiment was billeted. The Appleton men in Company A went to Vacon; Fond du Lac's company headed to Broussey; soldiers from Oshkosh's Company C marched to Maligny le Grand. Lieutenant Bahr and a few fellow officers were quartered with an elderly French woman, while the enlisted men were quartered in barracks and barns that were in questionable condition. Having yet to quarter or sleep under combat conditions, the men naturally compared the training

The battalion's first barracks in France. "1st idea of place very discouraging." Arthur Bahr Collection.

quarters to what they had known back in the states. Later, these accommoda-
tions would seem like a palace. Corporal Robert Holterman in Company B
kept a concise diary of his time in France. After the company's arrival, his
scratchy entry read, "1st idea of place very discouraging, muddy unclean billets,
lived on hardtack and corn B. [beef] for a number of days. Rainy."[23]

In every war and in every army, officers lived better than enlisted men, and
such was the case in the 150th. "[O]ur room is cold and damp, and the only fire
in the house is a fire place in the next room, where the old lady burns little
twigs, and when they blaze she blows it out so the wood don't burn up so fast,"
Bahr jotted in his diary.[24] Enlisted men, in contrast, sometimes had no source
of heat and bunked in one large room and often slept on the floor. "I am in a
room with ten other fellows," Lloyd Ray in Company B told his cousin Alva,
"we have a large fireplace. Our bunks are on the wall resembling a lumber
camp—without the bugs [lice]—Ha Ha."[25] And Walton B. Cooper with the
Appleton boys wrote his mother on November 17 that his French accommoda-
tions were acceptable despite living with farm animals, "Most of the boys stay
up stairs and sleep in the hay," he told her. "There are eighteen of us sleeping up
there in the hay, which makes a pretty good bed."[26]

A far more serious problem than sleeping with animals was the lack of tobacco. After a week or two in France, their supply of tobacco was almost gone,
and American supplies, including cigarettes, had yet to reach them. Before the
war, smoking pipes and cigars was widespread, but there was strong anticigarette

Robert Holterman kept a diary during his time in France. This photo was probably taken in Germany in 1919. Courtesy of the Fond du Lac County Historical Society.

activity in many states. In fact, cigarettes were referred to as "white slavers." Despite the discovery of a link between tobacco use and cancer in 1912, the use of tobacco was growing among males, especially cigarette smoking. During time on the Mexican border, Bull Durham "roll your own" cigarettes became popular with the Guardsmen. By 1917, men were smoking one of the three preferred brands: Lucky Strike, Camels, and Chesterfields. The entry of the United States into the world war accelerated the use of cigarettes until it was almost universal among the men of the AEF. General John Pershing is said to have cabled Washington, stating "[T]obacco is as indispensable as the daily ration; we must have thousands of tons without delay."[27] Some believed cigarettes were a "psychological escape" for men in combat and helped boost morale. In 1918, the War Department purchased the entire output of Bull Durham tobacco.[28]

Then, as now, supply and demand dictated price. When American tobacco was available, it was in high demand and therefore costly. One soldier complained that a package of Bull Durham that had cost five cents back in Oshkosh, now cost thirty-five cents (roughly equivalent to $6.89 in 2018) in France.[29] Desperate for a smoke, the men turned to French tobacco. French soldiers smoked pipes or Gitanes or Gauloises cigarettes, the latter made with dark tobacco from the Middle East and wrapped in rice paper. The tobacco was cured by the fire-flue method and had a strong flavor and aroma. "The French tobacco is black and strong," wrote one doughboy in the 165th Infantry. "I exchanged a gold Franc for a French cigarette with the money and the fag nearly choked me."[30] The doughboys preferred air-cured American tobacco, as it was far milder and more aromatic. This prompted a flurry of letters home asking folks to send cigarettes and tobacco. Back in Oshkosh, the former members of old Company F decided to help their comrades in France by raising money to buy tobacco. They held a dance and solicited donations for the "Tobacco Fund" for Company C. After Edward Haslam mailed Company C's Frank Ruechel a carton of Camel cigarettes, he wrote back to thank him, saying "I certainly enjoy to smoke a cigarette, as it is hard to buy them here."[31]

The vast majority of the doughboys had not traveled far beyond their hometowns. Their knowledge of the world came from school lessons, newspaper articles, and the occasional magazine or book. The Guardsmen were something of an exception, for they had all seen service along the Mexican border, but that was about the extent of it. Many men in the 150th were born of immigrant parents, and their surnames read like the roster of a unit in the German Army. Company C's Frank Obersteiner, for example, had been born in Austria, and the family came to Wisconsin when he was young. When parents talked about Europe, it was probably limited to the family and the place they grew up, and not about customs and life in general. The contrast between France and America was striking and seemed very different to the Wisconsinites. They were continually amazed at the "novelties of the Old World," as one man termed it, and French life was a subject in countless letters. The substantial manure piles in front of French homes astounded them, and the fact that inhabitants wore wooden shoes and "sounded like a team of horses coming" was to them a humorous part of French culture. What wasn't so quaint was living side by side with farm animals in the homes where they were billeted. "The next room to the living room is the cow barn here they have cows, sheep, goats, chickens, pigs, they sure have things handy," wrote Lieutenant Bahr. The manure piles finally became intolerable. "Had the whole company out cleaning up the town this afternoon," he noted, "and it sure did need it."[32]

Men in all the companies sent home tales of French life. Company C's Arthur Davis wrote home to Theresa Davis about French citizens: "They wear heavy clothing in spite of the fact that the winters are very mild with but little snow," he explained. "The women wear heavy stockings, flannel dresses and big wooden shoes and do all kinds of hard work and are very strong." As for the men, Davis pointed out that they "wear large trousers and most of them wear a strip of cloth about a foot wide and six yards long around their waists." Davis and others admired their ability to perform hard, manual work. "But for all their rough looks they are very good Christians and when Sunday comes they all dress up in their best clothes and go to church and worship."[33]

Like all young men, the doughboys had romantic visions of beautiful foreign women. It didn't take long, however, for reality to change their minds. "That newspaper stuff about the pretty French girls running up to kiss you in the streets is a lot of bull," wrote one soldier. "In the first place there aren't any pretty French girls, or anyway they have all gone to Paris."[34] After being in France for several months, Lorenzo Reed had to express his frustration. "The fellows back home think that it is easy to cop off a dame over here," he disgustedly wrote to his friend Jack Rouse back in Oshkosh. "[A]ll I've done is to talk at a distance to these fair dames. The people back home have it all wrong. . . . The girls back home have it all on these ten to one."[35]

As the weeks went by, they gradually realized that the long and terrible war had deeply impacted the French population, and that they had suffered severely. The people the Badger men saw were elderly, children, or disabled and discharged veterans; there were few young men. The daily chores in villages and farms were all carried out by women and children, and many of those wore the black bands of mourning. Lieutenant Bahr learned from a French officer that the elderly woman he was billeted with was a refugee and had lost her home and possessions to the Germans, giving him a different perspective on what the

French women were a common topic in letters home, especially the devastating impact of the war on their families. John Matschi Collection, Oshkosh Public Museum.

French experienced since 1914. It was a sobering revelation. It was also apparent to the men that France was poor, but its peasant farmers were hardy and tough. This perception actually boosted their enthusiasm and eagerness for defeating Germany, for the general feeling was that "The Germans can't be so good or they'd have licked the French long ago."[36] As well, they heard of atrocities supposedly committed by their enemy, and they would repeat this throughout their letters. "And a lot of the children they just took and cut their hands off," Arthur Bahr wrote to the mayor of Oshkosh in February, "or either they would make them put their hands on the ground, and then they would jump on them with their heels and crush the hands of the poor innocent little children."[37] After writing about atrocities, Guy Gross said, "The graveyards are filled with the graves of women and children murdered by the Huns."[38] Whether true or not, stories like this increased their resolve to do what they had been sent to do: defeat Germany.

Leo Uelmen, a Campbellsport soldier, expressed this opinion to his parents: "[T]he U.S. is a paradise along side of this country, I wish they would send some of those people that kick about America over here."[39] The men received hometown newspapers and read them in detail. Articles about "slackers," as those who did not support the war were called, or worse yet pro-German sympathizers, deeply angered them. Just like the GIs who would follow twenty-seven years later to fight Nazis, the doughboys had a soft spot for French children, for they had little to eat and many were orphans. They gave the kids food and francs, and photographic evidence shows the Badger men sitting with French children. Later, the 150th "adopted" a little girl they called "Miss Rainbow." Their generosity and compassion continued after the war, and ex-doughboys helped subsidize orphans through financial contributions.

Each day the autumn weather turned a little colder and a bit grayer. The men barely had shelter and few warm clothes, and not many supplies were arriving in France. On November 16, their first mail from home caught up with them, putting everyone in good spirits as they found out what was happening there. Hearing from wives and parents and reading about day-to-day activities at home was a heady elixir that boosted morale. On Thanksgiving, the men were given a fine meal of turkey, dressing, mashed potatoes, bread, butter, applesauce, and coffee. After living on "sowbelly and hardtack" for more than a week, Bahr recorded in his diary that his men "sure were happy when they saw all these good things."[40]

Since arriving in France, the men had heard unconfirmed reports that they were to be used as replacements in other armies. This idea, referred to by the British as "amalgamation," was to insert American troops into British units to make up losses.[41] President Wilson and General Pershing were totally opposed

Leo Uelmen of Campbellsport was a faithful writer, sending home detailed letters of his experiences. Courtesy of Dean Uelmen.

to it, as was the entire American command structure. They were keenly aware that the American public would never accept that their young men, fighting in the nation's first major overseas war, were simply to be used as replacements in a foreign army, something along the lines of mercenaries. This arrangement, the British claimed, would be fast and efficient because all the existing divisional and supply organizations could immediately be put to use. However, General Pershing and the French and British leaders knew Germany would soon be bringing almost three hundred combat-experienced divisions from Russia to France. President Wilson and Pershing agreed that amalgamating American troops at the divisional level would be acceptable, given the imminent threat massing to the east, as long as American officers still commanded their dough-boys. It was the right thing to do, but this did not filter down to the enlisted men.

Despite the War Department's hectic pace and the award of hundreds of contracts for military goods ranging from M1917 uniforms to rifles, there was not enough equipment to meet exploding demand. Shipping space was in short supply, French ports could not handle the influx of American ships and goods, and the French transportation network was unable to rapidly move the arriving equipment and food to supply bases. Everything the soldiers needed was in short supply, so some American divisions were given British uniforms and British food. This was not popular and reinforced the amalgamation rumor.

Aside from drilling and cleaning the town of manure, there was not much for the battalion to do without machine guns. "We hike and drill as usual," wrote Bill Heiss to his brother. "War isn't very exciting to us over here . . . [we] are about 6,000 miles from nowhere."[42] Lloyd Ray said that all they had for amusement was a sixty-two-year-old Frenchman down the street who spoke both French and German, "He's a great entertainer," Ray declared.[43] The weather didn't help their spirits. "We are having another spell of bad weather, as it rains every day, and is cold besides," said Arthur Bahr, "mud, mud, mud, is all you can see."[44] Companies C and D would be assigned to assist the infantry from the Ohio National Guard, so when several companies of Ohio's 166th Infantry arrived, the men helped them settle in. The Appleton and Fond du Lac companies, A and B, were often attached to support the 165th Infantry, the famous "Fighting 69th" from New York. Company officers tried to get to know the infantry officers they would soon fight alongside. The machine gunners would come to refer to the infantry as "our battalion boys."

Small pocket books, such as the *Soldiers' French Course*, provided a basic guide to the French language, including common phrases such as "Is there any-one here who speaks English?"[45] But for most enlisted men, as well as officers, using any type of a pocket guide was beyond their ability. "I am learning con-siderable French," George Luther told his parents in January, "which surely does help me to get along with the French people."[46] Any soldier who could speak French was in great demand. Knowing the language certainly helped when the company had to buy and haul firewood, which the French were quite reluctant to sell. Company C had two men fluent in French, and that helped pass the time and get extra food—eggs, vegetables, and bread. Despite the slowly improving supply situation, the enlisted men's rations were meager and consisted primarily of "sowbelly and hardtack,"[47] pretty much the same thing that Civil War soldiers ate fifty years earlier, so supplementing with French food was necessary. Some of that old American Army standby, hardtack, was actually left over from the Spanish-American War of 1898. Officers, on the other hand, ate quite well. Early in his diary, Arthur Bahr frequently noted the hearty meals he shared with his fellow officers, going into details about what his French housekeeper served."[W]hat we had today: Breakfast, a bowl of hot milk, eggs, hamburgers, bread, butter, jam, and coffee. . . . I don't think I will starve, do you?"[48] Several months later, Private Art Kroll wrote to his father, "We generally get rice for breakfast and I put that [jelly sent from home] on it just like I used to do at home."[49]

On December 6, 1917, the unit received orders that they were being assigned to a new area for additional training from French officers. Elements of the 150th moved out at 8:00 a.m. on December 12, just before the weather turned nasty. As Christmas approached, their morale started sinking: France was a long way from Wisconsin. The men cut a small pine tree and made a miniature Christmas tree, which they decorated with little trinkets and personal items.[50] The day before Christmas, the remaining battalion men were told that their destination was a place called Rolampont.

The day after Christmas, the division left Vaucouleurs and headed for Rolampont for more training and equipment issue. It was a march no one would ever forget. The Rainbow Division soon learned that modern war meant a hell of a lot of walking. World War I infantry marched amazing distances, and they did it repeatedly. Supplies moved by truck, train, and horse-drawn wagon, but infantry typically walked. An American division, larger than its European counterpart, stretched for many miles when on the march. Divisions shared the road with other units, so mix-ups and wrong turns were common and caused delays. Divisional movement was often done at night to minimize enemy observation, and the complete blackness frequently resulted in lost units.

The official U.S. Field Service guide used by officers stated that an ordinary march by infantry should cover twelve to sixteen miles a day, and a forced march should cover sixteen to thirty miles.[51] But conditions in wartime France severely challenged that assumption. Soldiers were tired and frequently had foot problems caused by ill-fitting boots, worn-out socks, or from standing for long periods in wet conditions. Because they were not able to eat high-calorie meals on a regular basis, or were dehydrated due to clean-water rationing, they didn't have the fortitude of well-fed, well-rested men. What is more, soldiers were often forced to carry more than the regulation gear because of inadequate transport. French roads were not ideal under the best of conditions, and during rain or spring thaw, any place not adequately drained became a quagmire. Sticky, claylike mud clung to soaked leather boots like massive, heavy over-shoes. Dirt roads that had seen heavy military traffic for years were in abhorrent condition, and American divisions had even more supply trucks and artillery, which made everything worse. Despite these difficulties, soldiers were tough and soon became conditioned to the rigors of campaigning. However, even young, physically fit soldiers able to cover the regulation twelve to sixteen miles were totally worn out by the time they stopped for the night.

The Wisconsin companies were widely acknowledged as superb on marches, with tremendous stamina and speed, and were often placed in the lead to set the pace, but as a whole the 42nd Division and even the 150th was not ready for wartime marches. "The men were not hardened to long hikes even under fair conditions," said one history source, "they had not entirely straightened out the kinks of the cramping ocean voyage."[52] The Rainbows marched to LaFuche, rested ten days, and then started on the final leg for Rolampont, which some of the Badger boys called "Rollin Pont" in doughboy slang.[53] The soldiers had barely started to march when they ran into a blizzard. In places the drifts piled up three to four feet deep, and the temperature dropped to below zero. Some soldiers had no overcoats, and their lightweight shoes literally fell apart in the wet conditions. Like General George Washington's Continental Army soldiers in 1776–77, some men were forced to wrap rags around their feet when old boots fell apart. But they kept going.

At night the lads piled into barns, haylofts, villages—any place they could find that was at least somewhat out of the winter weather. As they walked, their leather boots and leather soles became saturated with water. When they stopped for the night, the tired soldiers took their boots off in an attempt to dry boots and socks and air their feet, but during the bitter cold of the night the wet boots froze solid. In the morning, it was impossible to put the rock-hard boots back on. "Here we were billeted in an old barn, with no fire of any kind to dry our feet," explained the anonymous Company C scribe. The men were ingenious and found a way to keep going, "[W]e stuffed them full of straw and burned the straw,"[54] thawing the boots enough to put on and lace up. Cook wagons could not keep up, so there was no hot food. Exhausted though they were, a good night's sleep was impossible.

Hard as it was, the winter march had a positive impact on the entire division, for soldiers who endure adversity as a unit, who pull together and help each other not because they are ordered to do so but because they must do it to survive, often bond in tight cohesion. During the Valley Forge Hike, as the march was called, the men drew on unspoken and unknown strengths. The shared hardships solidified them as a division. It was a tough hike and a harsh introduction to the realities of soldiering.

Arriving at Rolampont, the battalion thawed out and regained its strength. The village had seen its share of war and was anything but picturesque. They were now close enough to the front lines that when the wind was right, they could literally smell the battlefield. By this time, the men knew each other very well. It was one thing to soldier together at home, with clean barracks, monthly drills, and adequate food; it was quite another to soldier in a foreign nation at war. Forced marches, harsh conditions, and lack of nourishment and sleep brought personalities into clear perspective. Being this close to the battle lines, it's not hard to imagine that they wondered how comrades would do when put to the ultimate test.

Mail and holiday packages had caught up with them shortly after Christmas, and news from home always comforted everyone and immediately perked up spirits. "Dearest Mother," wrote Walter Thorne on January 9, "Just received your most welcome letter and was sure glad to here from you. . . . I was sure glad to get [the Christmas box] and you can also thank the kind people who sent me those presents and they sure were appreciated, you bet. Got quite a few boxes from the girls and friends this year, but here we can not return their kindness, only by saying thanks."[55] Henry Kieckhaefer wrote on January 8 [1918]:

> We received our Christmas boxes from the people of Oshkosh and, be-
> lieve me, they were appreciated for they brought Christmas cheer and
> remembrance to this far off corner of God's forgotten earth, and everything
> was something the boys were in need of. So if you know anyone that had a
> hand in sending them, please give them our most heartfelt thanks. It
> certainly shows though we are many miles away, we are not forgotten by
> the good people of Oshkosh and believe me the boys of old Company F
> will surely put the old town on the map every time they get a chance. Yours
> Ever, Cook Henry Kieckhaefer.[56]

Along with mail and packages came the welcome news that the three machine gun companies would no longer be assigned to the infantry but instead would come together and remain an independent Machine Gun Battalion. Moreover, they learned a fourth company would join the 150th, the former Company I of the 4th Pennsylvania National Guard would become Company D. (Keystone men also bolstered the 151st Machine Gun Battalion.) The soldiers of the Keystone State came from the city of Reading, a community similar in size to the Fox Valley cities. The area was heavily Germanic, an industrial city surrounded by farms. The inclusion of the Pennsylvania unit was a good match and gave the 150th four strong companies, two for each infantry regiment.

The battalion was finally issued machine guns, the big French Hotchkiss Model 1914. They were issued ammunition carts, too, but no mules to pull them. Draft horses and mules were in short supply in 1918. In all the armies, draft animals pulled artillery pieces and ammunition caissons and supply wagons. The animals were not only worked extremely hard in muddy, difficult conditions, they were inadequately fed and were subject to toxic gas and enemy fire. It could take a year or more to train teams, so replacement animals were always in short supply. Without mules for their ammunition carts, the companies ended up pulling the heavy carts themselves. "[I]t sure was some job for the men to pull them by hand," Lieutenant Bahr admitted in his diary.[57] Men in any unit that depended on animal transport had to manhandle their equipment whenever animals were unavailable.

The companies were now within the distant sound of artillery. Day after day they were exposed to the distant crump and reverberations like summer thunder on the horizon. It was a steady, somber sound that was now part of their days. If in those restless hours between sleep and consciousness, they thought about their ability to kill, to hold up to the demands of combat, or regretted their decision to enlist, it did not make it into letters and diaries. The closest any man came to expressing what soldiers must think before going into combat was Art Bahr, "[I]t gives a man the shivers when you think of all those men in the cold and muddy trenches, day after day."[58] As yet, the men had no gas masks or helmets, something at the time that didn't seem all that worrisome. Aircraft, those graceful bi-winged craft that screamed through the sky at an amazing 150 miles per hour, remained a thing of wonder. The doughboys watched in amazement as French and German planes engaged in daily dogfights in the skies above, and they often remarked that they witnessed fights above, or saw the wreck of an enemy craft.

The army's intention was to give all American divisions thorough training for upcoming offensives, which leaders assumed would begin in 1919. The 42nd Division's training routine began in earnest and once started, was demanding: bayonet and gas drill; grenades; digging trenches, building shelters and laying wire entanglements; visual and mechanical signaling; maneuvers and terrain problems; and optical range finding. "We worked like tigers crawling and rolling over field and rock piles," explained Lieutenant August Arens to a friend in Appleton. "Not a man let out a word of complaint all day. They know we have to win this war." When the men of his company heard of a ship being torpedoed [this was probably the USS *Tuscania*], he said "when our men heard the news it made them all the more anxious to get busy and clean them up."[59] These things were never-ending, and the thought of hand-to-hand fighting, of taking an enemy bayonet in the belly, was a powerful incentive. The men were being transformed, although they might not have looked at it that way. The soldiers were coming to know which men were the rocks, the ones to be counted on no matter what. On the other hand, they learned who were the complainers and the weak links. In the short time they had been in this foreign land, differences and irritations that at one time seemed important and meaningful must have seemed trite.

While on the Mexican border, the Wisconsin men were introduced to and used machine guns, but it was the lightweight British Lewis machine gun. The Lewis was a fine weapon, one that used an ammunition drum that could be changed quickly. But the Lewis was not a stationery gun of the type required for prolonged fire support. The first twelve divisions of the AEF to arrive in France were issued well-used Hotchkiss guns.[60] Germany, Russia, England, and the Balkan nations had all adopted the Maxim gun and its variants; France did not. There were two disadvantages to the Maxim. First, it used long cloth belts to hold cartridges. The cotton belts had to be kept dry because the fabric swelled when it was wet, often to the point where the gun could not extract cartridges from the belt, and then the gun jammed.

The Hotchkiss used thin metal strips to hold cartridges and, while they might bend, they were impervious to moisture. Second, the Maxim used a relatively small diameter barrel, which was kept cool during firing by water contained in an outer jacket. The gun had to have a ready source of water for refilling the jacket because as the gun heated, the water turned to steam and evaporated. The steam jet from the jacket could easily give away the position of even a well-camouflaged gun, especially in cool or cold weather. Because a Maxim barrel moved forward and backward slightly as part of its operating mechanism, the seals that kept the jacket water tight could leak. During combat, the water jacket could be pierced by shrapnel or bullets. Without water in the jacket, the barrel quickly overheated and burned out or warped. While the gun would continue to fire for a short while, it would soon be out of action.

The Hotchkiss, on the other hand, used a thick, heavy barrel. Because of its mass, it took a much longer time to heat up. Cooling fins on the breech area, which looked like fat donuts, increased the mass and thereby aided cooling. Soldiers could apply a wet cloth or sponge to the fins to speed cooling, but during frantic, extended combat it was possible for a barrel to actually turn red from firing heat. When that happened, a cartridge could "cook off" or fire before it was fully in the chamber, with potential for wounding or blinding gunners. Worn or hot barrels could be changed in the field; crews were supplied with extra barrels, a barrel wrench, and thick asbestos mittens.

Corporal Robert Holterman seated behind his Hotchkiss gun. His squad shows Private First Class Michael W. Retterath (*standing*), Mechanic Herbert R. Rosenow (*left*), and Mechanic Lawrence L. Stolfuss (*right*). They are wearing captured Austrian hats. Courtesy of Bryon Historical Society, Inc.

The French gun did not fire as fast as the German Maxim (*Maschinengewehr*). The Hotchkiss had a sustained rate of fire of about 450 rounds a minute, but this rate was seldom used. Instead, crews fired in bursts at a rate of 200 to 250 rounds per minute. This resulted in less heat buildup and a lower rate of ammunition expenditure. Crews preferred to have good stockpiles of ammunition close at hand, and it was not unheard of for one gun to go through 75,000 to 100,000 rounds in an engagement. The disadvantage of the Hotchkiss was that it weighed 110 pounds. It was grueling for gun squads to keep up during an advance, especially over broken ground. Squad members had to lug dozens of heavy wooden boxes of ammunition, often over long distances. This was necessary because the unit's mule-drawn ammunition carts could not move too close to the area of combat. Unlike men, mules could not seek cover or lie down in shell holes and were therefore at risk from long-range machine gun, artillery fire, and poison gas.

The Hotchkiss was a gas-fired gun, meaning a small amount of gas from a fired cartridge was bled off to a cylinder below the barrel. The gas moved a piston in that cylinder, which was connected by a rod to the bolt. The gas pressure propelled the bolt backward, and a spring forced the bolt forward and back into position. As it went forward, it picked up another cartridge from the metal clip. This happened almost instantaneously. The Hotchkiss fired an 8mm diameter bullet, but its bullet was longer and heavier and made of solid bronze rather than jacketed lead. This gave the Hotchkiss bullet superior stability for long-range firing and greater penetration. The front sight was a blade, and the left rear sight was a notch graduated in meters. The Hotchkiss could effectively fire out to 3,000 yards, or almost two miles, and its maximum range was about 4,800 yards.

The French gun was not well-liked at first, for two reasons. The first reason was its miserable weight. The second was that to everyone's dismay, the gun sat much higher off the ground than other machine guns, exposing the crew of three to enemy fire. The fact that machine guns were always priority targets for enemy guns was not lost on the men. Later, American field ingenuity remedied this problem. As training progressed, the men recognized that the Hotchkiss was utterly reliable. They almost certainly heard stories about how, at the great battle of Verdun in 1916, some Hotchkiss guns had endured sustained fire without cleaning or breakdown. This no doubt made an impression on the battalion men as they learned to use this important weapon. It was an easy gun to maintain as it only had thirty moving pieces, with no pins or screws. It was fast and easy to take apart and impossible to reassemble incorrectly. The men grudgingly came to accept it. The iconic Hotchkiss was featured on the cover of *Collier's* magazine on May 4, 1918; the famous illustrator Herbert Paus showed U.S. Marines firing the big gun at enemy aircraft.

Machine guns dominated the battlefield. With an almost constant fire, at seven or eight cartridges fired every second, the Hotchkiss used astonishing amounts of ammunition and needed constant resupply. Because the Hotchkiss used rigid 24-round or 30-round ammunition clips rather than long cloth belts of 250 rounds like the Maxim or Vickers, the clips helped control excessive consumption of ammunition. Some Hotchkiss guns were modified to accept a type of belted ammunition, but photographs show U.S. troops using strip-fed guns. The long clips were carried in twenty-eight-pound boxes (288 cartridges), which were stacked into the accompanying mule carts. All the men in a machine gun squad knew how to use, repair, and clean the Hotchkiss, but some soldiers were designated as "runners." Their role was to bring the orders and information back and forth, and ammunition runners carried boxes of ammunition from the mule carts to the gun in an unending chain. Other men in the company were in a support role, either tending animals, cooking, or keeping the men supplied.

The Ford trucks everyone hoped for never came. Instead, the battalion relied on mule power, and animals arrived during the winter. Ever since its founding, the U.S. Army had used mules to carry packs and pull wagons and artillery. Aside from cost, there were many solid reasons why mules, the offspring of a male donkey and female horse, were preferred over horses. Mules are tough with fantastic stamina, able to endure far harsher conditions than a horse. A hard-working mule required about one-third less grain than a horse, and it was fine with eating plain hay. The animals rarely foundered from overeating or drinking too much water. The sure-footed mules had far fewer hoof and leg problems than did the horses, but when they did occur, they were less severe. Some thought mules were smarter than horses. It was a well-known fact that mules could be cantankerous, but much of that was exaggerated. "Had a little episode with a mule the other night or rather his hind feet," Corporal Walter Thorne in Company C told his mother in March. "I guess the mule found out I was a pretty tough proposition anyway, as I only got a scratch on my leg and a bump on my head."[61]

A good teamster was prized, and the army looked for men who had grown up on farms or had prior experience handling draft animals. While most of the men of the 150th were familiar with animal power, not everyone understood how to make a mule work, or how to care for it. If a teamster knew how to be calm, gentle, and firm, he realized his mule would get him and the valuable cart through the worst conditions imaginable. Harvey Stich drove a cart and proudly declared to his sister-in-law, "Hilda, me and my mule are true friends. And we get along well and happy."[62]

Carts carried more than just the guns and ammunition. They held tools like rasps, augers, punches, hammers, chisels, a spoke shave, and axes. In short, enough tools to perform basic repairs to the cart or build and repair shelters. Mules were a vital part of the battalion's ability to perform its mission, so carts also contained spare bridles, reins, and draft equipment such as traces, extra shoes for the mules, shoe nails, tongs, and a farrier's hammer. Although each gun had spare parts like extractors and springs immediately available, it wasn't practical to carry all the necessary repair tools with each gun. These were kept in the carts, as well as accessories such as blankets to screen the muzzle flash during night firing.

Each unit needed a range finder, too, and that was carried in a cart. This tripod-mounted optic was used to accurately estimate distance. Because the guns regularly fired at extreme range, meaning in excess of fifteen hundred yards, it was vital to know the range as closely as possible to determine the gun's elevation and bullet deflection. At distances in excess of six hundred yards, due to the extreme bullet trajectory, misjudging the range by a mere fifty yards would result in bullets that fell short or went over the target. Using the optical range finder, the platoon officer or squad leader would accurately establish the yardage to known reference landmarks in front of each gun. For example, he would ascertain the range to a barn or other structure, or to a geographic feature such as the crest of a hill or the edge of the woods. A card was placed by the gun that would note something like "1,800 yards to tree line." Once the yardage was recorded, the range finder was taken back to the cart for safekeeping.

When the officer received an order to fire on a target using a map coordinate, a whole host of factors came into play. Officers performed complex mathematical calculations with pencil and paper, factoring bullet trajectory, deflection for wind and other factors like rain or snow, and whether the bullets were to be rained down on one specific area or walked across and through a defined zone. If firing was done at night, common because enemy movement took place under the cloak of darkness, or in concert with other guns, it was even more challenging. A gun that was off only a quarter of an inch at the muzzle could throw bullets hundreds of yards off target at long range.

As January passed, it was clear that learning the fundamentals of heavy machine fire and operation was demanding. It took a considerable degree of knowledge and experience to quickly and correctly set up and establish firing coordinates, especially at night or under the tremendous stress of combat. The enlisted men had to know every detail and every operation and part of the Hotchkiss; how to quickly load, clear jams, keep the gun clean, and keep it in a constant state of readiness. They had to be able to do this in total darkness, during times of deep exhaustion, and while under fire. The only way to achieve that level of expertise and confidence was to practice over and over and over in varying conditions.

The army endorsed what they called "scientific machine gunnery." Accurate, intense machine-gun barrages could be quickly called down on the enemy if gun crews understood those mathematical principals. War meant, and still means, inflicting the maximum number of casualties on the enemy as possible. The greater the volume of fire that could be speedily brought to bear, the greater the enemy's losses. When the opponent was close and in view, machine gun crews went to work and swung the gun freely as necessary. During these combat situations, machine guns were most effective when shooting at the enemy in the flank or at an angle, especially when in the ideal range of two hundred to six hundred yards. This allowed bullets a greater probability of hitting multiple targets. The closer the enemy, the less effective the fire was and the more vulnerable the highly trained crew was to aimed rifle fire. However, when the targets

Learning the operation of the Hotchkiss gun and how to provide accurate, effective fire. William Pechmann Collection, Oshkosh Public Museum.

were out of view it called for "indirect fire," and that required much skill to
prevent firing on friendly units.

Correctly done, grouped machine guns could rain down a destructive hail
of bullets in a given area, called "the beaten zone." Bullets would plunge down
silently at a steep angle, often without warning. The only escape from the bullet
storm was to be in a dugout. The psychological effect of a machine gun on
troops was significant. Corporal Elmer Grabinski, in the Fond du Lac Company,
wrote to his mother in the summer of 1918 and tried to explain this. "We did
some bombarding the other and I shot over six thousand rounds myself," he
told her. "We had them pretty well scared."[63]

As riflemen, they had learned to pick their target carefully and, with aimed
fire, destroy it. But with a machine gun, they would be called on to fire at targets
they could not even see. "Harassing fire sometimes by day but most often by
night, is directed at certain areas at irregular intervals, to destroy the enemy,
lower his morale and cause him to suffer great discomfort." The battalion learned
that the British used this class of firing to a greater extent than the French did
and achieved excellent results. "Two or three times a week they stage extensive
'shoots' in conjunction with their artillery," the manual stated, "They usually
select a time when the enemy troops are being relieved and new divisions are
coming into the sector. It puts the enemy in the frame of mind that they want
him to be in while he is in the sector." And, they were never to allow an enemy
machine-gun to fire without vigorously retaliating and had orders to fire five
shots for every one fired by the enemy gunners.[64]

To achieve this, machine-gun squads had to correlate the target through
map reading and correctly orient the gun to a compass heading. The gun had to
be carefully laid and leveled, and the tripod had various adjustments to achieve
that. Once set, the gunner could maintain the same angles and elevations, ad-
justing or resetting occasionally to allow for the vibrations from firing or as the
earth settled or shifted. A brass disk on the tripod was divided into sixty-four-
hundred "mils," and the barrel was aligned to the mils that the officer or crew
sergeant determined through his computations. A key to accurate firing was
correctly determining the range of a target. Anything out to six hundred yards
was easy; beyond that distance required the use of a range finder. Ranging or
test firing was discouraged because it gave away the element of surprise. Once a
target was identified (for example, a rear supply area) and range determined
and angles calculated, many guns fired simultaneously to maximize the element
of surprise and the devastation. Guns were relocated after firing because the
more a gun fired, the higher the probably of discovery. A typical fire order to an
emplaced gun crew might read:

1. Range 1500—3 right
2. Reference point 11 o'clock
3. That lone tree
4. Target at 3 o'clock (or the target 10 mils to EL)
5. Battalion of infantry
6. Fixed (or search 10 mils and distribute 70 mils)
7. Commence firing.[65]

Early on, the men learned that machine guns were always considered high-priority targets. For that reason, the training stressed that every effort was made to keep guns well concealed, even to the point of keeping them in a bunker until ready for use. Enemy spotters and gunners looked for machine guns, but it was difficult to locate an expertly camouflaged site. Writing from his hospital bed in March, Albert Lange, in the Fond du Lac Company, told his friend Otto Zoeller that when a German aircraft flew low over their position, they withheld their fire even though they had a good chance of bringing it down. "[W]e had orders not to shoot . . . so that we would not reveal the machine gun positions. This is exactly what they want to know for as soon as a machine gun is located the artillery is sending them over thick and fast."[66] Only inexperienced crews placed their guns in exposed or easily discovered positions, and those crews quickly paid the price in blood. A single machine gun could be ruinous to exposed infantry, so its destruction was paramount. The Germans were known to mass their artillery on suspected or known machine-gun positions, firing all cannon at the same time. Infantrymen stayed away from these positions for that very reason, and sometimes machine gunners were referred to as "suicide squads." Nonetheless, at least one Wisconsin soldier made a point of explaining that wasn't the case with their battalion.

Officers and sergeants had far more demanding lessons and received detailed instructions on all phases of gun operation. In turned, they passed the training to the men in their respective companies and squads. They were responsible for locating and positioning the gun—often a decision that could result in life or death for the crew—and gave firing coordinates based on map coordinates or verbal commands. During offensives and when hectic combat conditions prevented or hindered communication, squad leaders took charge. Sergeants, in many ways the real backbone of the army, worked and lived directly with their men day in and day out, and on them fell much of the responsibility for ensuring that each Hotchkiss and its crew performed flawlessly. "You can take no chances whatever of firing into our own troops," said the training manual under the subheading of "Direct Fire." "A single instance of this sort of carelessness will do harm beyond calculation, for it will shake the confidence of our men in your reliability as a machine gun officer."[67]

"The gunner is able to produce very nearly the same results when fatigued as when fresh and fire conditions are excellent," the manual continued. They had been trained as riflemen in the Guard, but their impact on a battle was far greater as machine gunners. "If firing about 300 rounds per minutes, roughly speaking, 25 men are equal to one machine gun. At long ranges, the fire of one machine gun equals from 30 to 50 marksmen," said the training manual.[68]

The soldiers discovered that they would be night owls, too, for their guns would be brought forward under the protective cloak of darkness. They would often be called upon to fire at night because the enemy was more vulnerable by night. "His working parties are mending wire or trenches or digging; his carrying parties are on the move; relief usually takes place at night; in fact all the world will be taking advantage of the possibility that cover from view may be cover from fire."[69]

More than anything else, it was impressed on the men that when a gun crew received a fire order, they had to react quickly and accurately for their comrades' lives depended on their response. Indeed, a battle might turn on the fire from one gun. At the least sign of an attack developing, the gun should be taken back to its "battle position" and laid ready to fire. "Guns taken from position within eight hundred yards of the front line, must always be in their battle-position during the "stand to," the manual continued. The Guardsmen knew their Hotchkiss and how to use it, but they would discover that infantry officers did not always grasp the power of massed guns.

As General Pershing observed the overall training progress of his few divisions in France, he concluded that the French training was of minimal value. The French were not interested in learning anything new, he claimed. In Pershing's view, they only wanted American soldiers to adopt the same tactics used since 1914, which he believed had not worked for four years and would not lead to victory. Pershing instead advocated spirited attack—"the rifle and the bayonet"—and believed strongly in individual marksmanship. From the French standpoint, Pershing's ideas of attack were folly, or at least naive. "Spirited attacks" with the bayonet had succeeded only in bleeding France of a generation of her young men. The doughboys' robust energy and willingness to come to grips with the enemy was extraordinary, to be sure. The other thing about the Rainbows that impressed the French was their accurate rifle shooting, something the French did not emphasize with their soldiers. Although marksmanship was commendable, battle-tested French officers diplomatically tried to convince Pershing that marksmanship and vigor was simply no match for

German defenses.[70] Thoughts about Pershing's decisions or the opinions of French leaders did not make it into the letters.

With nothing more than a steady schedule of training, the Wisconsin men grew bored. "The boys, by this time, had become quite efficient with the Hotchkiss gun," explained the Company C scribe,[71] and they had their helmets and other necessary equipment. Training was frustrating. "[I]t is hard to learn from [the French]," Bahr noted with some annoyance, "as they keep right on talking and we don't understand them."[72] How soon would they be sent into action? Lack of small comforts like a cheery fire at night, warm clothes and adequate blankets, and mail from home were bad enough, but it was boredom that exasperated them, not the work. The men of the 150th were tough, and by twenty-first-century standards, used to hard life. Physical labor in a mill or farm helped prepare them for campaigning. Factory workers put in ten-hour days, six days a week, and much of the work was by sheer muscle power. Daily life at home was even more demanding for those living on farms, with no break in work except for Sunday church and a few picnics and socials throughout the year. For many, campaigning in France was not any more physically challenging than daily life. There was, however, one enormous distinction. Back in Wisconsin or Pennsylvania, the men went home to eat, relax, and sleep at the end of the day. In France, the men were constantly cold, their boots and clothes wet, they were often hungry and functioned on minimal sleep. This was succinctly expressed by Leo Uelmen, who simply told his mom and dad, "soldiering in cold weather is not very pleasant."[73] Aside from the first flurry of mail shortly after arrival, now even the comfort of a letter from home was lacking.

At long last, American underwear, uniforms, and M1917 trench boots and socks arrived in quantity, and everyone bathed and cleaned up. Even if the uniforms did not fit properly and were made of low grade, itchy wool, which was a common problem in the AEF, they knew they were wearing the products of their own country, made by the hands of American citizens. Better food arrived, too. It all helped morale immensely. Wearing worn, filthy, clothes, and threadbare socks day after day, their bodies unwashed, was both a psychological weight and a physical problem that contributed to a sense of fatigue. After the heavenly opportunity to get clean, the men were rejuvenated and ready to tackle Germans. Words sent home during the winter expressed the unshakeable conviction they were ready for whatever came their way. Arthur Bahr could see the men in his platoon becoming hardened in many ways. "I could see the men eating their dinner on manure piles with the Hogs gathered around waiting for a hand out. I often think of what the folks at home would say."[74]

5

Into the Trenches!

If you folks at home only knew what it is to fight in the trenches.

Harvey Stich
to Hilda Stich,
May 16, 1918

Tourists head to Lunéville, a beautiful part of the Province of Lorraine southeast of the city of Nancy, for many reasons. The rolling hills stretch away and offer a fine vista, a scene to rest the eyes, mind, and heart. Strolling visitors admire striking eighteenth-century chateaus of the French aristocracy, and everyone wants to purchase an example of the exceptional ceramics the town is known for. The Vezouze and Meurthe rivers come together in this city of twenty-thousand, so it is a pleasant spot to have coffee and pastry at a sidewalk cafe. In summer, the countryside presents a series of soft green, seemingly endless undulations. The mounds and hollows are ghosts of a war fought long ago, and grass veils the tragedies. Impressive but cold stone monuments and memorials mark this little corner of France where fathers and sons now sleep. It was here that the first American soldiers saw action against the kaiser's troops.

The longing to enter combat as a remedy for boredom was soon fulfilled, for the division was sent to a section of the front near the city of Lunéville. Not all parts of the line were active; some were known as quiet sectors and, by mutual agreement, neither side was aggressive here. In active sectors, meaning areas where the two sides regularly or even daily fought, raided, or shelled each other, the Western Front remained a horrid land of churned soil, shell holes, and constant death. The scarred trunks and clawlike branches of dead trees stood bleak against the sky. But in the quiet sectors the resilience of nature showed, for grass, small bushes, brambles, and young trees grew amid blasted trees and shell-pocked ground, signaling life in an otherwise dismal setting. Amid battle-scarred trees, tiny green signs of hope sprouted in a sea of brown mud. Such was the case at Lunéville. Behind the lines were the stark remnants of wrecked villages, farms, and churches. They stood as ghastly sentinels, scenes of destroyed life that were forever embedded in memory, and this was what the battalion men saw as they passed through towns and villages.

Regardless of active or quiet, one thing was constant: filthy, sleep-deprived soldiers were required to constantly dig or shore up trenches. Since trenches were essentially ditches, water, snow, and ice collected in the bottoms, and there was no way to drain them. Boardwalks and rubber boots helped keep the men's feet somewhat dry, but soaked clothing and boots were a fact of life. In active areas, concealed snipers used rifles with telescopic sights and watched for any movement above the trenches; it was almost suicidal to venture a look above the trench in daylight. Sentries used periscopes or stood behind steel plates with very thin slots to watch No Man's Land. At night, small groups of soldiers from both sides patrolled No Man's Land, repaired barbed wire, and occasionally raided each other's trenches to capture prisoners and cause general mischief. Whether active or quiet, both sides were plagued with limitless numbers of rats that fed on the soldiers' food and on corpses. Letters often mentioned the endless struggle with these marauding creatures.

A quiet sector was thought to be an ideal setting for introducing American divisions to combat, under French direction. There had been tactical changes by the time American forces arrived. Trenches were no longer haphazard affairs. Rather, trenches were carefully planned and engineered. They were composed of a series of connected command posts or strong points normally held in platoon strength—roughly thirty to forty-five men—each commanded by a lieutenant. Behind that, out of range of light artillery, was the "battle zone," a series of deeply fortified, fully manned trenches. Well beyond the battle zone, out of reach of anything except the very largest artillery pieces, was the "rear zone" where reserves were billeted in relative comfort of basements, barns, homes, and other structures that offered protection from the elements. This variation resulted in fewer casualties, allowed soldiers more rest, and enabled defenders to take a heavier toll of attacking forces from the comparative protection of the second line of resistance.

Lunéville itself was set amid the rolling wooded hills of Lorraine, a place "altogether too beautiful to be the scene of battle."[1] Many sections appeared untouched by battle, trenches wound through the woods; the overall geography was not unlike parts of Wisconsin. The area had not seen true and heavy combat—large scale offensives—since 1914. French divisions were periodically sent to "quiet" sectors to rest, and Lunéville was one those areas. There was an informal agreement between the French and Germans here that neither side would shoot, shell, or use gas; thus it seemed the perfect place for the Rainbow Division to be introduced to warfare by their French companions. Their living conditions were not bad either, at least when they were in the reserve areas. Bill Heiss told his family back in Appleton that in his quarters, which he shared with a few comrades, they had chairs, a sink, and a bed with a straw-filled tick. "[T]here are no springs and it's a little short," he explained to them, "but the fact it's really a bed makes it good to sleep in." The weather was improving, and he said the Company A boys were in a fine mood, whistling, singing and eating French fried spuds.[2]

The battalion was to go into support trenches for a while, and then move into the front line for seven days. Companies A and B were assigned to support the 165th Infantry, along with the 164th French Infantry, in the Forêt-de-Parroy. Companies C and D were attached to the 166th Infantry and French 14th Division in the St. Clement sector, near Benaminil.[3] The companies and their platoons were spread out to effectively cover the various sectors and to minimize casualties in action. A company could be devastated by a heavy barrage of artillery, leaving the infantry without machine guns.

As units approached the front, the distant rumbling of artillery grew increasingly louder. They had yet to understand the difference between artillery shells— What was the distinction between gray, white, and black artillery smoke? The overhead shrapnel bursts seemed harmless, but what was that pattering noise?[4] When should they dive to earth for safety, and when should they continue walking? What were the distinctions between those fluttering noises as artillery shells passed through the air? Should one duck at the zip-and-crack of rifle bullets? It must have been almost surreal. The men experienced a combination of excitement, eagerness, and fear; a gnawing feeling of dread of the unknown and whether they would meet the test of bravery. They were all green, untested, and untried, just novice soldiers—and they knew it. All were determined to prove themselves, to make a difference, to not fail or show cowardice in front of their comrades.

As if the apprehension of battle and possible death were not enough of a worry, the Oshkosh boys headed into their first combat assignment without their beloved captain, Gustave Schwandt. During a training exercise, Schwandt was wounded when a grenade exploded prematurely.[5] "[W]e are losing a prince of a man," Herman Sawall explained to his wife, "and everyone in the company feels bad about it." Sawall knew his wife was worried about him, so he tried to give her strength, put her at ease, and minimize the danger he faced. "Now be brave and don't worry," he encouraged her. "After our duty is done, we will return safely to the ones we love best. You know we are defending the greatest flag on the earth, Red, White and Blue."[6]

To get to the front and the supporting trenches, replacements had to negotiate a labyrinth system of communication trenches that ran perpendicular to the front lines. These were not straight lines but wound in a zigzag fashion to prevent enfilading fire if a trench were overrun by the enemy. Trenches were narrow, muddy, and often had side branches and other dugouts that made negotiating them challenging, even under the best of conditions. As if that weren't enough, the soldiers carried their packs, weapons and ammunition, equipment, and anything else that needed to be taken forward. To do this in the daylight, when a man was familiar with the routine, obstacles, and general layout was grueling enough; a man would often be exhausted by the time he reached the line. To walk down the trenches for the first time in the black of night was beyond daunting.

Replacement was always done in darkness to minimize observation by enemy artillery spotters and aircraft. The 150th and the infantry it supported went up to the line at Lunéville on a night "so dark that you could not see your hand ahead of you,"[7] recorded Company B's Herbert R. Granger. Another Fond du Lac soldier, tall, lanky Robert K. Holterman, underscored the difficulty of moving forward. He noted in his diary that one night it was so black as they worked their way through the woods and trenches that they almost could not find their post,[8] something not all that uncommon in the maze of communication and support trenches. Some men had purchased small flashlights, but it was strictly forbidden to use them near the front. Any observed pinprick of light could bring down a storm of enemy shells. Men were jumpy and nervous in the blackness, worried that German raiders might be sneaking up. If a soldier was separated from companions at night, he might have to wait until morning or run the risk of being shot by friendly fire on his own side.

Arthur Guy Empey provided a compelling glimpse into what soldiers experienced in active sectors. He was an American National Guard soldier from New Jersey who joined the British Army in 1915. Wounded in 1917, Empey was discharged and returned to the States, where he wrote a best-selling book, *Over the Top*. His description of soldiers entering the trench paints a vivid picture:

Next evening, we took over our sector of the line. In single file we wended
our way through a zigzag communication trench, six inches deep in mud.
This trench was called "Whiskey Street." On our way up to the front line
an occasional flare of bursting shrapnel would light up the sky and we
could hear the fragments slapping the ground above us on our right and
left. Then a Fritz would traverse back and forth with his "typewriter" or
machine gun. The bullets made a sharp cracking noise overhead.[9]

Walking in pitch blackness in an unknown area under the stress of front-
line combat was bad enough, but added to that was the incredibly tough task of
walking in thick, clinging, claylike mud. It stuck to boots and formed great
clods. "Mud was ankle deep," Granger wrote in his diary. "Dam near broke our
necks going down the trenches. The dug out leaked like the devil. About six
inches of water in the joint."[10] It was all so new, so unreal. Many first-timers to
the trenches retched uncontrollably from the poisonous atmosphere—the
smell of death, unwashed bodies, latrines, and rotting equipment. Lieutenant
Hugh S. Thompson from Chattanooga, Tennessee, was assigned to the division's Iowa men in Company L, 168th Infantry, 84th Brigade. "The sight that
greeted us brought an immediate and positive reaction," he wrote about his
first sight of the trenches. "'[D]esolate' was the only name for it. A mass of
rusty barbed wire was strung on crisscrosses of posts.... Ghostlike trees were
splattered with shell scars."[11]

Adrenalin high, no one slept that first night. As if that wasn't bad enough,
the next morning they found that a party of trench-raiding Germans had hung
a large white sheet that read, "Welcome, Rainbow Division." It was evident
their opponent was well-informed, and that the Germans meant to intimidate
their inexperienced enemy from across the Atlantic. Shortly after dawn, German
artillery greeted the rookie Americans with an introductory barrage. "First off, I
want to tell you it's no place for a healthy man," penned Private Frank Coffers
in Company C to his cousins in Oshkosh. "I didn't mind their shrapnel as much
as their gas. That's the only thing I dread about the trenches . . . when the alarm
is given for gas, believe me, it doesn't take us long to put on our masks."[12]

Another Company C soldier, Private Henry Witt, went into more detail
about the introduction to trench warfare when he wrote to friends living on
Eighteenth Street in Oshkosh. "[T]he shells were playing a merry tune around
my ears at times . . . it's no joke to be in the trenches," Witt flatly stated. Perhaps
to soothe the folks back home, a sentence later he added that "it takes nearly a
direct hit to do any harm" because the dugouts were "fifteen to thirty feet underground. That makes them shellproof . . . if it wouldn't be for the rats and lice, it
would be a pretty good place to sleep."[13] And Lieutenant Bahr wrote to a friend

that a big German shell landed squarely on top of his dugout the first time he was in the trenches. "I thought that I was a dead one—or would be very soon. I had to pinch myself to see if I really were alive. One good thing about this war is that close does not count."[14]

There was a routine to life at the front, and soon everyone began to understand it. Lunéville was not a quiet sector, and letters home avoided the harsh truth about life and death in the front lines, due to both the censorship and because the men did not want to unnecessarily worry family. Harvey Stich wrote to the wife of his older brother Alfred in Oshkosh: "Well Hilda you may know by this time of the year that the 42nd Div. are at the front and doing their bit for the country. If you folks at home only knew what it is to fight in the trenches."[15] It is good the folks at home did not know the gruesome details, although word passed from person to person, and family members knew their sons and brothers were in harm's way.

The Wisconsin men had much in common with the *Dreckfresser* (dirt eaters) on the other side of No Man's Land. Like their foe, they had to contend with the weather and the mud and the army. Soldiers from ancient time to the present could find common ground with the misery of life on campaign. But there was more to it than what nature threw at them.

Their enemy in *feldgrau* (field gray) and the doughboys in khaki shared the same Germanic heritage. In many cases, the doughboys were not even one generation removed from the Fatherland. They appreciated the same food: sausage, potatoes, dumplings, cabbage, and pork, the hearty fare of the German *volk*. Many Wisconsin and Pennsylvania lads could converse in German, for it was not just the language of their parents but was spoken in their respective communities. Both doughboy and *Dreckfresser* grew up in a culture that revered beer as the preferred drink at all social events. Both participated in societies and clubs, called *Verein*, which in addition to the main focus of the organization also furthered Germanic culture. And soldiers in both the American and German armies sang together in lusty if not off-key songs that took their minds away from battle and loneliness. Like a church congregation singing familiar hymns, the joining of comrades' voices brought them together for a brief time of conviviality. These things did not make it into the letter or diaries.

In spite of their shared heritage and common traits, the two sides were worlds apart. It was the old battling the new. Not every doughboy had a high school education, but their lack of formal public schooling did not prevent them from embracing the ideal and promise of America. They were not subject to a ruler or dictator like the kaiser who handed down orders and decrees, nor were they bound by societal status or family name. Instead, they were governed by a political system that reflected the will of the people, a system that ensured that no president could ever become a despot. As loyal Americans, they had freedoms and opportunities denied to citizens of other nations. Through hard work, education, and countless opportunities and choices, these citizen-soldiers could create a good life for themselves and their children and grandchildren, one that was far better than life in Europe. What they saw of France reinforced that the United States was indeed the land of promise. No domineering kaiser would take that away. All the Wisconsin lads had heard the stories from Belgium, saw posters alluding to murder, rape, and savagery by German soldiers. "It is a scar they will always carry," said Appleton's Sergeant Edward Lutz to his mother. "The boys are all stirred up already from what little they have seen."[16] This war was a fight of honor, a battle of ideologies. In this clash of blood and steel, they would prove their devotion to America, their homeland, and forever sever ties with the Old World.

The French expected the Americans to be satisfied with Lunéville, to settle in and learn how combat actually took place on a day-to-day basis. Both the Rainbows and the Germans quickly ended the informal no-shooting agreement. The Rainbows had come to fight, to pay a debt owed to France since the American Revolution; they needed to show their martial spirit to the world. Instead of sitting back, the Rainbows began aggressive patrols. This change was best illustrated by an incident recalled in a postwar account. When some infantry saw Germans washing their clothes in shell holes on No Man's Land, they opened fire, wounding several. "A French officer came rushing to the outpost in a fury of excitement. What did the Americans mean! They had done a terrible thing! Now the Germans will be angry." The doughboy response was, "What the hell . . . I came out here to kill these Boche, not to sit here and watch 'em wash clothes."[17]

The enemy quickly retaliated. On the night of March 2–3, an especially dark and murky night, the unit was on the receiving end of artillery fire of "great intensity," including large-caliber guns.[18] The infantry had a lot to learn, and the men of the 150th now saw their first casualties. On March 13, 1918, Granger wrote the terse line in his diary, "Seen three men of the 165th Inf. Carried out," and on March 15, "Seen a dugout with 22 men of the 165th Inf. C.C. buried in it."[19] It soon became worse than that for the Fond du Lac men.

In all armies, soldiers were rotated between front line, support, and reserve trenches. The stress of the front line was very great, and a week was about all a man could reasonably be expected to bear. The men of a heavy machine gun company were not expected to go "over the top" like regular infantry during offensives but instead had a major support role. Nonetheless, they sometimes participated in the numerous patrols and raids. These actions were done under the cover of darkness and were nerve-racking and frightening. Not only was there the chance of running into the enemy in the blackness but there was the added anxiety of finding their way back to their own trenches. Sentries were nervous and scared, and there was the constant fear they would open fire on a returning raiding party, mistaking them for German raiders. The Hotchkiss gun was not designed for rapid battlefield mobility, so the gun squads were typically not expected to actually enter the enemy trench. Their task was to support the infantry doing the raiding, so they set up their machine guns to provide covering fire or in the event a fight started. "[O]n several nights when we had to set up the machine guns in 'No Man's Land' and stay with it until morning, taking it down just before daybreak so as to get back to the trenches before a Dutch [German] sniper could get us . . . I can assure you that I was glad when morning came."[20]

German snipers with excellent telescopic sights mounted on accurate Mauser rifles were a real threat. The Guardsmen of the 150th were good rifle shots and had won numerous competitions, but they had no experience with telescopic sights. At first the Guardsmen did not realize how a scope increased a rifle's lethal range—and the danger that posed to those who thought they were far enough away to be out of range. "The first day in another fellow and myself were being shown around the trenches," wrote Arthur Davis to Carl Okerberg in Oshkosh, "when a rifle ball whizzed between us. That was our first experience."[21]

The division was stationed at Lunéville to be introduced to warfare under French guidance, and they did learn the routine and guidelines for staying alive. Machine gunners had frequent, unscheduled drills. During these practice alarms, they had to bring their guns quickly out of the dugout, set them up swiftly, and be ready for firing. It was tiring and physically taxing, but the squads learned teamwork in a combat setting. Time in the trenches could be monotonous, which was hard on eager young Americans anxious to show what they were made of. After the war, Isaac Walters, a new lieutenant assigned to the Appleton company, said, "We learned to apply our knowledge of Machine guns, determine how and when to use them and how to conserve ammunition. Also we determined the cool, level-headed officers and men in our organiza-tion."[22] The latter statement is revealing. Not every soldier performed well in combat, and some men who seemed inadequate in other ways had fortitude and courage when facing the enemy. These things could not be determined through any other means except combat.

With troopships bringing robust American soldiers to France every week, the German high command believed they had until summer to break the dead-lock and win the war. Germany was by this time not actually led by Kaiser Wilhelm. Instead, the nation and war effort was led by the team of General Paul Von Hindenburg and General Erich Ludendorff, with the latter directing the war effort. Ludendorff believed Germany had a real but brief opportunity to prevail against her enemies due to a slight advantage on the Western Front. Transferring soldiers, artillery, munitions, and supplies from Russia, Ludendorff and other generals believed they were poised to regain the initiative in France. An aggressive, hard-minded man, Ludendorff was concerned not so much about the doughboy's fighting ability but that American troops would reinforce the line and thereby make available more French and British troops. This additional manpower might prevent the Germans from breaking through the Allied line and into the open country beyond. Like France, Germany was by this time out of manpower and had drafted teenagers and older men. The high command then planned a massive offensive, which they named the Michael Offensive. It would be known as *Kaiserschlacht* (Emperor's Battle).

The 150th had had met their adversary in combat, survived, and learned a bit about their opponent. "We have a lot of fun with Fritz," Sergeant Leo Moquin wrote to his cousin Loretta from his hospital bed after being wounded at Lunéville. "He is some smart boy sometimes."[23] The time at Lunéville ended just as spring began. But on March 21, 1918, the Germans launched their immense offensive against the British sector to the north in an attempt to force Britain out of the war by isolating its army. Although General Ludendorff had no real strategic objectives for his massive attack, he did have surprise and a slender numeric advantage. The opening of the immense Michael Offensive was heralded by a massive artillery barrage, the most dreadful smashing of power the Western Front had yet witnessed. German artillery maintained a regular barrage on trenches, rear areas, batteries, and road junctions. "A flaming curtain went up, followed by unprecedentedly brutal roaring," wrote Ernst Junger, a German officer, as he watched hell descend on his enemy. "[T]he gigantic roaring of the innumerable guns behind us was so atrocious that even the greatest of battles we had experienced seemed like a tea party by comparison."[24] The opening barrage of the Michael Offensive went on for hours, seemingly one continuous explosion.

In conjunction with the artillery, the Germans tried a new tactic. Instead of massed infantry, the Germans used what they had learned fighting the Russians: fast moving, specially trained troops called *Stosstruppen* (storm troopers). The special assault units exploited weakness in the lines. When they found it, they used signal guns to show the route for forces following behind. *Stosstruppen* traveled light, carried adequate ammunition and bags of grenades, and a special portable, lighter-weight Maxim machine gun designed for squad use. For the first time in the history of warfare, infantry was supported by waves of ground-attack airplanes. In four years of war, seldom had attacks changed the trench lines more than a few thousand yards. In five days, Ludendorff's *Stosstruppen* advanced thirty-seven miles. It appeared that the stalemate had come to an end, and the Allies were deeply concerned.[25]

In order to keep the British and French from attacking their flanks as they advanced, the Germans shelled the trenches at Lunéville and other points with high explosives and poison gas. The 42nd Division had left the trenches in shifts as their replacements moved into the line. Because machine guns provided defense and covering fire in the event of an assault, some of the 150th were caught in the opening of the *Kaiserschlacht*. The leading units of the division had already marched at an unhurried pace about fifteen miles to Gerbéviller, but without radio or other means of communication they did not know the larger strategic picture and were not aware that some units had been caught in an attack. They heard the roar of artillery in the distance, but the divisional leadership assumed the artillery fire was just another German welcome. The column continued to march away from the sound of the guns.

The 150th had been in the trenches about eight days and were looking forward to a chance to clean up, sleep, and receive mail when the Germans punished them in a most horrific way. The machine gunners bore some of the heaviest casualties in the division, with fifty-six men killed or wounded, most of them in the Fond du Lac company. The men had been enduring a nonstop drizzly rain for some time. Because the men were green, they did not realize that the weather was perfect for poison gas because the damp held the destructive gas close to the ground for a long time.

About dusk on March 22, enemy artillery opened a three-hour barrage that included almost everything in their cache of weaponry, including the dreaded *Minenwerfer*, or "The Flying Pig," as the men called it. "They make a hole in the ground and about five feet deep," wrote Albert Lange to his friend Otto Zoeller.[26] Unlike other forms of artillery that soldiers could hear coming, Flying Pigs were silent, and they carried a massive explosive charge. But it was poison gas that resulted in mass casualties. Letters reveal that gas masks were in short supply, so the men were issued used masks (probably battlefield salvage). Huddled in dugouts to escape the shelling, the men received orders to remove their gas masks. Unbeknown to the officers and sergeants, the dampness held a significant amount of mustard gas, and they suffered the effects. Axel Watson wrote a letter home from a hospital bed fifty miles from the lines and described some of the results of the gas attack. "The morning we left there was an awful mess of dead mules which were killed by gas. These animals were supposed to be fitted with gas masks when the order comes for them, but I guess in their hurry forgot to put them on the animals."[27] Watson was able to rejoin the company a month later. Loss of their animals was a serious blow. Holterman simply recorded in his diary: "33 of [Co. B] gassed," and the next day, "6,000 gas shells, more gassed,"[28] with a note the company lost four dead and thirty-five wounded. Holterman was badly gassed and was taken to a hospital at Neufchateau for three weeks. He did not rejoin the company until late April.[29]

Another soldier serving with the Fond du Lac company, Corporal Frank Wheeler, wrote to his brother Charles from a hospital bed, stating that the gas attack "was some experience for me and if I can help it, I don't want any more like that." He went on to describe the situation: "We were all down on our knees ducking the hardware for over two hours and all that time we had our gas masks on and we were nearly suffocated in them, so after the shelling had stopped we crawled out of our holes for fresh air, but that was not to be found . . . inhaling [the gas] and paying not the least attention to it. . . . I am fine and dandy now and wishing they would let me out of bed. All I want now is to get a crack at the Germans . . . for what they did to us."[30] Part of this anger was because the men had to endure poison gas attacks and artillery bombardments. There was no way to retaliate, nor could they see their opponent. Sergeant Leo Moquin, also wounded by gas in the attack, told his cousin Loretta Moquin, "I almost met my Waterloo. . . . All the boys in the hospital are anxious to take a good wallop at the worst man that ever lived [Kaiser]. . . . Lucky I had a good gas mask (English make) that protected my breather and eyes." In closing, he encouraged her not to worry and told her, "I am getting three squares a day and a nice bed to sleep in."[31]

Moquin was wounded far more severely than he let on. When Lieutenant John Smith of Fond du Lac returned home in the autumn of 1918, he told a reporter from the *Daily Commonwealth* that Moquin and Corporal T. Edward Sullivan were badly gassed that day because they were carrying a wounded member of the company through the gas. In his opinion, their exploit was deserving of a "war cross" (Distinguished Service Cross).[32] Moquin was discharged from the hospital June 26, but doctors thought he was far from recovered. He was reassigned to clerical work at Post Headquarters, where instead of hammering away with a Hotchkiss, he "hammered away on the typewriter." When we wrote to his cousin Loretta in mid-July, he was still hoping to return to his buddies.[33]

Despite the brutal introduction to warfare, the battalion's resolve remained firm. Even though Guy Gross admitted his company got "hit pretty hard" and lost comrades, he wrote to Mrs. Frank Shaurette in Stevens Point, Wisconsin. "You see trench life is a hard life, and a fellow can stand only a couple weeks of it at the most. We can hear the roar of the big guns and the pop, pop of machine guns and rifle fire from here [i.e., reserve]." Despite hardships and grief, "I'm mighty glad that I enlisted," he told her. "If every man in the good old U.S.A. knew what I've found out in the last six months there wouldn't be an unmarried man who would hesitate a second [to enlist]."[34]

News finally reached the headquarters of the 42nd Division that the offensive was a serious threat to the British line. General Pershing immediately offered the French high command the use of the U.S. Army to help block the German drive. On March 27, the Rainbow Division turned around and started for the Baccarat Sector to relieve the French 128th Division, which would then be sent north to aid the hard-pressed British. The Rainbow men referred to this episode as "the rest we never got."[35]

The first deaths in any unit are the most shocking, the hardest to bear. The death shatters the men's feeling of invincibility or even gaiety. For the people at home, the loss of the hometown boys changed the war from abstract to reality, and they were no longer untouched by world events. In the Fond du Lac company, the first casualties were Robert Thill and Pearson Brown, both victims of pneumonia, and Alvin Bohlman, a mechanic. Bohlman was on a working party when shrapnel burst above them; he was struck in the right side by a ball. He lingered in a hospital for seven days before dying. One of his companions, Sergeant Earl Zoch, wrote to Bohlman's sister, Martha, and explained that "Although naturally the loss is felt more keenly at home, little need be said as to the feeling of the boys in the company. Alvin was always a favorite amongst us and everything possible was done for his last moments."[36]

The conditions in front lines tested even those in robust health, and Leo Uelmen wanted the folks back in Campbellsport to know that his friend Pearson Brown died as a result of active, front-line service. "The next day after the last bombardment he was on detail to go after our eats," Uelmen wrote to Herman Pass. "When he came back . . . he told me that he was beginning to get sick to his stomach. I advised him to go to the doctor. . . . That was the last time we were together. . . . He certainly was a game boy, a fellow that we all had confidence in, which means a whole lot when you are at the front."[37] The *Campbellsport News* published a moving editorial on April 4 under the title, "Our Hero," stating that Pearson "Died that future generations might be insured the freedom we have enjoyed . . . the future generations for which he died shall know that Private Pearson Lyle Brown, only son of Lloyd M. and Elizabeth E. Brown, died a Hero."[38]

6

Baccarat

Have been in the trenches again and sure was a busy lot of fellows
this trip. But we made it pretty darn lively for the Dutch.

Harold Smith
to his parents,
June 6, 1918

Alsace-Lorraine, in the foothills of the Vosges Mountains, is a lovely part
of France. The region around the village of Baccarat is agricultural, with grain
fields and rolling pastures interspersed with pleasant wooded hills. The topog-
raphy forms a serene setting, almost like a landscape painting. Baccarat, home
to about five thousand people, spans the Meurthe River and is known for the
manufacture and cutting of high-quality glass and crystal. The river flows from
its source in the mountains and winds its way northwest. This tranquil setting
conceals the violence that once took place there. The trenches, dugouts, shattered forests, and bombed-out buildings have all disappeared.

Baccarat is south of Lunéville, about where the trench line turned south toward
the Swiss border. It was considered a key hinge in the line. This sector, with its
pine woods and undulating hills and fields dappled in the soft green of spring,
seemed an idyllic setting. The 83rd Brigade held the subsector of Merviller. The
area consisted of "numerous small towns and villages closely connected by good
roads."[1] The men replaced the French 128th division without incident on April

11 and settled in. The Rainbow Division was the first American division to occupy a sector all its own without French support and under an American commander. Although this deployment followed their baptism at Lunéville, and the men were tired from their stressful first time in the trenches, Company B's casualties, and then the long hike, they nonetheless remained eager to engage their enemy. "We were in the trenches some time," Corporal Walter Billborg told his brother, Iver, "and I sure have a game squad, not a yellow one in the bunch. All they want to do is eat and fight. Our lieutenant said it was a good bunch of boys, they acted like veterans."[2]

It was at Baccarat that the division earned the name *les tigres* (the tigers). And it was here that the men honed the battle skills necessary both to survive and to become effective combat soldiers. The experiences would serve them well in the next few months. Those wounded at Lunéville were now ready for revenge. When the division's three machine gun battalions were assigned to an area like Baccarat or Lunéville, the battalions and their companies were separated. Company platoons were assigned to positions where they were able to support the infantry companies, and the squads were placed in a rotation.

The April weather was fine, and there was no large-scale German offensive activity in the Baccarat sector. Not unlike some other sectors of the front, "By mutual agreement the fighting had been reduced to a point where it was almost negligible," said a 42nd Division Intelligence summary. "It was a common thing for soldiers to go across No-Man's Land and barter chocolate for cigarettes and even to discuss the military situation and the prospects of getting home soon."[3] "This is a rather quiet sector," Arthur Bahr penned, "but there are plenty of Boche snipers around so a man must be on the alert all the time."[4]

While the men tended to be casual about snipers in their letters for the sake of those at home, snipers were a real threat. An officer in the 151st Machine Gun Battalion, Lieutenant Nellis P. Parkinson, wrote about an incident in the 151st sector. His deep dugout had steps that led up to a steel cupola, which was like a squat tower. The camouflaged cupola had a very thin slit that enabled a soldier to safely keep watch over No Man's Land. Because the lines had not changed for years, both sides knew the location of gun emplacements and observation points, such as the cupola. Parkinson related how a private on watch narrowly averted death when a German sniper placed a bullet through the slit. The sniper's bullet hit the bottom of the slit and thereby expended most of its energy before it entered the cupola, and the soldier was not injured. Such a shot required extraordinary marksmanship. Another time, Parkinson was walking through a trench where there was a seemingly insignificant space because the parapet was just a little low. As he walked through this area, his head was exposed for just a fraction of a second. A sniper was patiently watching the spot through his rifle scope, and when Parkinson passed through, the enemy's bullet narrowly missed his head.[5]

The lines had not changed much around Baccarat since the first year of the war. The machine gun battalions were assigned to predetermined defensive positions, and the battalion's platoons would be rotated through these positions: some platoons were in reserve, some resting, and some on active duty. Corporal Walter Pochojka explained to his parents why he was not always aware of casualties in the 150th: "Our company didn't stay in one crowd but was scattered all down through the trenches."[6] The companies of the battalion did not come together as a unit again until they were relieved. A platoon would man these points for a few weeks and then be relieved. The defensive positions, usually well behind the front line, were carefully spaced and, if possible, kept hidden. Gun positions were designated on maps by a number-and-letter combination, such as "A-10" or "B-4." One gun squad was assigned to each position, and a gun was usually manned in two-hour shifts. Guns were sometimes kept in the dugout if artillery was active. Each gun position had a range card that told the exact distance to landmarks so there was no guessing if firing commenced.

The day was long and monotonous; one hour before dawn was "stand-to," where all men were alert for an attack until full dawn. The second stand-to was one hour before sunset until one hour after dark. Those men not on watch could rest or were put to work. Dugouts already existed, but they were in need of repair. As well, most of the defensive positions had fallen into a state of disrepair, so repair was a priority. In between, the men entertained themselves with killing rats, writing letters, or even sniping, although this was discouraged because it exposed the highly trained gunners to avoidable risks. Even so, these eager young men did it anyway because they had come to France to kill Germans. Before being assigned to the 150th, they were infantrymen and recognized as excellent marksmen with the Springfield rifle. When not manning the Hotchkiss, though, they often picked up a rifle. "[A]ll you have to do is watch so the Germans don't get you at night and in the daytime you bail water out of your dugout," Raymond Smith explained to his mother. "If you have any time left, you stick your head out of a rifle pit and see if you can find a German sniper. You can sleep if you want to, but who wants to sleep when he can do anything else."[7]

Rats were common in every trench, in all sectors, and on both sides of No Man's Land. The men's letters home told of the "sport" they had trying to rid dugouts of the repulsive animals. "The minute it becomes quiet in a dugout," recalled Lieutenant Parkinson, "the rats would peek out from a dozen holes and steal forth, foraging for scraps of food. We wondered why the poison gas did not exterminate them, but they seemed immune."[8]

Shortly after arriving at Baccarat, the Rainbows made things lively. They were not about to sit around and be content to live and let live. One day when the Germans were sitting in their trenches playing cards and "enjoying the rest and freedom from disturbance, a shell came over from the French lines, then another, and another." Confused and angered by this violation of the Baccarat rules of warfare, the Boche were determined to get to the bottom of this change. When night came, a patrol ventured out from the German line. Upon return, the patrol reported that instead of French troops being opposite them, the Americans were there. "No further explanation was necessary."[9]

The French high command needed to know as much as possible about the disposition of enemy divisions to ascertain movement and strength. The only way to obtain that information was by patrols and raids to capture or identify units opposite them—a task the Rainbow infantry excelled at. "For reconnoitering about 4 or 5 men is sufficient," wrote Sergeant Frank Obersteiner, a chair maker at Oshkosh's Buckstaff Company in civilian life. "[A] patrol is sent out for information and should not fire upon any opposing patrols. Combining patrols, one is sent out for the purpose of attracting their [enemy] attention by sparring fire or any way of attack."[10]

Infantry companies sent patrols into No Man's Land each night. Each machine-gun squad would receive a daily order telling when a patrol was expected to come in. They were provided the day's sign and countersign, something like "Epernay," with the countersign, "Epinal." Sometimes a gun squad was sent with the infantry to provide fire if needed. Magnesium flares would periodically burst over No Man's Land, floating slowly down, illuminating trees and bushes in a harsh, eerie light. Combat patrols were so aggressive that they drove the Germans from their front-line trenches, and soon the Rainbows dominated No Man's Land. Daylight raids were planned and were so successful that the doughboys occupied German trenches for as long as three days. "We aren't fighting steady and sometimes it's quiet as peace," wrote Bill Heiss, "we put one barrage on the Dutchmen & it was great sport. Never enjoyed anything so much in my life."[11] The machine gunners seldom saw the effect of their effort, but they knew it was effective.

Just as the 150th's machine guns sent barrages onto enemy lines, so did the German guns. One day, Lieutenant Parkinson of the 151st Machine Gun Battalion remembered, "[M]achine gun fire which fell around us drove us to shelter. They swept the hill for fifteen minutes with perfect enfilades fire through our trenches. Had we not quickly taken shelter, we would have suffered heavy casualties." And another time, he recalled, "Once a machine gun bullet falling at high angle from long range punctured a tin wash basin held by Raymond Proffit just as he picked it up to start shaving."[12]

One-sided skirmishing could not long last. The Germans in the trenches opposite the battalion were combat experienced and were not going to let the duel continue without reprisal. German patrols occasionally penetrated reserve areas, but they had a much greater surprise in store for the doughboys. If the men thought they had familiarity with enemy artillery and gas from their introductory tour in Lunéville, they had an awakening at Baccarat. With Ludendorff's third offensive now underway in the north,[13] it was essential that the Germans keep enemy troops preoccupied so the Allies, in turn, could not pull troops to use as reinforcements in other areas or mount an attack the German flank. One way to achieve that was by concentrated artillery bombardment. "By way of illustrating the density of the bombardment," wrote the unknown author in Company C, "the boys counted 2,000 big shells that landed in the city of Montigney."[14] Writing to his wife in early April, Gust Schroeder first asked her to send more tobacco and some toothpaste, then told her the trenches weren't so bad. "The main thing is to keep down, for when the German boys start sending those box cars through the air it means get down if you don't want to get hit."[15]

The men wrote frequently about artillery and sometimes tried to make light of shelling to ease the minds of the folks back home. Writing from the hospital while recovering from poison gas, Leo Moquin wrote, "Oh yes you've got to hear this one this happened while I was at the front. Two of the boys were hurrying along a road that lead to our trenches. A big shell some fifty feet away spattered a few things but didn't hit the boys. One of the boys stopped walking, looking in the direction where the noise came from said, 'how often does a shell like that hit a fellow?' 'Only once I think,' was the answer. This fellow wasn't just sure."[16] This was probably a running joke that traveled the front and might not have actually happened to a Company B soldier. However, Moquin most likely passed it along so that readers back in Wisconsin felt a little better about their soldiers.

Despite the dominance of machine guns, about 70 percent of all casualties in all armies were the result of artillery. Germany had started the war with many heavy cannon, and as the conflict went on they added to the arsenal; the enemy's guns were superb. Shells burst into large, jagged chunks and countless tiny splinters. To best understand this, imagine a brick being hurtled with great force through a plate-glass window, and those on the other side of the glass being showered with razor-sharp slivers and shards. Many memoirs described the grisly results from the jagged, odd-shaped splinters. Another type of shell was designed to burst in the air. Called "shrapnel," the shell was filled with lead balls about a half inch in diameter. When it exploded above them, the balls showered on the men below.

As if the spinning chunks of steel and lead balls weren't bad enough, there was another effect of artillery: the explosion created a fearsome force or blast wave. The small shells from 77mm field guns were bad enough, but it was the massive shells like those from German 150mm and 210mm artillery pieces that literally sucked the air out of the soldier's lungs when the shells exploded. The concussive blast wave from big shells stunned men and produced a fearsome blast surge that could rip off a soldier's clothes and his flesh, causing terrible disfigurement. Multiple detonations, especially over a short period of time, reduced the mind to numbness. A soldier's vision became clouded as the brain was buffeted by shock waves, and they lost the ability to think clearly. The brain literally could not send signals to the body, so soldiers were unable to react even if they somehow knew they must. The heavy geyser of dirt thrown up by the large shells could easily bury a man, and he would smother because his shocked brain could not send signals to the body. Unable to dig out, he would suffocate. A doughboy in the 1st Division described a bombardment like this: "The earth shuddered. The mist rolled and danced. Sections of the trench began to give way. . . . The air was filled with mud, water, pieces of duckboard, and shell splinters . . . the concussion from one blast knocked me forward on my face. Before I could get up, I was half buried by another explosion."[17]

Suffering a sustained bombardment was a horrific experience. One of the most descriptive recollections was written by a German officer. "It is easier to describe these sounds than to endure them," wrote Ernst Junger in his best-selling postwar book, *Storm of Steel*. "[H]uddled in my hole in the ground with my hand in front of my face . . . you must image you are securely tied to a post, being menaced by a man swinging a heavy hammer. Now the hammer has been taken back over his head, ready to be swung, now it's cleaving the air towards you, on the point of touching your skull, then it's struck the post, and the splinters are flying—that's what it's like."[18] Private Wilfred De Roseria was a runner in Company C, a soldier designated to take messages between trenches or command points. Runners were not envied and had a high casualty rate. "De Roseria was knocked down by the concussion of a shell that landed 10 feet from the edge of the trench. He staggered to his feet and started forward when another shell landed five feet away from the trench half burying him."[19]

During the war, a new term was invented for the effects of artillery: shell shock. The men mentioned it often in their letters. Some soldiers bore artillery bombardments better than others, and there was no predicting who might be affected. A soldier's nerves could be so damaged, his mind so altered by the constant state of shock and noise that he would convulse or shake uncontrollably. In severe cases, the man could not talk, walk, or carry out any function. The brain was damaged, and sometimes the medical service and officers had a callous disregard for shell-shock victims. But the men who endured shelling understood.

"One day in a train I was with some troops who were suffering from shell shock," said Henry Coe Culbertson, the president of Wisconsin's Ripon College, to an Appleton audience in November 1918. "They suffer as if it were a fearful case of St. Vitus Dance [i.e., Sydenham's chorea, or chorea minor, a disorder characterized by rapid, uncoordinated jerking movements primarily affecting the face, hands, and feet], shuddering and twisting continually, the most pitiable sight I have ever seen in my life. They stutter when they talk. They jump and almost collapse at the noise of a door slamming or the whistles of an engine."[20] Treatment for shell shock was limited. Over time, some victims recovered while others lived in agony, almost as an invalid. After the war, Wisconsin's shell-shocked machine gunners remained casualties.

In four years of war, preparatory bombardments against a well-entrenched enemy had proved ineffective at annihilating the adversary. The reason why is simply because as the war progressed, soldiers dug deeper. The deeper the dugout, or "cellar," the safer the men were from shrapnel and blast waves, but they were not pleasant places. "These cellars were cold, damp, and smelly and overrun with large rats—big black fellows," wrote Arthur Guy Empey. Some of the largest artillery pieces, usually a land-mounted naval gun, fired delayed-action shells that could penetrate twenty to thirty feet of soil before exploding. A direct hit from a heavy shell like that might collapse a bunker, but in that case there was nothing soldiers could do anyway. It was far safer under the ground than on top. Sustained shelling, even underground, was still a terrible experience, to be sure, and as the earth shuddered it was impossible to talk. Experienced men knew that if they were deep, the storm of steel would pass. The armies persisted with artillery bombardments because they destroyed trenches and had shock value. Like all combat soldiers faced with bombardment, they were powerless to fight back. The machine gunners just had to endure. While they waited it out, it strengthened their desire to settle the score. Another difference between Lunéville and Baccarat was that the Germans used far more poison gas, both phosgene and mustard-gas shells. Clouds of poison gas were so thick that the men were forced to wear gas masks much of the time.

There were three main types of poison gas, plus several in the secondary category. Of the three primary agents, phosgene, mustard, and chlorine, the men most feared mustard gas. Inhaled, it brought an agonizing death as it seared and burned the lungs away. It reacted violently with any moist area, such as armpits and groin, and swelled the eyes shut. Skin had to be protected by clothing or with a special salve, called SAG ("gas" spelled backwards). Mustard gas raised incredibly painful blisters on skin, and the blister filled with a thick yellow liquid. Unless the gas was removed quickly, it would literally eat its way through skin and organs, causing incredible pain and agony. Sometimes symptoms did not appear for several hours, and by that time the gas had saturated the uniform and worked its way to the skin. The gas mask was a critical part of a soldier's equipment, but it required that the men be as clean shaven as possible so that the mask fit tightly. As much as they might detest shaving, for clean water was at a premium in the trenches, it was essential—even if it meant a painful dry shave. Soldiers often purchased their own shaving kit, which they viewed as an improvement over the Gillette safety razors they were issued. "About the only thing we are a little afraid of is the gas," Private Henry Witt confessed in a letter to his parents in Oshkosh, "[the masks are] a little uncomfortable to wear. It is hard to breathe and they fit so tight on the face they hurt if we have them on any length of time."[21]

Everyone carried a gas mask, even French civilians in the rear areas. Without a mask, death was almost certain. "Gas travels quickly," wrote Empey in *Over the Top*, "so you generally have about eighteen or twenty seconds to adjust your gas helmet."[22] It was an absolutely indispensable part of the doughboys' gear, and the AEF had adopted a version of Britain's Long Box Respirator, although some soldiers preferred the French M2 gas mask. The Long Box consisted of a rubber mask with glass eye-pieces held in place by elastic straps across the rear of the head. A rubber hose led to a filtering canister, good for about thirty minutes before it had to be changed. The mask pinched the nose shut with a clip and required the wearer to breathe through the rubber hose connected to the canister. Air was filtered through the canister material, which required effort. The mask was tight, hot, and most of the time almost unbearable. The lenses clouded with condensation and limited vision and did not stay centered on a man's face. This often caused the men more anxiety about being surprised and bayoneted by an enemy he could not see than did the fear of gas itself. But without the mask, a soldier would die an agonizing death. It took serious willpower, mind over matter, to keep the mask on for extended periods of time. During these gas attacks, the men huddled in their dugouts with moistened blankets nailed to the door frames to reduce the amount of gas entering.

When gassed, men had to make their way to reserve areas for treatment. Mustard gas often blinded the victims by swelling the eyes. This forced gassed soldiers to hold hands in a long chain as they were led to rear areas. Once there, the victim took off his uniform because it was inundated with the poison vapors, and the men washed. Guy Gross was gassed in a March 22 attack, and after time in the hospital, told his parents of his experience. He was moved "about a mile away where we laid by the roadside until morning. I couldn't rest as my eye commenced to smart something fierce and by morning I was as blind as a bat and had to be led to the auto that took us to the hospital. I was unable to see at all for four days but can see almost as good as ever now, thanks to our Red Cross nurses. The treatment we are receiving is sure great, it couldn't be better. My face and the lower part of my body is burned somewhat but is coming along dandy."[23]

There was no antidote and not much help for a suffering soldier, other than rest and clean air. Unless severe, most gassed men recovered enough to rejoin their units after a few days or weeks. Many men in the 150th were wounded in this way, but because gassing did not draw blood, soldiers did not consider this a true wound. "[I]t is of no great importance," wrote Sergeant Obersteiner to his mother after being gassed, "it is more illness than wound. . . . I believe that in a week or so I shall be back with the Company." Unfortunately, the long-term effects of inhaling poison gas impacted the men's health for years after the war ended and sometimes caused an early death from respiratory disorders.

Special gas masks were made for horses and mules, too. The ammunition carts of the 150th were pulled by mules, as were their rolling kitchens and supply wagons, so it was important to protect the animals. But trying to fit a mask over the nose of a terrified, rearing mule was dangerous to the handler and not always successful. Yet, relatively few draft animals died from gas during the war, even though the Germans frequently targeted the animals because they were so indispensable.

The Germans planned a gas storm of enormous power. In total secrecy, the enemy brought up one hundred special gas projectors, a type of mortar that threw a huge poison gas bomb. At midnight, one sector of the line was attacked and totally enveloped the Rainbows with a "tremendous concussion." Combined with artillery, the impact was immediate and overwhelming. "The violence and magnitude of the attack in this small area cannot be overstated," said one postwar history of the unit. Their adversary combined the gas with an assault by storm troopers in order to hit the doughboys as they were reeling from the sudden blow. Despite the intensity of the combat that quickly became a fierce and bloody hand-to-hand melee, the storm troopers were repulsed. A few days later, the Rainbows retaliated, and the 150th assisted with a massive and sustained machine-gun barrage. The ferocity of the reprisal caught the Germans by surprise and unprepared, and doughboys penetrated three lines of resistance. No quarter was given.[24]

Aside from combat, accidents were all too common among the tired and inexperienced men. While at Baccarat, one of the oldest Oshkosh men, Paul Fauck, died from an accidental gunshot wound from his pistol. Elmer Bullis wrote his friend Bert Washburn, "We gave him as good a funeral as we could.

We did not dare all go: only 1 man from each squad . . . the burial took place in a little cemetery in sight of the Boche trenches. We put a nice neat fence around his grave & a cross at the head with his name & tag on & hung his helmet on the cross & covered it with flowers of which this country is alive with them."[25] Burying a friend known for years, and realizing the grief his family would have to endure, was a sobering, sad experience beyond words. Giving a friend a proper burial was a responsibility they all shared.

Back in Wisconsin, newspapers reported on the enemy's great spring offensive. It took time for telegrams to arrive announcing casualties, but as soon as information was available, it was published and posted. In Fond du Lac, "great crowds stood around bulletin boards there all day. In one family two sons were seriously wounded."[26] The war was no longer an abstract idea; it had become a neighbor, a family member, or a friend. Sergeant Heiss wrote to his brother about the casualties in the Fond du Lac company. "Yes, we're still with them but our company is luckier. So far we've made it without a man getting a scratch."[27]

By early May, the German threat subsided and the danger of offensive action at Baccarat was over, but the men began to suffer from another malady: trench fever. This infectious disease was carried by the body louse, which harbored the rickettsia bacterium organism. Men came down with a fever, headache, sore joints and muscles, especially in the shins, and skin wounds on the back and chest. The worst part was the first four or five days, and after that the soldier improved, although the fever often returned. A full recovery took two months, but it was impossible to prevent it.

When the companies were rotated into support or reserve areas, they were still well within the zone of battle. Reserve areas were usually out of range of short-range artillery, but larger guns occasionally shelled these rear areas. As new soldiers quickly learned, men in the open that could be seen by the enemy, either from aircraft or other observation points, would invariably result in shelling. For that reason, even in support they learned to limit their time in the open. Regardless, they had to maintain a condition of readiness because German raiding parties could get into rear areas. "Our guns are in position every night," George Luther explained to his parents, "and during the day they are set up for antiaircraft use—shooting at enemy planes."[28] Despite the condition of readiness, in reserve they were closer to the field kitchens and had better food than when manning front-line positions.

As well, when in reserve they also had a little free time to walk to the little villages for whatever diversions they could find, and one was drinking. "You sit down [in a cafe] and if the chair doesn't break you are very lucky," Ben Golz in the Oshkosh company carefully explained to a friend. "Then you pound on the table with a glass or bottle and after a while an old woman comes in and hollers

When not in the front lines, the men stayed in villages. The boy on the left is probably one of the "mascots" the 150th financially adopted. John Matschi Collection, Oshkosh Public Museum.

something at you. You tell her as best you can what you want and then she will bring you a bottle of wine and charge you fifty or seventy cents for it. Of course you pay it, but it's a pretty steep price."[29] The men had no bona fide furloughs that enabled them to leave the zone of battle. "I have been in France eight months," George Luther disgustedly wrote to his parents, "and I have failed to see any one yet that has received one day's furlough, say nothing about seven."[30]

At last the Baccarat tour was over, and they headed to a rest area. The 42nd Division was relieved on June 21 by the French 61st and U.S. 77th Division, and by June 22 they were out of the trenches altogether, marching toward a well-deserved rest and clean-up. The men wanted four things: a wash, food, sleep, and mail from home. Combat soldiers wore the same uniform and underwear for weeks, sometimes months. They lived in dirt and mud; it was ground into their uniform, hair, and skin. They barely had enough clean water for drinking and seldom could wash decently. This condition of filth affected their morale, and finally getting clean was often mentioned in letters. Sleep at the front was intermittent and seldom sound, so men caught an hour or two whenever they could. The chance to truly sleep was deeply longed-for. While the battalion could be fed and receive new uniforms and the all-important news from home, there was one thing they could not purge: body lice.

"[T]he men were smudged up and beloused as only trench warfare can smidge and belouse a man."[31] Elmer Bullis told his friend, "We even got something that crawls & stays right with us, in the trenches & out. They go by the name of Cooties."[32] Although the battalion had largely escaped battlefield casualties, they were engaged in a nonstop battle with the parasites, a fight they could never win. The cooties drove soldiers to distraction as they bit and sucked blood. Whether officer or enlisted man, they could not sleep because of the incessant itching and crawling. After a uniform was cleaned or deloused in rest areas, within a day or two, new eggs hatched and it started over.

Harold Smith wrote his parents, "Have been in the trenches again and sure was a busy lot of fellows this trip. But we made it pretty darn lively for the Dutch."[33] The 150th had been in the line 140 days with the 83rd Brigade, although not all those days were in front-line positions. More than any other American division, the Rainbows were considered hardened troops capable of any assignment. They were proud that they had been tested and passed the trial, had grown confident in their fighting abilities, and considered themselves bona fide veterans. "A fellow gets so blamed used to it that he sure misses the hum of the shot and shell," Smith said. "We have learned to tell a gas shell by its sound as it comes through the air and also the report it makes when it burst."[34] Now more than ever the men of the 42nd Division were anxious to prove their worth and take revenge for what they endured, and for what they had lost.

The Guardsmen were tired after two months on the line, but they left the line knowing they had done a fine job. No soldier slept well or enough on front-line duty, so they caught up on sleep and ate decent food, which they often referred to as "a good feed." They had time to bathe, received clean underwear and socks, and read their mail. And, they were finally paid—in French francs. "Every body was celebrating for fair," recorded Herbert Granger. "Some were fishing and swimming."[35] He also wrote to his sweetheart, Addie Olson, "I am willing to admit France is O.K. in the summer," he confessed, "but is no place when the rain starts." Soldiers on campaign lived outside no matter what the weather was, so it was a frequent topic in letters. Although they had shelter in buildings once in a while, rainy weather made their lives miserable. He explained to Addie that the company was in a rest area and there were baseball games, a concert, and a track meet for recreation. The night before, Granger wrote with apparent pleasure, "we saw real moving pictures (made in America). Tonight five American sisters are going to play here."[36] While they men often wrote appreciatively of the Red Cross and occasionally about the Y.M.C.A., the latter was not always held in high regard. "The only thing we can get at the 'Y' is writing paper, a few cookies the size of lemon snaps (eight for twenty cents) and soap. . . . I know what I am talking about."[37] Other than that, life seemed good.

There were parts of France that were not scarred and torn, and they still seemed glamorous, at least from what little they could see from their marches and train cars. In all wars, stories are passed from unit to unit, becoming increasingly descriptive and enhanced with each telling. The soldiers of the 150th were young and wanted to know more about the wonders of life—especially those Paris beauties they heard about. Their rest was short-lived, and there were no trips to Paris. The division was ordered to entrain at the towns of Thaon-les-Vosges, Châtel-sur-Moselle, and Charmes.

Time was not on Germany's side, and Ludendorff knew it. The new offensive tactics worked, to a degree, but logistical problems that had plagued all sides could not be overcome. The Germans found there was no way to exploit a breakthrough before their troops became exhausted. The British had learned how to contend with the new infiltration tactics, and as a result there were high casualties among the *Stosstruppen*, who could not be easily replaced. The British had not been driven to the coast and had mounted an unyielding defense, but there were limited reserves of German manpower. If they were to act, they had to do so soon, for every month the Allies grew stronger as 250,000 spirited and eager American troops arrived in France. After engaging American troops over the winter and spring, the German assessment indicated they faced a serious new adversary: "The individual soldiers are good. They are healthy, vigorous, and physically well-developed men of ages ranging from 18 to 28, who at present lack only necessary training to make them redoubtable opponents."[38]

Nor did events at sea favor Germany. Despite remarkable seamanship and bravery, the submarine campaign had failed. The U.S. Navy destroyers were exceptionally aggressive. American warships convoyed merchant and troop ships across the Atlantic with efficiency and assertive patrolling, shepherding their merchant charges so closely that U-boats did not have much opportunity to attack. Britain had finally developed an effective counter-measures to the U-boat, a sonar device that enabled destroyers to hear and "see" underwater (titled ASDIC, Anti-submarine Detection Investigation Committee). Of significance, they at last had a bomb that exploded underwater at preset depths and could crack a U-boat's pressure hull. Together, these improvements ended the threat to supply lines. Militarily it was impossible for Germany to achieve a sweeping and decisive victory. Nonetheless, German leaders remained confident that it was possible to strongly position Germany for armistice negotiations—as long as Germany held as much French territory as possible.

Just before the Rainbow Division came off the line and moved into reserve, General Ludendorff continued offensive operations, this time against a section of the French-held line. On May 27 he launched a powerful attack in a new sector: the Aisne, between Soissons and Reims. The offensive, code named Blucher-Yorck, easily broke through the defenses. German forces eventually reached Château-Thierry, a village on the Marne River, much farther away than they had anticipated. This newest German attack strained resources on both sides. French and British reserves were inadequate, and they simply did not have manpower flexibility. Now, the very thing that Ludendorff and his generals feared became reality. The American 2nd and 3rd Divisions played an important part in stopping Blucher-Yorck. On June 6, U.S. Marines showed what Americans were capable of when they blunted the German thrust at Belleau Wood.

Taking Paris was not the objective of Blucher-Yorck, but it placed German forces threateningly close to the capital. The French government drew up plans to evacuate Paris and move to Bordeaux. But France never considered an admission of defeat, and morale in French divisions remained strong. France now had doughboys from across the Atlantic, and German leaders faced the prospect of fighting against the big, fresh American divisions.

The men of the 150th, like most soldiers in all armies, were unaware of the big or strategic picture, especially when they were in the front lines. Once they were in rest areas and mail caught up with them, they had hometown newspapers to read and the army's *Stars & Stripes*, so they could form an understanding of what the situation was. However, at the front they were in isolation, especially if they were in combat. Their world was what they could see around them, and sometimes they were so tired that they didn't even know what day of the week it was. The men took each day as it came. As the battalion moved out for another assignment, they were aware that the army was heading west and north . . . and not toward Germany. But one thing they did know was that they were keen to see Germany crushed and were eager to fight. "Some of the sights a fellow sees around here fairly make his blood boil," Guy Gross wrote to a Mrs. Frank Shaurette in Stevens Point. "Some of the towns . . . with beautiful buildings, churches and homes are nothing but large heaps of sand and plaster . . . the graveyards are filled with the graves of women and children who were murdered by the Huns when they first invaded France and Belgium in 1914–15. . . . I'm glad Uncle Sam got into this war when he did. I hate to think of what might have happened to our beloved country had Germany pulled through this war victorious."[39] And Harvey Stich explained it in a little different way to his sister-in-law, Hilda. Stich's view was uncomplicated, but really quite superb because it was so straightforward. He said that the war was necessary because "the Germans blowed everything over and took the little girls' and boys' fathers and mothers away."[40]

Another thing that made the men's blood boil was reading articles in their hometown newspapers of incidents of pro-German activity, or failure or resistance to fully support the war by buying bonds. It truly angered them. War was gruesome business, they now understood. Home was four thousand miles away, and they wanted to return there, and that meant more fighting. To read of anti-war activities, whether true or exaggerated, was close to intolerable.

French railroads were overburdened. Moving by rail was not always possible, and often the trains took only a division or selected units of the division part of the way. To reach a destination, the men often had to cover long distances on foot, which they referred to as "hiking," and the Wisconsin men were proud of their ability to walk. Each gun company was officially assigned seven saddle horses and two or three riding mules. When they were available, they were reserved for officers and messengers. Everyone else walked. Troops were needed everywhere to block probable German thrusts, and their new destination was the Valley of the Marne between Vitry-le-Francois and Châlons-sur-Marne.

A soldier was required to carry quite a load on his person whenever the unit changed locations. Generally he always wore a gas mask on his chest, and in addition, wore a haversack containing his personal possessions, and that weighed about forty to sixty pounds. This included a mess kit, spare underwear, socks, and clothing, reserve rations, personal items and toiletries, a blanket and overcoat, and any souvenir or other item he couldn't live without. On his web belt, he carried a holstered M1911 Colt pistol and four spare ammunition clips, a one-quart aluminum canteen, and a first-aid pouch. On the outside of the haversack was his entrenching tool. The weight resulted in aching shoulders, back, and hips. Some items could be carried in the carts or supply train, but every man had to carry his own gear. Their M1917 boots were heavy due to the construction and steel hobnails and heel plate, and if it were muddy, each boot picked up additional weight.

Making time on a march required the men to be physically fit. On June 20, the battalion covered twenty-six kilometers (sixteen miles) through a driving rain, "but not a man fell out . . . we were drenched with the rains [but] kept on." In another long day's march, they covered seventy-two kilometers (forty-five miles). It was summer, and the sun was high and hot and the days long. "We do all our hiking by night," Harold Smith told his parents in early July, "as it is terribly hot."[41] On June 28, they hiked thirty-five kilometers (twenty-two miles), covering that distance in only seven hours. After a short stay of a few days, they headed out again and marched well into the night, arriving at Suippes at 4:30 a.m. on July 4. "[We were] tired and foot sore so the greater part of our Company spent our National Holiday getting what sleep they could, which was not very much as we were only seven miles from the lines."[42]

7

The Lousy Champagne

I would like to have the good luck to get back & live my short life
with my family.

Elmer Bullis
to Bert Washburn,
June 9, 1918

The best wines require a combination of good soil and sun, the right grapes, and the accumulated understanding of how to turn the raw ingredients into a superb drink. Despite the appeal of wine, not as many tourists come to the rural area northeast of Paris, unless they are heading to Reims to see the magnificent rebuilt cathedral or other attractions. The scenery is not compelling, the endless rows of grape vines breaking the rather arid nature of the place, but it is steeped in history. When the land was known as Gaul, Roman troops garrisoned the region. Their famous roads, which enabled legions to quickly traverse their empire, bisect the countryside. It was down the ancient road axis that German commanders chose as part of their attack in the summer of 1918.

Having yet to experience the devastation and grief resulting from heavy casualties, the cohesive 150th remained eager to come to grips with their enemy. "Our old company has had awful good luck so far," acknowledged Sergeant Bullis to his friend Bert Washburn. "We have been in the trenches 3 times & been on

2 raids & only lost one man."[1] Letters reveal the battalion was eager to engage in battle. In the Appleton company, Bill Heiss exclaimed to his brother, "They'll wish they'd never started anything. It may seem hard to shoot the Germans but we could do almost anything to them after what we've seen and heard."[2]

They were sent to France to fight and kill Germans, but they also needed the promise of relaxation and were somewhat annoyed because France was all work and no play. The siren songs of France beckoned. Harold Smith serving in Company C reflected on this in his letter home. "Well since the last time I wrote we have made another move. That is all we have been doing here of late.... You see we will not stay in one front any length of time at all. We travel from one front to another. Give a few heavy raids and barrages and move on to another place almost all foot travel at that." Although feet might be sore, spirits were high. In the next sentence Smith proudly told his family, "Besides a few minor casualties and sicknesses the Old Co. F bunch cannot be beat. We hold our own no matter where we go or what we under take to do."[3] That was certainly true, for the Rainbow had gained an enviable reputation as excellent fighters. This was due not just to the infantry but was in no small part helped by the Machine Gun Battalions. The Hotchkiss guns of the division's 149th, 150th, and 151st battalions were force multipliers and influenced outcomes on the battlefield. Infantry needed the power of the barrages and interlocking fields of fire that the machine gun companies now knew how to quickly establish. The infantry knew they could count on the support of the gun companies no matter how tough the conditions, and it gave them confidence. The big guns would be behind and beside them, a formidable barrier.

While army regiments were normally composed of young, physically fit men in their prime, National Guard units had men of varying ages. This diversity tempered the companies and provided a degree of maturity and emotional stability. Some of the men in the 150th were older than what was considered a normal age for combat soldiers. The demands of combat were physically and emotionally demanding and exhausting. Activities that did not tax twenty-year-old men like Bill Heiss, Harold Smith, and Frank Obersteiner, might be incredibly hard for someone in middle age. Yet, there is no record that the older ages of some National Guardsmen diminished their effectiveness. At forty-five, Elmer Bullis was the oldest man in Company C, and perhaps in the 150th. He was fondly referred to as "Dad," a name given with respect rather than ridicule. Bullis had worked at the Hollister and Amos Lumber Company in Oshkosh before the war, and had also been a lumberjack in the Northwoods during the winter. At five-foot-five, he was small, wiry, and tough. His professional portrait, taken after the Border Expedition, shows a face lined by time and responsibility. Bullis enlisted in the National Guard in 1904 at age thirty-one, and by 1918, was a sergeant. Noncommissioned officers—sergeants—were the backbone of the army. Through a combination of know-how, personality, and experience, they kept the men of their platoons in line and functioning as a well-disciplined team. This could be challenging in a National Guard unit where everyone knew each other pretty well and friendships often started in childhood, for it could be awkward to discipline a friend. It took a special type of person to be an effective, respected sergeant. Bullis was in the class of respected sergeants.

The relentless campaigning was no doubt hard on Bullis in many ways, especially so because he was a father with a family that depended on him, and he had been away since the Mexican Border days. In a beautiful, careful script, Bullis wrote to his friend Bert Washburn back in Oshkosh on June 9, 1918, asking him to visit his wife, Maude, who evidentially must have been beside herself with loneliness and worry. "That would take her mind off from me being away. I know she puts in a good many lonely days," he explained in the letter. Feeling the pang of solitude in a foreign country at war and a deep longing for home, he continued, "I have seen all the war I ever want to see & all the country. I would like to have the good luck to get back & live my short life with my family. I have been away so much that my children don't hardly know that they have got a Daddy." Maude had recently given birth to a baby boy while he was in France, "I am one of the proudest old boys in this world," he wrote. Bullis then joked that, "My head has expanded so since I got the word that they had to make another helmet for me."[4]

Germany's General Ludendorff's early June offensive, called Operation Gneisenau, started with promise but promptly had been blunted by a French counterattack on June 11. Even so, the territory gained positioned elements of the German Army only fifty-six miles from Paris. Ludendorff was grasping at straws. Despite massive losses since spring that could not be made up, he remained convinced he could still isolate the British Expeditionary Force in the north if he continued the attack toward Paris. He believed a new assault would draw British forces from Flanders. At least some German leaders understood or believed they did not have much choice, as their manpower was limited and would continue to diminish as the Allied forces grew. Some generals were imbued with new confidence that their last attack had the Allies reeling and believed the German Army would burst through or around what they perceived as weakly held Allied line. Others, however, were circumspect and advocated peace because surprise was unmistakably gone, and the Allies knew how to cope with German storm troopers. Nonetheless, the decision was made. Ludendorff's First, Third, Seventh, and Ninth Armies, a total of forty-three divisions, would attack in what was labeled Operation Marneschutz. To the Americans and Allies, it would become known as the Second Battle of the Marne.

It was now a different kind of battle than the attrition of four years of fixed trench warfare. The armies were now in untouched countryside, the French capital relatively close to some elements of the German Army. The German plan was a two-prong attack centered on Reims, a major rail hub for the Allies and a transportation center that the Germans desperately needed. Their supply situation in the Marne area was tenuous, and they were eager to acquire the rail center. East of Reims, Ludendorff would send forward twenty-three divisions of the 1st and 3rd Armies, and west of the ancient city of kings seventeen divisions of the 7th and 9th Armies would attack. This action, he believed, would split already weakened French forces and pull both French and British divisions south from the Flanders area. Once that happened, a major offensive in Flanders would certainly reach the English Channel and isolate the British, thereby putting Germany in a position for peace negotiations.

Opposing the Germans was a combination of French, British, Colonial, and two Italian divisions, plus eight American divisions, all divided into five army groups. These forces were arrayed in a shallow crescent from Soissons to Reims. Farthest to the east was the French 4th Army, which consisted of forty divisions, including the 42nd Division, under General Henri Gouraud. American divisions fighting under French command was a form of amalgamation, but it was a necessity. When the division was moving to the Champagne region, the Wisconsin men heard they were to practice for a big raid planned for the Reims sector. The raid was to be large enough to concern the Germans that an offensive against their flank was brewing. The operation was canceled and the men told to prepare to blunt a coming attack. "We accepted this responsibility as though it were a charge to defend the integrity of our country, whose birth was that day being celebrated."[5]

Letters and diaries reveal that the Guardsmen knew an attack was coming, and so did everyone else. The Germans had grown careless, most likely from weariness and the loss of experienced staff. From information obtained from German deserters, air reconnaissance, and simply understanding his enemy, French General Ferdinand Foch prepared to blunt the attack. But far more significantly, once the assault was stopped, the Allies would themselves go on the offensive.

The 150th was now in the region of France known as the Champagne. When the men heard "Champagne," they no doubt thought of bubbly sweet wine, a drink most likely few had tasted. But they took an immediate dislike to the area. It might have been superb for growing grapes, but to the soldiers it was anything but attractive. "The heat was sweltering. The chalk plains glared white in the blazing sun, their baldness relieved here and there by the red poppy and the blue of the cornflowers."[6] The men began referring to it as "the lousy

Champagne," a phrase with double meaning since the men were filthy and lousy.[7] The ground was hard and chalky white with scrubby little pine trees, definitely not picturesque. "[N]ot a vineyard, not a garden, and not a field of wheat. . . . It was very white and desolate. The scrubby trees were dwarfed and gnarled," wrote Walter Wolf of the 84th Brigade in his postwar history of the division.[8] After resting on Independence Day, the Wisconsin men moved forward with their assigned infantry on July 5 to second-line defensive positions. As was normal, Companies C and D was assigned to the Ohio boys in the 166th Infantry, and A and B were attached to the New Yorkers in the 165th Infantry.

The weather remained uncomfortably hot, and the doughboys sweated in their M1917 wool uniforms while waiting for something to happen. The army did not issue summer-weight (cotton) uniforms to the soldiers in France. Instead, the wool tunic and flannel shirt were standard. The stand-up collar was particularly galling because the fabric was low grade and therefore coarse. Granger's diary kept tersely noted, "nothing doing." For shelter, Fond du Lac's Company B had a dugout in an old chalk mine that was a half-mile long and forty feet deep.[9] The area had many cellars for storing and aging wine, and they made suitable bunkers. At least it was away from the intense sun. "[I]t is large enough for three hundred [or more] bunks. It has twelve stairways . . . it is cold enough to wear an overcoat at all times and it is also very damp and unhealthy, but the worst part of it is we have no water . . . it is just like working in a flour mill all the time. It sure is a fright."[10] The Oshkosh company was in reserve, well behind the lines, and had relatively shallow trenches for cover. The Appleton men and Bucktails had the luck of the draw to be up front with the French.

One design of the Hotchkiss gun that the men truly did not like was that it sat up rather high and thus exposed the two- or three-man crew to enemy fire. The tripod could not be lowered enough to conceal the gun. In typical American fashion, they set out to fix this problem. Within a few hours of seeing the dilemma the gun crews faced, an ordnance sergeant named John Walbilic came up with a simple and ingenious way to lower the height and make the guns easier to move. The sample was tested by the men and proved a fabulous improvement.

The men took the test gun mount back to headquarters and showed it to the divisional ordnance officers, where it was examined. In characteristic U.S. Army fashion, the new mount was not well-received. The officers said they "would make note of [the] design and send it to some board which would meet at some time and advise us of their action. We could see that the mounts would be forthcoming in time to be used in the next World War after the war-to-end-wars." Taking matters into their own hands, the enlisted men went to the supply officer and requisitioned steel strips and bars, bolts, washers, and chain, stating it was needed to repair French artillery chariots. They took the raw materials to the mobile machine-shop truck and went to work on the unit's mounts, completing them all. "This permitted [the men] to take shelter behind low objects and conceal themselves in wheat-fields. It only weighed about two pounds and one man could carry the gun and mount assembled together." This homegrown solution would soon prove to be a great advantage.[11] While none of the letters speak to this modification, a change like this would have quickly worked its way through the division's various units.

General Gouraud wanted to maintain as much secrecy as possible, so the men had to limit daytime activity and were not to show themselves. While they waited for the German assault, they cleaned weapons, picked lice from shirts, repaired trenches and dugouts. Long periods of waiting are common in just about every army in every war, and it was not different for the battalion. The machine gunners tried to occupy the time, but for some it was agonizing. Young Harvey Pierre used the time to write to Dr. D. S. Runnels in Appleton. "Still laying away in a quiet sector and waiting for our turn to stick the punch on Kaiser Bill's jaw, that made John L. Sullivan famous," he confidently told the doctor. "[I]am hoping our turn will soon come. We've got him coming now and don't think it will be long before he shows that he is all yellow and a big bluff. All we ask now is that the people back home wake up to the fact that we are in it at last and do everything they possibly can to help us."[12]

Harvey's brother, John, was also busy writing home. He told his dad that he had taken confession from the now-famous Father Francis Duffy of the 165th Infantry, the Fighting Irish, but there was something else he needed: tobacco. "There is something that I want and can not get it. A few cigars and a carton of Camel cigarettes. A man with a Camel on his person sure must have a guard or two with him for his life is in danger." Tobacco helped calm the men and gave them something to do in the long hours of inactivity, and of course became a habit that was tough to stop. Perhaps John wasn't quite as spirited as his younger brother, for he ended his letter by saying, "[A]fter this war a keg of powder is the only thing that will make me leave [the good old U.S.A.] and that would be upwards."[13]

When German forces were closing the ring on Paris in 1914, the goddess of war changed sides and the Germans were defeated. Four years later, Athena once again smiled on the Allies. The French had captured a group of Germans in a raid, including a sergeant. While the French knew an offensive was coming, they did not exactly when. Under interrogation, the sergeant revealed that the attack was scheduled to start at ten minutes after midnight on July 15. Perhaps

Appleton's Harvey Pierre was killed during the Champagne battle. The city's Veterans of Foreign Wars Post was named in his honor. Courtesy of Veterans of Foreign Wars Post 2778, Appleton, Wisconsin.

the Germans reasoned that July 14, Bastille Day, would be a day of rejoicing and drinking, and thus French soldiers would not be at their best the following day. Once that information was revealed, the German lost the crucial element of surprise.

The French plan was to create defenses in great depth, and to pull the bulk of their troops from the forward trenches, placing them in second-line trenches and dugouts two miles to the rear to await the attack. Volunteers remaining in the front trenches would delay the enemy but, more significantly, signal the German's main route of attack. Some of the Rainbow elements were ordered forward to the intermediate trenches to reinforce the French units. General Gouraud expected the decisive action to take place before the second defensive line, which actually consisted of seven lines of resistance. Here, German forces would be decimated. So thorough was the defensive line that the "Plains of Champagne were one bristling area of prepared defenses."[14] Gouraud impressed on the troops that the coming battle was the climax in the epic struggle that began in 1914: the Germans would be stopped, or the men would die and France would fall under German domination. Captain Lothar Graef sent an order to his company, later to become famous, that said in part, "This position will be held to the last man and the last round of ammunition . . . THERE WILL BE NO RETREAT."

The Rainbow Division occupied a front about five miles wide and ten miles deep, with French divisions on either side. Through the center ran an important macadam road, the old Roman road called the Châlons-sur-Marne, a critical axis of attack for the enemy. To the right of the road, were the 84th Brigade and the 151st Machine Gun Battalion; to the left, the 83rd Brigade, supported by the 150th. Lieutenant Hugh Thompson, waiting with the Iowa men in the 168th Infantry, looked out on that hot and dusty landscape and described it like this: "A flat expanse ahead was divided by a snake-like road of white. . . . The desolate plain was crisscrossed by gray-white parapets and dotted here and there with patches of stubble and scrub pines. Myriad poppies, blood-red against the chalk, danced in the shimmering waves of July heat."[15]

Word came down to the various units holding the trenches that the German bombardment would begin between shortly after midnight, and that General Gouraud ordered a preemptive shelling at 11:45 p.m. to catch the enemy off guard. "[T]here came a crash that fairly lifted men from their feet. All the hidden guns belched forth their death calls as one voice and the air was filled with tons of screaming steel," catching many German units in the open and without any cover. From horizon to horizon the night was filled with flashes of red and orange from French and American artillery. The official story of the Ohio Infantry stated that, "Hell was being manufactured that night."[16] Two

Appleton soldiers, Tom Miller and Harvey Pierre, were reconnoitering in No Man's Land just before midnight. "It is so quiet we sense that something is wrong," Miller recalled twenty-five years later to newspaper reporter Don Anderson. "Suddenly all hell breaks loose. The noise and fury from thousands of those big guns, laid hub to hub, is simply indescribable. Beneath a sky that was aflame and on ground that literally rocked, we crept back to trenches that were leveled off."[17]

While the doughboys watched the inferno unleashed on their adversary, German artillery responded with the most intense barrage anyone had ever experienced. German General Georg Bruchmuller had devised a way to pre-register guns by firing just a few shells. Prior to this, it often took many shells to sight in artillery, consequently giving the enemy advance warning that a bombardment was imminent. Rather than spread the impact along the entire length of the enemy sector, Bruchmuller had all the cannon in a given area focus their fire on just one smaller stretch of the enemy's line. As a result of this method, the Germans were able to surprise and pound their enemy with an inferno.

The bombardment of high explosive and poison-gas shells defied description, far worse than the drubbing at Baccarat. "[D]eadly H.E.'s [high explosive] set with instantaneous fuse which broke on contact sweeping everything above ground with a veritable hail of jagged fragments, the most destructive form of artillery fire known to infantry in the open."[18] Nathaniel Rouse, a private in the 165th Infantry, wrote in his diary, "They started to shell us about 12:05. Oh my God, how they shelled. I hope never to have to go through it again. Oh God, what a night. They shelled us something terrible. I had my gas masque on for 4 hours straight."[19]

The Company B troops, safe in the old chalk mine, waited. Herbert Granger jotted in his diary, "Germans sent over one of the heaviest barrages for twelve hours we were ever thru. . . . They made three direct hits on our dug out but it only jarred out the candle."[20] The Oshkosh company was in reserve and was spared the full fury of the opening. "The Germans started sending over shells of every size," recalled the nameless soldier-scribe in Company C who, after the war, recorded the company's exploits. "This barrage lasted 12 hours and . . . most of the men had small holes dug in the ground for protection it seems almost a miracle that we had only ten casualties in the Company."[21] In Bahr's platoon, ten men became casualties. "Treichel got shell shock," he jotted in his diary, "Pvt. Zindler was killed and the same shell hit Cook Kiecheafter [Keickhafer] in the leg. . . . This sure was a heavy bombardment on our lines and a man don't know when he will get hit."[22] "We had a very severe bombardment," wrote Private Art Davis to his sister Frieda in Oshkosh, "we got an awful lot of gas. I think that gas lasted at least seven hours. We had to keep our masks on that long. . . . [O]ur company was lucky, for we did not have many casualties."[23]

Lieutenant Thompson with L Company of the 168th (Iowa) wasn't so lucky. "We started for the trenches and had made but a few yards when the woods became a torrent of whizzing, roaring, flashing, deafening hell," he recalled in the 1930s. "The darkness was now violet and now splotched with green, yellow, and red flames of fire. Gravel rained on our helmets, trees fell, we choked on swirls of dust. . . . Now shadowy, now vivid forms huddled against the walls of the fire trench. . . . A green flare cast a sickening pallor into the roaring, belching yellows and reds. 'Jesus, it's gas.'"[24] Thompson, unable to escape the torrent of steel, was badly wounded by shards in the shoulder, lower back, and hip.

The full wrath of the horrendous barrage fell on the thinly held first-line trench, and the Badgers were thankful they were part of the second-line surprise reception that awaited the Germans. When the artillery fire slackened, German divisions moved forward across a sixty-five-mile-wide front, including the area facing the 42nd Division. They confidently expected to roll over dazed men, dismembered bodies, and crushed defenses, take Reims, and head toward Paris. Companies A and D were in the front lines, and now their gunners joined the infantry coming out of the dugouts and holes.

Unlike attacks in World War II that included tanks and other mechanized forces, offensives in 1918 were still composed principally of massed infantry. The Rainbows faced thousands of Prussian soldiers in field-gray uniforms and distinctive *stahlhelm*—"coal scuttle" helmets the doughboys called them—who walked toward what they assumed were just the shocked remnant of their adversary. Well-equipped, they moved steadily forward with the supreme confidence. Prussians were considered the best in the kaiser's army. It surely must have been an impressive and frightening sight to watch the wide fields fill with Germans. "At dawn they came over, thousands and thousands of them," said Tom Miller.[25]

Artillery bombardment, however severe, seldom killed every man if infantry were sheltered below ground. Such was the case with the sacrificial French soldiers in the first-line trench. The French *poilu* had defied odds, and many had survived. Shaken and covered with chalky dust, they cleared their weapons and fought the first wave before being overcome. As part of their heroic stand, they alerted the main defense line and indicated the route of attack. The next line of defense was well beyond the first trench, and the German infantry had to cross two miles of hell. Over those long, seemingly unending 3,600 yards, the courageous Prussian guardsmen hunched their shoulders, tucked their heads into their collars, and tightly gripped their long Mauser rifles as they started across fields severely cratered by their own artillery. French and American artillery opened fire, and the Germans were, in turn, hammered by a wave of exploding steel, but rifles and machine guns were silent. When the leading formations were within one hundred paces, the American and French troops opened fired. The impact was devastating.

Machine guns were especially demoralizing against an attacking force when gunners withheld their fire until the enemy was close. The psychological impact of the surprise fire from the multiple guns could cause panic, as well as mass casualties. Platoons from companies D and A were well-camouflaged with nets and grass and had been well-placed in the second-line trenches on July 11. Two Company D guns were placed one hundred yards in front, giving devastating enfilade fire.

The men exercised control and waited until the leading Germans were quite close.

> They were allowed to come within one hundred yards of our lines before a single shot was fired at them. But when the hundred yard line was reached, it was one roar and spit of fire and they were mowed down like hay. It sure was terrible. But wave after wave as they came got the same dope. Machine guns and small rifles just cut them off the face of the earth. . . . Oh, it was one grand, glorious victory for all who partook in it. We had a number of casualties in this company, but the boys are all well and happy, happy because of the victory won by us. Will close with love to all,
>
> Your son,
> Harold L. Smith.[26]

One of the Bucktails who manned the two forward guns was Willis P. Snyder. They were "all nearly crazy with the awful bombardment," he wrote after the war in a detailed description of what happened. "We hadn't been told the first line trenches had been abandoned," he recalled. When his squad saw "thousands" of men coming through bushes, they at first thought they were French because many were wearing French uniforms. Smith, the corporal in charge of Willis's gun, yelled that they were German and started firing but was immediately killed by a bullet. Willis took over. "I couldn't very well miss them, they were so close." The other gun was out of action, and then the enemy was upon him and he fought hand to hand. Willis was the only man to survive from the two forward guns. Two days later, Company D's Captain Brooks took a detachment forward over ground "carpeted with dead Germans." They found the gun intact and buried the two crews.[27]

Kurt Hesse was a German officer in No. 5 Grenadier Regiment, 36th Infantry Division, and faced the prepared defensive positions. Although farther west and therefore not in front of the Rainbow division, his recollection is telling. "[N]ever have I seen so many dead, nor such frightful sights in battle. The Americans on the other shore [of the Marne River] had completely shot to pieces in close combat two of our companies. They had lain in the grain, in semicircular formation, had let us approach, and then from thirty to fifty feet had shot almost all of us down. This foe had nerve, one must allow him this boast; but he also showed a bestial brutality. 'The Americans kill everything!'. . . . A day like the 15th of July affects body and nerves for weeks."[28]

In some cases, the enemy's second wave had to literally climb over their dead and wounded comrades in order to press forward the attack, certain the Allied line would break. The heaviest attack fell on the men of the 165th Infantry and their attached machine-gun company.

Seven times the Germans came. Without well-trained storm troopers, they used outdated infantry tactics. It seemed like the same form of madness that had caused the British soldiers to be slaughtered at the Somme in 1916. In spite of the carnage, German troops reached the Rainbow line and the lads fought hand to hand with bayonet, knives, grenades, and shovels. "Some got to our trenches," recalled Appleton's Miller, "and as most of our machine guns were blown up, we joined the Fighting 69th in driving them out."[29]

The Appleton men fought side by side with the New Yorkers in the 165th Infantry. "That day the Badgers showed the fighting qualities of their totem," Father Duffy recalled:

> Several of their guns were put out of action at the outset of the fight, and practically all of them one by one before the battle was over. In each case Captain Graef, Lieutenant Arens and the other officers, together with the surviving guns, set themselves calmly to work repairing the machines. Corporal Elmer J. Reider fought his gun alone when the rest of the crew was put out of action, and when his gun met the same fate he went back through a heavy barrage and brought up a fresh one. Privates William Brockman and Walter Melchior also distinguished themselves amongst the brave, the former at the cost of his life. There were many other like Melchior who, when their gun was made useless, snatched rifles and grenades of the fallen infantrymen and jumped into the fight. As specialists, they were too valuable to be used up in this way and an order had to be issued to restrain them. Afterwards, Sergeant Ned Boone, said to Father Duffy, "Father, after this I will stand at attention and salute whenever I hear the word Wisconsin."[30]

Casper L. Schommer was manning a gun. "I've never seen so many men come after me in my life," he wrote to his cousin John Schommer from Walter

Reed Hospital in Washington, DC. "When they came I was at my gun and I sure hung back on the trigger and swung the gun back and forth. Out of 70,000 rounds of ammunition at my gun I only used 18,000 rounds from 5:30 in the morning to 1 in the afternoon. When the Boche gave up there were over 1,700 dead lying in front of our 14 machine guns."[31]

The fighting was of the most desperate kind. Hand-to-hand combat in the trenches was a murderous, gruesome affair, more reminiscent of a medieval battle than warfare in the twentieth century. Rifles were used as clubs to break bones and smash faces and heads; bayonets were like spears, stabbing and slashing. Trench shovels with sharpened edges cleaved like the battle-axes of old. Blood spattered faces, uniforms, and hands. For soldiers involved in this most brutal and personal combat, they tried to kill whatever soldier was in front of them who wore an enemy uniform. There was no time to think, no time to look about and survey the scene; if it wore the enemy's uniform, it must be destroyed. Afterward, an infantryman in the 165th, Martin Hogan, related: "They broke furiously upon our line . . . [it] became a dizzy whirl of hand-to-hand combats. . . . Clubbed rifles were splintered against skulls and shoulder bone; bayonets were plunged home, withdrawn and plunged home again. . . . Our front line became a gruesome mess."[32] The troops of the 150th Machine Gun fought side by side with the infantry. "A bunch of [Germans] ran up dressed in French uniforms . . . and got close enough to throw grenades at a gun-crew of the 150th Machine Gun battalion, killing two Wisconsin gunners, and putting the gun out of action," said one report. "Another Wisconsin man, mortally wounded but still at his gun, drove them away, and died firing."[33]

With machine guns knocked out, the gunners grappled with their foe in the chalky dust. Sergeant Elmer J. Reider in Company A, known to his comrades as the "Original Elmer," won the French Croix de Guerre and a gold Wound Chevron (title changed to Purple Heart in 1932) for his exploits that day. When his Hotchkiss was knocked out of action, Reider crawled back, found a working gun, and single-handedly dragged the big weapon back to the emplacement and resumed firing. When the Germans were too close to use the gun, he threw grenades, helping stop and then drive off the determined enemy.

Original Elmer wasn't the only battalion soldier to show exceptional heroism in Company A. Private First Class William L. Brockman, along with Private Willis P. Snyder of Company D who had manned one of the forward guns, were singled out for the second highest award for gallantry. Both men were awarded the Distinguished Service Cross; only the Medal of Honor is higher. This beautifully sculpted two-inch bronze cross was established by President Woodrow Wilson on January 2, 1918. "While manning a machine gun against the enemy, and after all his comrades had either been killed or wounded, Snyder remained at his post and, in the hand-to-hand fight which ensued, forced the enemy to retire, and, although wounded he attempted to carry back his wounded comrades." "The Distinguished Service Cross is presented to William L. Brockman, Private First Class, U.S. Army, for extraordinary heroism in the action near Auberive, France, July 15, 1918. Private Brockman continued to operate his machine gun against the attacking enemy after all other members of the crew had been killed. Then, going forward to rescue a wounded comrade, was himself instantly killed."[34]

"Appleton Co. A was up in the first line of trenches," wrote Fond du Lac's Roy Watson, "and the way they piled up the Germans was something fierce. The Germans never gained an inch of ground and it certainly cost them a pile of men."[35] Another Fondy soldier, Elmer Grabinski, praised the men in Company A. "The Appleton boys did the trick," he told his parents. "They deserve all the war crosses [Distinguished Service Cross] in France."[36]

The Fond du Lac and Oshkosh companies held in reserve had few casualties, but one of the wounded was E. J. Stark, a wagoner. As the Germans shelled rear areas, Stark was hit by a shrapnel ball and wrote to his parents from the hospital. "Dear Mother," he began, "I had a little bad luck [but] I am getting along fine." Despite his wound, Stark was worried about his mule, perhaps because he was hoping he didn't have to pull his cart by hand. "[T]hose centimeters [shrapnel ball] lamed one of my mules but he will be alright by the time I am, and then I will get revenge at the Boche."[37] An Oshkosh soldier, Arthur Davis, elated by the victory, related a story to his sister, Theresa. "I was in a small dugout with a top about eighteen inches thick," he told her. After enduring hours of shelling by himself, he'd had enough. "[A]t 9:00 I made a dash for the large dug-out about 2,000 yards away and it was some dash, too. When the shrapnel would burst over my head, my helmet felt like it was no bigger than a fifty-cent piece, but I made it o.k." Davis didn't want to go into detail about it because he said she'd have already read all about it in the newspaper. "We call it the battle of Chock Hill," he told her, "which turned out to be a famine as we did not get anything to eat for twenty-four hours for the reason that they could not fetch it through the rain of shell that the Boche kept up. There is one glorious thing about it all—we beat them and we beat them bad we are going to do this as long as they last. . . . With love and kisses to you and mother and dad."[38]

After the battle, Private Edward Steckbauer wrote enthusiastically to his mother in Oshkosh: "Well, at 4:30 the Germans came over and what our boys didn't do to them is not worth mentioning they simply mowed them down like one would mow down grass . . . it seems [we] . . . put a crimp in their plans."[39] Another member of Company C, Harold Smith, sent a glowing report back to his parents that same day, "when the 100 yds. line was reached it was one roar and spit of fire and they were mowed down like hay. It sure was terrible. . . . Machine guns and small rifles just cut them right off the face of the earth. . . . Oh it was one grand glorious victory . . . the boys are all well and happy."[40]

The battalion soldiers were dead tired and dirty, some were wounded, but the biggest grievance and predicament, as Art Davis told his sister, was that they had had no food for twenty-four hours. "If only we could get something to eat we would be alright," explained the anonymous scribe in Company C.[41] Men wrote home about food, or sometimes the lack of it, with special emphasis on bread; its quality, comparison to bread at home, or its taste. There were no K or C rations like the GIs of World War II, so they were likely eating their reserve rations. They existed on probably less than two thousand calories a day, which for men living outside and performing tough, stressful, physical work was totally inadequate to keep them healthy and vigorous. They scrounged where and when they could, and when possible, visited *estimates* behind the lines, but once up front they were totally dependent on the supply system. Even so, they could not cook because lighting a fire within sight of the enemy was a guarantee that shelling would follow.

Each company had a mess sergeant who had the responsibility of feeding his company. He was in charge of a mobile, mule-drawn, kitchen with a wood-burning stove and oven, and the intent was that soldiers receive a hot meal every day. That seldom happened at the front. The army had standard recipes for the company sergeants, who drew rations from the supply column. The food was selected to provide active men with the calories they needed. However, the mess sergeant and his mobile kitchen often could not keep up with the column for a multitude of reasons, or, during rapid advances, were simply unable locate the company. Even without these challenges, the kitchen could not move too close to the front because if the enemy saw smoke from the kitchen, shelling would certainly follow. Men were detailed to bring the prepared food forward in special containers, but during battle this was impossible, and the men subsisted on their reserve rations or other food kept in their packs. One characteristic of a veteran soldier was that he had at least some food with him. When the companies were in reserve areas or pulled out of the line for rest, the mess sergeants did a good job and often augmented the standard fare with fresh food obtained from French sources. Many of the Wisconsin men noted in their letters that they put on weight while in France.

Food aside, the battalion had not just endured the caldron of battle, they had emerged victorious and rightly proud of their performance. Not everyone, though, was well and happy.

Company A had the highest casualties, and one of the badly wounded was John Pierre. Two weeks after the battle, he wrote to his mother from the hospital where he lay. "I am finished I guess with the front but one thing I can feel thankful for and that is, they left me my arms, legs, body and face so what more do I want to feel thankful for? All they did was took a nice slice of the upper part of my leg." He tried to be cheerful, perhaps because he knew his brother was among the dead. "A nurse just gave me a piece of butter-scotch candy," which was worthy of note because candy was a rarity. "The reason I got it, was she made a tear fall while fixing up three shrapnel wounds. They were small, but oh my! I told her she could do that every day for a piece of candy like that."[42]

Among Company A's dead was the "fine and gallant" Harvey Pierre, as well as William Brown, William Hageman, William Brockman, Carl Norenberg, William Schafelke, Arthur Kositzke, and Edward Weinfurter. The article in the *Appleton Evening Crescent* stated, "For here in this vicinity as well as Appleton are young men who belong with the Rainbow Division which has been, and is, in the thickest of the fight and blood is now being spilled in the allied cause." The article noted that thirty-two-year-old Carl Norenberg had married Eva Hancock just two weeks before the company left for Camp Douglas in August 1917, and that Eva had just had a baby that spring.[43] William Hageman and Edward Weinfurter were neighbors and buddies and had enlisted together in 1917. They died together, and in 1921, their bodies were returned home, and their burials were conducted at the same time.[44] Casualties were light in the other companies, especially the Oshkosh unit, which was in reserve. "When one stops to think that most men simply had small holes dug in the ground for protection," the company narrator rationalized, "it seems almost a miracle that we had only 10 casualties in the Company."[45]

The Germans withdrew in late afternoon on July 15. They had gained territory to the west but had failed to break the Allied line anywhere along their line of advance. This was the highpoint of the last German drive. When the offensives began in March, some Allied generals feared that four years of stalemate were over and that Germany might in fact be victorious. When it ended on that hot day, everyone knew the war had at long last reached a turning point, and that American troops were a force to be reckoned with. Some German companies left 60 percent of their men dead in front of the Rainbows. The 42nd Division casualties were 43 officers and 1,610 enlisted men.

The battles east and west of Reims were a momentous victory. Not only had the immense German offensive been stopped, their enemy had suffered grievous losses: 168,000 casualties. Despite the victory, General Ludendorff was still considering resuming the offensive. But on July 18, French General Foch unleashed the divisions he had assembled in secrecy and struck a sledgehammer blow at the enemy near Soissons. The German Army of 1918 was not the same force it had been a few years earlier. Not only was it worn out and its best soldiers casualties, but the German leadership had grown careless and consumed by their own self-assurance that the Allies were close to being finished. Foch's offensive caught them totally by surprise, pushed the Germans at Soissons, and pressured them at Reims and other points along their line. The attack threatened their main supply route in the already poorly supplied Marne region. The Germans forward divisions were vulnerable and thus were forced to withdraw.

As a result of the battle, and the fast-paced repositioning of divisions for the counterattacks, Allied divisions became tired and mixed up, units confused, and orders failed to reach some companies. There was a sense of urgency in the air. The 150th received an order to move out and leave their guns and ammunition behind. After marching about two miles, the order was rescinded, and they were told to return and pick up their guns and ammunition. The Company C writer noted with disgust and dismay that German planes were everywhere.

In the dark of midnight on July 18, the 150th packed up and moved to their staging area. "We certainly were a tough looking bunch coming back, all white with chalk dust," said Roy Watson, "but we are now camped along side of a river, and the boys are busy washing, and swimming. The weather is fine." The swim, however, had a tragic ending for the Pennsylvania company when Private Nelson Bowers drowned.[46] Lieutenant Bahr also found time to pen a letter to Oshkosh's mayor, A. C. McHenry. "[T]his company . . . is ready to do or die. . . . I do really believe this is the beginning of the end. . . . I feel proud to be able to take part in this great war for democracy."[47] Bill Heiss was staying near a large impressive chateau with formal gardens, the home of an old couple who had an attractive daughter, and of course the young woman became the fixation for most of the soldiers. "She's about 20 years old and some looker," he told his brother Tim. "She's always sitting in the window sewing and the fellows hang around all day." They didn't have much time to get to know one another, and that was frustrating. "The lady and the girl are trying to parly with me but I can't get this French at all. They understand about as much English." And then it was time for the battalion to move on.[48]

The 150th was to move about twenty miles by train to the southwest, to Château-Thierry, and on a fine moonlit night they began boarding. It was a night perfect for aircraft. When the war started, the men were in awe of airplanes. By this point, however, they hated them; it was terrifying and seemed impersonal. They noted frequently that German planes were seldom challenged by American or French aircraft. "The hum of motors above us seemed to increase every minute and it seemed as though there were a hundred of them directly over us," said one Oshkosh soldier. Search lights were playing the sky, and anti-aircraft and machine guns tried their best to stop the unseen foe. "[I]t sent a chill down our backs, for we knew it meant only a matter of seconds before they would unload their cargo of death on us and go back and get some more." The bombs missed the Oshkosh company, but the Appleton and Fond du Lac units were not so fortunate.[49]

A. J. Kraemer offered a detailed description of what happened that night when he wrote his cousin, Alex. "We had just nicely commenced loading when we heard a mass of planes heading our way." Like the "droning of a giant bee," the planes came ever closer, he explained. "Everyone ceased talking and lay real quiet . . . all of a sudden we heard a whizz-bang and up goes our engine . . . and one hit the car next to us. Then we did jump: no shoes, shirt or socks, and believe me, we did run . . . to the center of a wheat field and there we stayed, waiting and praying for daylight. We lost a few men. . . . Every time I hear one of them planes it sends what they say a very, very funny feeling all the way through."[50] In his typical terse way, Herbert Granger noted: "bombed train and burned depot 20 wounded and 1 killed Thot [thought] all hell had broke loose."[51] One of the dead was Roy Watson, who had just rejoined the company after recovering from poison gas.

Company A's mess sergeant, William Lang, was hit by shrapnel. His best friend, George Vermeulen, was the first to reach Lang after he was wounded. "Don't bother with me because I can't live, and just look after the others," he told Vermeulen. But Lang was taken to the Hospital No. 13 anyway, where he died the following morning. Vermeulen explained to Lang's sister that he "fixed him up and put a new uniform on him," and he "was buried with all military honors in a regular army coffin and a big American flag over the coffin. . . . The French people here come up every Saturday and Sunday and place flowers on the graves."[52]

The planes returned later when the train was near the town of Esbly, there to be greeted by the unit's machines mounted on flat cars. Tracers flowed into the dark sky but, luckily for the battalion, all the bombs missed. When things were sorted out, the 150th rode for twenty-four-hours to reach La Ferté-sous-Jouarre, a trip that in peacetime took three hours. Once all the companies and their mules were gathered, they headed northeast toward Château-Thierry. They marched down the Marne Valley, green meadows and yellow wheat fields. After a brief break by the Marne River, two days later they set out for Château-Thierry on the Soissons-Château-Thierry Road. For families back in Fond du Lac, Oshkosh, and Appleton, and towns across the state, the name Château-Thierry would forever bring grief and heartache.

8

Château-Thierry

Believe me it was all the hell any body wanted.
Herbert Granger,
diary,
July 28, 1918

Today the town of Château-Thierry does not show the scars and pain of the horrendous battle that took place there a century ago. It is a pleasant, quiet community of perhaps fifteen thousand people, situated on a bend of the famous Marne River. At one end of the town square is an attractive church, a Protestant memorial to the herculean efforts of tired American soldiers who fought there in 1918. The American Memorial Church, as it is called, was built by American donations in 1922 as a way to remember the fallen. Exquisite stained-glass windows depict French and American historical figures united in a bond of friendship spanning the American Revolution to World War I. The windows recall that the town of Château-Thierry was once the epicenter of war. It was the place where the war caught up to the 150th Machine Gun Battalion.

Despite the initial success of General Foch's July 18 offensive, the Allied attack faltered. The German Army, weakened by its spring offensives, remained formidable. The massive Marne salient or bulge looked something like a backwards capital *D* anchored by Soissons in the west, Reims in the east, and with

117

Château-Thierry at the tip of the bulge. The German high command realized that their hold on the Marne salient was uncertain, but they were not yet ready to give it up without a fight. If they could stop the Allies at the natural barrier of the Ourcq River, part way into the bulge protruding into the Allied lines, they would gain time to move tired, depleted divisions to their old defensive line on the Vesle and the Aisne Rivers. As well, forcing the Allies to fight held out the promise that they might hold on to the larger gains in the north, won during the first phase of the Michael Offensive. For these reasons, they were fiercely determined to hold at the natural Ourcq River barrier and compel the Americans and French divisions to batter themselves bloody. Unknown to the Germans, or to the 150th moving into the battle zone, General Pershing had at long last succeeded in his desire to have created a true American Army. This force would be under the command of American generals and consist solely of American divisions, and plans were being prepared for an all-American battle. The war had moved to a new phase.

General Foch and other Allied leaders believed that Germany had been given not just a bloody nose but a real drubbing and might collapse with continued pressure across the salient. Near Château-Thierry, the American 1st, 2nd, 26th and 28th Divisions, and the French Moroccan, 164th, and 167th Divisions pursued the enemy in their assigned section of the salient. In other areas of the salient, British and French divisions assaulted the Germans. Leaders supposed that that their adversary's morale had been dealt a severe blow, and the average front-line German soldier was exhausted. The generals reasoned that if the foe were attacked relentlessly—before he could rest and refit and think things through—the initiative would clearly be with the Allies. While the latter was true, that the advantage had now passed to the Allies, the former was not. The German armies in the Marne salient had recovered quickly from their surprise on July 18. A short history of the Rainbow division published the year after the war, admitted that "the morale of the Boche was still high—as high as ever, in fact . . . [he was] prepared to try to delay even a dashing American effort to drive him out."[1]

German resistance increased, and they were aided by the terrain, which consisted of ravines and hills. The enemy established numerous ingenious ambushes that took a heavy toll on the advancing infantry. Before the Allies could recover and retaliate, the Germans retreated and set new traps. At first no one could determine if the Germans planned to stand and fight, or whether the opposition was only strong rear-guard action meant to delay Foch's attacking divisions. Continuing to strike was an opportunity to pummel the enemy and force him to abandon badly needed supplies and weapons. If the German Army meant to make a new defensive line, the sooner it was attacked the weaker it would be.

The 42nd Division was chosen to take its turn as the tip of the spear and moved forward to replace the exhausted 26th "Yankee" Division on July 25. This part of the enormous Second Battle of the Marne, as the campaign came to be called, would continue through August, and would be referred to as the "Battle of Château-Thierry." It began July 26 and ended August 3, an episode that Colonel Douglas MacArthur, in the Rainbow's 84th Brigade, later called "the six bitterest days and nights of the war."[2]

A convoy of small French trucks, called camions and driven by Indonesians, arrived to move the machine gunners forward. This was a sure sign that they were headed toward "the furnace," as one soldier put it, because trucks were used only when the men were needed quickly. Emergency rations were also issued. The field kitchens and supply wagons, along with their ammunition carts, had to make their way forward separately. It was a rough, unpleasant trip in the canvas-covered vehicles. Many recollections recalled the constant, cloying stench of unburied dead.

Those converging, muddy roads were heavily congested with American, French, and British troops. In fact, they were in chaos. "I doubt if Fifth Avenue in good old New York has been a busier thoroughfare than that road leading from Château-Thierry to the front that night," chronicled the anonymous Oshkosh author.[3] Units were mixed up and lacked cohesion from forced and night marches. The Marne Valley roads led through the shattered village of Château-Thierry. As an Ohio soldier in 166th Infantry passed through the town, he recalled, "[W]e saw ghastly evidence of the Huns' departure—the ruined homes; the ruthless destruction coupled with the terrible artillery bombardment has left the town a scene of desolation. Household goods all over the streets, trees down, buildings torn to pieces, marks of rifle and machine gun bullets on everything."[4]

When the vehicles stopped outside Château-Thierry, the men were ordered out, and the trucks immediately turned around and headed back. Everyone was eager to get off the roads and get moving even though the men were bone tired, as roads were prime targets for enemy artillery and aircraft. There were German supplies, uniforms, weapons, and other material scattered everywhere. The machine gunners were ordered to follow the fast-moving infantry, which proved to be almost impossible. "We were carrying our packs and our machine gun equipment with extra boxes of ammunition," recalled Lieutenant Parkinson in the 151st. "[E]ach man had no less than 60 pounds and some of them 100 pounds extra equipment to carry."[5] They straggled, despite the attempts of officers to keep them together. A cold rain had set in, but it would stop for a while and then start again. The men walked as fast as they could in wet uniforms and kit, boots and threadbare socks saturated and squishing water with each step, soles clumped with thick clay pancakes. Parkinson called it a "killing pace."

That wasn't all. Even as the Germans retreated, their artillery periodically bombarded the roads to impede the advance. "We soon crossed an open field and hurried to the next shelter of trees. . . . As we stopped for a minute to regain our breath the German began shelling heavily. . . . We forged on."[6] The American and French artillery responded in kind, always pressuring the withdrawing Germans. "Our guns were keeping up a constant fire . . . [we] started on a march which was to last all night . . . we marched through a woods nearly three miles. Here at times, it was almost necessary to don our gas masks, as the Germans were retreating so fast our men did not have time to bury the German dead. . . . This, coupled with loss of sleep was almost unbearable, but we grit our teeth and kept on."[7]

Behind the gun squads, the men in the support units did not have it any easier. Thousands of men, trucks, wagons, and artillery from both armies had churned the road into ever deeper mud. The cantankerous, exhausted mules were not always able to move carts and wagons through the thick mire and out of shell holes, so the men pushed and pulled their laden vehicles through the sludge.

At last they arrived at the front lines on July 27, taking over lines held by the exhausted 26th Division. The 150th was disorganized and disjointed, and worn out. Their assembly area was a short distance from the river, a forest called the Fôret-de-Fère and the adjoining smaller woods. Enemy artillery shelled the woods regularly "with pitiless accuracy." The Pennsylvania company once again found itself out of luck and was hit especially hard, with many wounded and dead. "No ambulance could be secured until 7:30 the next morning and the poor stricken boys must bear their sufferings as best they might," recalled a postwar history. One Bucktail said, "We found it hell in its hottest state."[8]

The main line of German defense was on the north side of the Ourcq River, but they had also built strong points on the south side to delay the Americans. The most prominent defensive point was in a large clearing around the Croix Rouge Farm, which controlled the main road leading to the river. This farm had to be cleared of the enemy before the 42nd could advance to the river. Germans excelled in defense and had put their battlefield expertise to work. The Marne Valley was a beautiful place, not unlike Wisconsin in some respects. It was a wooded region dotted with grain fields, thick forests, ravines, orchards, and stout old farmhouses with massive stone barns. Each farm had a courtyard enclosed by thick masonry walls. They were defending terrain they had selected. With an expert's eye, officers picked the most advantageously located farmhouses and turned each into a fort with dozens of machine guns so skillfully camouflaged that detection was exceedingly difficult. These guns were positioned so every angle of attack was covered by intersecting fields of fire. Well-hidden rifleman enhanced the defense. Despite the Allies superiority in infantry and artillery, the odds favored the Germans. Attackers faced a daunting barrier, hard to surmount with their limited weapons and inadequate communication.

The first phase of the attack against the Croix Rouge Farm was made by the 84th Brigade, 167th (Alabama) and 168th Infantry (Iowa), and the 151st Machine Gun Battalion (Georgia). Infantry units were committed to battle before the entire division was assembled. The defending troops in the Marne salient were commanded by Crown Prince Wilhelm, a seasoned and successful commander. The combat for Croix Rouge was without mercy, and the doughboy infantry incurred considerable casualties, and they had a rough time of it. Meanwhile, in the chaos along the road one platoon from Company A had gotten ahead of the battalion and tangled with retreating Germans. "[We] mingled with the Dutch," wrote Casper Schommer to his cousin. "I shot three of them with my automatic pistol, one of which was shooting liquid fire at some of our guys."[9] Everyone realized that this was clearly no small rear-guard delaying action; the Germans meant to stay until they were pushed out. The farm was cleared by July 27, the stage was set for the larger battle and a period of heavy fighting for the 42nd Division.

Beyond the Croix Rouge Farm was the small village called Villers-sur-Fere, and then wheat fields and orchards that led to the river. On the other side of the Ourcq was the main town of Fère-en-Tardenois. To the east of that main town was the village of Seringes-et-Nesles, and a bit farther east was Sergy. In between was the Meurcy Farm. Both were more or less directly in front of the 150th. The 165th Infantry was to attack and capture Meurcy Farm and Sergy; the 166th Infantry was to capture Seringes-et-Nesles. The 167th and 168th Infantry were to the right, and on the left of the Rainbow Division were French divisions. Beyond the immediate objectives were the Fôret-de-Nesles, and more villages and farmhouses. "[N]ow he was in a great natural fortress," explained the postwar history, "with the village of Sergy in the valley backed by bare hills that sloped up the plateaus eighty meters high."[10] All the fields and orchards on both sides of the river and the small tree groves here and there were overlooked by an enemy strongpoint on Hills 184 and 212. Observation balloons were always in view. With their excellent optics, Germans in the balloons could see the Americans as they moved north. Observers called down deadly artillery using detailed maps that included precise coordinates of all approaches, drawn before withdrawing. Enemy aircraft had total control of the air and their planes roamed at will strafing the advancing doughboys. Air superiority enabled the Germans to keep their observation balloons aloft to provide a superior level of control for their artillery. The number of aircraft, and their ability to strafe at any time was a frequent comment.

Before the battle, commanders changed the way the 42nd Division's independent machine gun battalions were to be used in the upcoming battle, a revi-
sion that would have profound consequences. Although an integral part of the
division, not every officer knew how to make use of the power of machine guns.
Infantry officers had minimal training on how to deploy heavy machine guns in
battle, and they had limited combat experience to draw upon. The true supremacy of a division's machine gun battalions came when they were massed and
centrally controlled. In addition, each company officer had to give their platoons
freedom to place and use the guns to achieve the specific mission assigned.
They did this because once battle started, there was no way to convey orders to
gun squads, other than by runner. For that reason, officers trained their sergeants
well and expected them to control their guns at specific, identified targets.

Infantry regiments already had guns assigned to them, but the order was to
give the infantry companies more machine guns from the battalions, and to
have those gun squads support their assigned infantry company and fire on
"targets of opportunity." This generally meant targets they could actually see.
Instead of keeping the battalion machine-gun units together to deliver concentrated and coordinated barrage fire from safer, well-established firing positions
behind the infantry, the battalion companies were divided and assigned to *accom-
pany* attacking infantry. Each machine-gun company had three platoons. A
decision was made to attach a platoon, or four Hotchkiss guns, to each infantry
company, and to have the platoons move forward with their guns as the infantry
attacked.

As a rule, the infantry was poorly trained in effective offensive tactics, and
those tactics they knew were outdated and of little value in this situation. The
machine gunners were never expected to advance like infantry, so their prepara-
tion was similarly limited. The decision to use the guns in this way was clearly
against the best practices advised by divisional machine-gun officers (each division had an officer assigned to advise the division on use of the battalion guns),
and went counter to what the French and British had learned and put in practice over the past four years. Neither were the men of the 150th used to this
new arrangement. The 150th had been trained and exercised as an independent
unit, and now, on the eve of a great battle against an experienced and courageous
enemy, that security was stripped away.

Powerful, crew-served weapons like machine guns and artillery were far
more devastating when carefully directed and controlled. Working together,
these weapons could influence the outcome of a battle. Once separated and
used individually, that supremacy and power was drastically reduced. After the
attack started, there would be no way to communicate with platoons as they
moved forward, other than by runner.[11] Because the gun crews would not be

in communication with battalion or divisional headquarters, it would be impossible to direct the guns to deliver concentrated fire on priority targets, or to create the lethal multigun barrages that hindered or prevented the movement of enemy troops. Machine guns moving forward with their infantry company could only fire on targets identified by the platoon leader or the infantry company commander. On a practical level, it also meant that a platoon sergeant did not have the same effectiveness of command over the squads and sections. What was worse, however, was that by advancing with the infantry, it exposed the highly trained crews to much greater danger, risks that should be avoided or minimized. Moreover, it would be physically hard to bring the 110-pound Hotchkiss guns forward under fire, in the mud, and casualties were sure to result.

The 150th remained sheltered in the Fôret-de-Fère, a cheerless place. Trees had been shattered by artillery and looked like forlorn skeletons against the somber rainy sky. The water-saturated earth was plowed by the explosion of shells and also full of fallen branches and tree trunks. The incessant rain made everything worse, and the 150th tried to get comfortable in the soaked woodland. Grouped by company, the men must have joked and made small talk as they looked to their gear and prepared to move forward, to engage the enemy in their first offensive. They probably looked at each other and wondered who would fall and who would be there when the battle ended. Letters and diaries do not reflect what went on in the Fôret-de-Fère, but it's not hard to image the men gathering in small groups, eating and sharing whatever they had because the rolling field kitchens did not keep up with the companies. The soldiers still wore the same filthy uniforms and underwear they had on at Champagne, now soaked with rain and caked with mud. The probing, seeking whine and explosions of enemy artillery shells still occasionally explored the woods, the buzz of razor-sharp shards chewed trees, dropped trunks and limbs, and tore flesh.

About 6:00 p.m. on July 27, Company A was ordered to join the Second Battalion of the 165th Infantry just south of Villiers-sur-Fere, a village of about one hundred buildings and a forward command for the division. The Appleton boys moved ahead but skirted Villiers-sur-Fere because it was under heavy artillery fire. Captain Lothar Graef could not find his assigned position in the dark, and the company walked until reached the banks of the Ourcq River. There, Graef asked a French sentry if they had seen any Americans; he said no. Graef knew something was wrong, or they were lost, and so he went back to the village. About midnight, he met Major Alexander Anderson, commander of the Second Battalion of the 165th Infantry. Anderson sent him back to the Fôret-de-Fère to rest and prepare, and Graef scattered his exhausted men because the woods were still under periodic artillery fire. They noticed Ohio infantrymen asleep, and so they spread their blankets among the Buckeyes. "I lay down next to one of the soldiers and pulled his blanket partly over me," recalled John Hantschel in 1943. "I was awakened . . . in the morning. I noticed that my right arm was bloody. Then I discovered that this fellow was dead. And so were all the other Ohio men lying there. We thought they were sleeping."[12]

After a few hours of fitful rest, Graef was awakened early the next morning, July 28, and told that the Appleton company had just fifteen minutes to get ready to join the attack, scheduled to begin at 3:45 a.m. The company was to move toward the Ourcq River and prepare to attack. Across the river was all German-held. What they suspected, but did not know, were to what degree the interconnected German defensives commanded the entire area. There was misinformation and confusion, as some believed the French had already crossed the river and taken the main town of Fère-en-Tardenois, which was in fact still in enemy hands. (French forces would soon take the town.)

The weary Appleton men, like the rest of the 150th, had had no breakfast as they scurried to get themselves together and reach their assigned areas. The Fond du Lac, the Pennsylvanians, and the Oshkosh men found themselves also in the same situation. All four companies had an assigned area and, while the circumstances differed, the overall experience was the same for every company. Orders were to keep five-minute intervals between platoons, which was tough in the dark and with muddy conditions. It was so dark that the platoons moved by compass. In the case of one platoon in Company C, they had just started when they found a ration wagon stuck in mud and its load of bread spilled everywhere. Since they had not eaten much except hardtack for several days, they stopped to gather as much as they could. When the mules could no longer pull the carts through the mud, the men were ordered to do it. "The Germans were following every move with their artillery," stated the recorder in the Oshkosh company, "[in] about one and one-eighth mile, I saw 5,000,000 German shells of all sizes and shapes."[13]

There were delays, and the attack was postponed. Sergeants John Hantschel and Iveaux Miller were sent back to find Company A's reserve platoon under the command of Lieutenant Keller.[14] The two men separated, each taking a half circle through the woods. At about 7:00 a.m., near the tiny village of Villier-sur-Denois, shortly after they parted, Hantschel was caught by artillery. "It certainly was a funny sensation when I went down and saw my leg shoot up in front of me and the warm blood flow over me," he recalled in a newspaper interview.[15] He lay there in absolute agony. Finally, shock and loss of blood rendered him unconscious.

Both the Americans and Germans had an evacuation chain designed to get medical aid to wounded men as quickly as circumstances allowed, and medical facilities and staff were part of every division's Sanitary Train. Each soldier carried a basic battle dressing pack on his web belt, but it did not include pain medication, so comrades did what they could soon after injury. Army records show about 40 percent of casualties could move to the rear without help, but the other 60 percent were immobile. Comrades helped each other as much as they could and often assisted the walking wounded back to the aid station.[16]

For those who were immobile, it was a long wait for help. Stretcher bearers wearing blue armbands worked in a constant stream. All of the unarmed bearers were volunteers who had attended a ten-week course on basic medical aid. Working in teams of four or six, these men were the first real help that a casualty received. They bandaged wounds, gave morphine shots, and put wooden splints on broken limbs. When conditions were too rough to carry an actual stretcher, the bearers often put the wounded on their backs. The men held stretcher bearers in high regard; everyone realized that they were not immune from enemy fire as they assisted others. The survival of seriously wounded soldiers depended in large part on how quickly they were evacuated to the first level of medical aid. At the Ourcq, getting help to casualties tested both the medical evacuation system and men's courage.

The first level of help was the regimental or battalion aid station, designed to support four companies. The stations had limited resources. The aid station for the 150th and the infantry was in a chateau in Villers-sur-Fere under the command of Major George Lawrence, and it too was under enemy fire. Once at the aid station, the priority was to stop or minimize bleeding, apply splints, and to take basic precautions against infection by cutting away dirty clothing around the wound, cleanse the area, give a quarter-grain of morphine, and administer antitetanus serum. They tried to treat shock and, when appropriate, gave soldiers food and water. But Hantschel was alone; it was dark when he awoke. The skies had cleared, and in the moonlight he could see Algerian soldiers burying the dead, and he cried out. Hantschel was placed on a stretcher for the long, jarring, painful trip to a hospital, much of the route under fire. His Algerian saviors dropped him several times as they sought cover from the probing artillery, which wounded Hantschel in the arm; he had also been gassed. At long last he arrived at the hospital, and there, Captain Ellis gave him a cigarette and some chocolate while he waited his turn with the busy, tired doctors. Upon examination, doctors realized he had "only a spark of life." He again lost consciousness.[17]

The wounded would be moved to a dressing station as the next step, and they either walked if they were able, or were transported by the division Ambulance Section. A steady stream of Ford ambulances and mule-drawn vehicles moved around the clock. The ride was awful, and many doughboys recalled the agony of the trip, especially if a man had broken bones, because the ceaseless jarring caused dreadful pain as the ends of the bones moved. There was a higher level of care at a dressing station, but casualties were still within the enemy's zone of fire. If a man was not too badly wounded, he could return to his unit after resting. The dressing stations served as collecting points, and the wounded were next moved to a field hospital, the last part of divisional medical care. For a wounded man like Hantschel, there were field hospitals at Epieds and Château-Thierry. The focus was on triage; casualties were sorted into "light" and "serious" cases, with gas casualties segregated for special treatment. Field hospitals did not have in-depth surgical facilities or X-ray capabilities and mainly treated the lightly wounded, who could stay up to two weeks. After triage, the badly wounded, like Hantschel, were again loaded into ambulances for a trip to an evacuation hospital. When Hantschel awoke three days later, minus his right leg, he was in an evacuation hospital.[18]

An evacuation hospital was set far enough behind the lines to be out of range of artillery, near a railroad line. These hospitals provided a full range of services. For the 150th, the hospital was at Étampes-sur-Marne near Château-Thierry. The first step was assessment, and casualties were operated on according to priority. A typical evacuation hospital had one thousand beds, and two operating rooms with ten operating teams who worked in twelve-hour shifts. Surgeons used either ether or chloroform to anesthetize the wounded. Nurses were women, but all other staff were male. Patients were cared for in wards, and nurses and orderlies attended to daily wound dressings and daily irrigation with what was called the Carrel-Dakin's solution, a low concentration of bleach and boric acid. This was necessary to prevent what was called "gas gangrene." French soil contained bacteria from centuries of mature fertilizer, and this caused terrible infections. The Carrel-Dakin's mixture flushed and killed the bacteria, but it was decidedly unpleasant. There were not many pain killers available: only morphine, codeine, and aspirin. Blood transfusions were risky and rare because identifying blood type was not possible in the field, and the science was still in its infancy. The wounded could stay at an evacuation hospital for up to two weeks.

From the evacuation hospital, the wounded were loaded into a hospital train for a trip to a base hospital. These special railroad cars had rows of narrow beds and were staffed by nurses and orderlies. Base hospitals were far from the fighting and were generally large, well-staffed and supplied, and quiet. Some of these hospitals were specialized and focused on particular types of injuries. Here the men received additional surgical operations, and recovered and re-gained their strength. When assessment showed they had recovered sufficiently, they were sent back to their unit, or in the case of severely wounded, back to the

United States.[19] Hantschel was sent back to America and arrived in New York on October 2, 1918, for a lengthy stay in a New Jersey hospital.

Conrad Paffenroth was wounded early in the battle, and from a base hospital he wrote home to his sister in Oshkosh. "This is sure a better life here in the hospital than out in the field where you sleep on the ground and then you are called upon at any minute to roll your pack and get ready to move. Here in the hospitals you are between white sheets and a nice nurse to take care of you and your troubles. Here you are sure of being let alone so you can rest." Company C's Lieutenant Jung was wounded at same time as Paffenroth, and the two visited often, which helped pass time. "[A]ll we have to do is eat and sleep— some life here, what I mean. I don't mind staying here until the end of the d— old war."[20] Not everyone felt that way. "These are the hardest sixteen days that I have put in in my life," Carl Schneider in base Hospital 43 complained to Rose Baier back in Oshkosh. "I have had more than enough bed now."[21] Part of the longing to get out of the hospital was because there was always the nagging fear that instead of being returned to their unit and rejoining their comrades, they might instead be reassigned to another unit.

The army used female nurses to help staff the hospitals, and Red Cross nurses were also sent to France. While the medical organization and methods the army developed was advanced and provided a high level of care, the enormous volume of wounded tested the modern system to its limits. Women nurses were essential and gave a boost to the morale of the wounded. Every once in a while a casualty would be treated by someone they knew, and that was the case with Oshkosh's Earl Day, who was severely gassed on July 31. While in base Hospital No. 3, he sent a letter to his mother, who lived on Oshkosh's Tenth Street. The gas, he wrote, "[m]ade me pretty sick for a few days but am feeling fairly good now. . . . Was somewhat surprised when I got to the hospital and found two of the nurses from Oshkosh. One was Frances Gunz and the other Mary Nigl, of Ninth Street." His family surely knew the Nigl's because Oshkosh's social life revolved around the neighborhood. Day closed his letter by saying, "Cannot begin to tell you about the battle. It was a bad one."[22]

The nurses knew how much their presence meant to the wounded, and they were proud of this important work. "When a convoy [of wounded] comes in we are terribly busy," Mary Nigl wrote to her friend, Minnie Prautch. "[T]here is joy in one's work to know that the patients can be relieved of their pain and made comfortable and when they are feeling better, it is a real picnic in the wards . . . they want to go right back to the trenches and repay the enemy for each pain they've had since they were wounded."[23]

Back on the battlefield, the men of the 150th were fully engaged. As in most wars, information was either not relayed or failed to reach some units, and such was the case with the Appleton unit. The attack was without coordination, and as the 165th and 166th Infantry moved forward, so did their supporting machine gun platoons. A heavy morning ground-mist shielded the doughboys from observation as they moved north toward the river, but the mist suddenly lifted near the river, and Germans immediately opened fire. In the case of the Appleton unit, the men took cover in a sunken road near the village. The land was open before them, and it swept up a long slope to the heights beyond. Lothar Graef was a leader in every sense of the word; his men admired him. His bravery was beyond question, and even though he was committed to the mission, he also cared deeply for the men he was responsible for. He was not one to order his men to do something he would not, and so moved forward with his squads. After the war, he recalled that perfectly sited, well-hidden "enemy machine guns swept the entire slope" and river banks. This accurate firestorm stopped the assault. Graef ordered his men to return fire, but the enemy machine guns and infantry were so well concealed that they could not be seen. Artillery was one of the few "weapons" that infantry could use to neutralize or suppress enemy fire. However, it was hard to contact batteries once the caldron of combat began. American artillery, still trying to get organized, was simply not effective.[24]

A soft breeze danced the endless sea of golden grain in rolling waves. It must have been mesmerizing for those men to watch the play of light and dark as the wheat rolled this way and that in the morning light, the pale heads thick with kernels almost ripe for harvest, eventually to be turned into the breads of French life. It was across these verdant fields that the 165th and 166th Infantry and its supporting machine gun companies were ordered to advance, for there was no other way to get at the enemy other than to move across the wet wheat fields. Beyond the wheat was the little Ourcq River, the north bank rising higher than the south so that it was possible for anyone on those heights to look down on the fields. In turn, each company moved forward, following a sporadic and weak creeping barrage, and entered the arena of battle that would forever change their perception of war, and perhaps of life itself. Twenty-five years later, Appleton soldier Tom Miller recalled, "It all seemed like a dream."[25]

The frightened men sweated in their steel helmets, sweat soaking into the leather liner and webbing. The air was ripped by artillery shells and the unbroken zip-zip-zip of machine gun bullets. When courage gave out and it was impossible to make the body move forward, the soldiers lay tight against the earth, faces pressed hard against the soil for protection, the rich scent of dirt filling their nostrils. The men closed their eyes against flying grit, and to blot out fear as the sounds of battle flooded the senses. There were other smells, too: the distinct odor of cordite, sweat, and the tangy, unmistakable metallic smell of blood. Their war had been reduced to this small world. The mission was to cross that miserable little river and kill as many of the enemy as possible. But right now, that enemy controlled and saw every movement. It was a perfect killing field. They were trapped under constant observation, their concealed opponent determined and amply supplied.

But neither was it possible for the infantry to just lay there until darkness covered their movements. It was up to the men to swallow their terror. Courage could be contagious and all along the line the lads moved forward despite the carnage. "The wheat was so tall and heavy with grain that walking through the fields was almost like walking through water," recalled Major Winn of the 151st Machine Gun Battalion.[26] The Germans facing them were determined to extract the highest price possible from the khaki-clad figures trying to cross the fields and river. They were skilled, good at what they were ordered to do, but like the doughboys they, too, were scared. In the clutter and confusion of battle, one thing was clear: these Americans were very brave, and very good soldiers.

The challenge facing the doughboys was far more acute than anyone realized. Despite the fact that the Americans were well-trained, admirably led, and eager to prove themselves, courage only carried so far. Large caliber guns pounded them without letup, relentless concussion and shrapnel. But it was the machine gun fire that everyone remembered when recalling the Ourcq. The Maxim had a unique and unforgettable sound. Some doughboys recalled it as "pup-pup-pup" and others as "metallic." The Germans had positioned their machine guns in front of their infantry and slightly on the flanks to enfilade. From carefully sited, flawlessly camouflaged positions, the German Maxim guns sent streams of 7.92mm bullets. Nothing above ground was safe. Any movement drew the attention of expert gunners who had years to perfect the art of killing. The wounded could expect little help, no pain-killing morphine shot from a medic. Everyone was hungry because they had no breakfast, but it was hot and a craving for water dominated their thoughts. A simple mouthful of water would have been a gift from the gods. The canteens of the dead were taken, but heat and fear robbed the men of whatever solace the few drops of tepid water provided.

Another National Guardsman, Arnold Hoke from Iowa, fought in all the 42nd Division's battles as part of the 168th Infantry. In a 1971 oral history with his granddaughter, he called the battle on the Ourcq River the "worst of all." Despite their massive casualties while on the offensive, Hoke explained that the Germans "still had a lot of good men left in their army." Like so many other veterans, he remembered the Maxim guns. His company, "lost a terrific amount of men from machine gun fire."[27]

Appleton's Lieutenant Allan Ellis in the battalion's Headquarters Company watched the opening attack from an observation post in the rear. "It was more like a movie battle than reality," he wrote in a short 1919 chronicle of his wartime experiences. "Our barrage advancing steadily, the men following at a steady walk, the Hun barrage dropping on them, many falling, the line advancing steadily and surely."[28]

Ideally, before a machine gun was placed, there would be a detailed reconnaissance of the area by the platoon lieutenant or sergeant. This would identify targets, ensure the guns could be hidden, and make their fire more effective. Doing this under fire was daunting, but nonetheless, First Lieutenant Isaac Walker of Company A took a runner, Private Jennings, across the wheat to find a suitable location for his gun emplacement. He said, "[we] drew a burst every time [we] crawled forward." But eventually the two made it to a small plum bush and from there could observe the village of Sergy. He sent Jennings back for the platoon, which managed to make it forward, and the guns started hammering back.[29]

Crews from the 150th got their guns into action wherever they could find a little cover from the withering fire. The previous modification of the mount, putting the gun lower, proved a godsend. One by one, the Hotchkiss guns started sending back their answer to the Maxim, and loaders fed strip after strip into the hot guns so the infantry could move forward. Their response interrupted the enemy's fire and helped the infantry. Keeping the Hotchkiss supplied with ammunition became an ordeal. The cases were heavy and awkward. Even though the runners traveled light with only Colt auto pistols and gas masks, casualties mounted. Courageous men dashed from hole to hole, perhaps finding cover in a damaged building. It was rough, uneven ground, plowed up by hundreds of shells, but the angry zip-zip-zip drove them on. They yelled, cursed, and cried. Soaked in sweat, it was commitment to their friends manning the guns, and to the infantry, that kept them going.

Lloyd F. Kindness, Company B, had just turned twenty at the time of the Ourcq River battle. He recalled at length in a postwar interview:

> [O]n the morning of July 28, 1918, we were advancing toward the Ourcq River . . . our company in formation of platoons entering a small town called Villers-sur-Fère. We had to run across a street so as not to be observed and draw fire from the enemy machine guns across the Ourcq. They were shelling quite lively as we set our guns up at the north end of town in an orchard. I left my ammunition by the gun and went back to the woods [Fôret-de-Fère] for more. It was about a quarter of a mile to carry ammunition. I walked and ran through the town got my ammunition and returned to the gun squad, dug in and stayed there a while. The wounded started to come in, mostly boys of the 166th Infantry [Ohio]. One boy passed nearby.

I remember he was badly shot up in the leg, with some seventeen bullet holes. He was being carried by two buddies. He looked up at the apples on the trees in the orchard, and said he wanted one. They got him one. He ate it. He rested on one fellow's shoulder and asked for a cigarette and went on talking and joking with the boys who carried him.

Kindness continued in extraordinary detail:

One of our boys came along with news of our company's first platoon who were up in the front line. He told us some of the boys had been killed already. He was wounded in the shoulder and looked pale. I could look towards the Ourcq and hear and see the enemy machine gunners, getting in their deadly fire on the 165th boys [New Yorkers] and our battalion boys on the south slope of the Ourcq. I could see them fall in the wheat fields. It was growing hot on this Sunday morning in July. I lay quiet for a while. Then after a while I got orders to go after more ammunition to the woods. Another buddy was with me. We ran and walked through the town which they were still shelling. We got to the woods and got our ammunition O.K. A shell had nearly put our kitchen out of commission. It was in these same woods. I'm glad it didn't hit but just shook 'em up.

The events of that day were embedded into Kindness's memory: "We started back to the gun. I was behind my pal about 30 feet. There was camouflage along the road. We kept under that as near as could be so we would not be seen. But to our surprise an enemy aviator had spotted us, and we were in for a run. There was a farm house about half way to the town."

Aircraft are often mentioned in recollections of the multiday battle, and the Kindness narrative is no exception:

This plane dove down at us and opened up fire. Well, we ran full speed to the farm and just made it. It was a very close call. We stood there and could hear those bullets sing and whistle outside as he raked the place. Finally he gave it up and left. Then we left too and went towards the town. We left just in time as they started to shell the farm heavily. I was told afterwards that the German dead were stacked up like cordwood in that farmhouse. I never saw them though while I was in there. Only a few lying along the road. In town the shelling was heavy. . . . I reached our gun O.K. with my ammunition. I was just going back to my foxhole when a big shell landed from our right flank. One of our officers came staggering out of the dust and gravel and smoke. He was badly shell-shocked. I have never seen him since

Two unidentified Company B soldiers. The man on the left may be Lloyd Kindness, the Native American in Company B who wrote vivid, detailed recollections of his experiences in France. Courtesy of the Fond du Lac County Historical Society.

Artillery was the biggest cause of casualties during the war, and at the Ourcq River battle, the 150th faced enemy guns of all sizes. Kindness continued his narrative:

> That shell landed about 15 feet from me so I got up and changed my position. Going toward the front there was a crossroad. I just got on the road running east and west when another shell came over. It must have been very close to me. All I could hear was "whizz-bang." I looked to my left and back a little. It had burst in the ditch among some infantrymen. I could hear screams and groans. I looked around and seen them lying there. The dirt and concussion dazed me also. Then I reached this other road, and ran into a hedge next to a ditch. I no more than got out of sight when a shell broke right in the middle of the road next to me throwing stones, dirt and smoke all over me. My company commander came around the corner on the run and asked "are you hurt, Kindness?"[30]

Losses in the Fond du Lac platoon were so severe that in late afternoon they were withdrawn to reserve positions in the woods.[31] But even there they were not immune from enemy fire. "All day long we were shelled, and many of the boys went to the dressing stations as shell-shock cases. The Ourcq valley was one awful place to be in. But we held up. I recall how bad the atmosphere was, with dead lying all around, also horses and gas."[32]

When darkness hid the men that first night, they settled into whatever cover they could find. "I [was] played out," recalled Cap Schommer in Company A. His gun had been damaged and useless, the elevating wheel having been shot away, so he had picked up a discarded rifle and went "hunting Boche." Finally, hungry, thirsty, and tired, he just could not go on. "I dug a hole and though there was heavy shelling, I slept the sleep of the exhausted." He was awakened at 4:30 a.m. and waited for word to advance, but soon saw a trench mortar shell coming toward him.[33]

> Before I could dodge, it fell within 15 feet of me and burst, a piece of it hit me in the ankle almost completely taking off my left foot.... I was bleeding pretty bad, so I took off my belt and used it as a tourniquet ... my foot was hanging on by a little of the bone which was left, and as the hours dragged slowly by and no help came and being in the open with occasional bullets whizzing over my dome, I tried to drag myself in a shell hole, but my foot wouldn't come along just right, so I took my trench knife, shut my eyes, and made a slash at it. It came off all right. I don't suppose I would have had the nerve to do it only I was almost crazy with pain.

Eventually stretcher bearers found him and he was evacuated. By the time he got to a hospital, infection had set in and his leg was amputated above the knee. "I consider myself lucky in coming back with only the loss of one measly leg," he concluded.[34]

Keeping the Hotchkiss guns moving forward with the infantry did not work as planned. Hill 288 offered ideal observation for the enemy and accurate fire arched down from the heights. Squads advanced with their burdensome guns under relentless fire. They had to repeatedly move their guns forward as the infantry attacked so the guns were "always in position to cover the attack of our infantry and stop an enemy counter-attack." Often, the guns were not ideally positioned, nor were they hidden or protected. "Probably we were too close to our own infantry to give them effective support fire," Lothar Graef diplomatically explained after the war. "If we had been in position ready to fire sooner instead of moving forward with them as long as we did we could have done more damage to the Germans."[35]

Squads trained over and over to be able to quickly get their gun into action. Through repetition they were able to do it without thinking. Putting the gun into action involved the crew running to a location selected by an officer, platoon sergeant, or squad leader. The first man put the forty-one-pound tripod on the ground, its front leg toward the target. He then leveled it as quickly as possible. The other members of the crew were right behind him and placed the eighteen-pound traversing mechanism. Finally, the fifty-three-pound gun was placed and secured. While this was happening, the man with the ammunition boxes pulled out the metal cartridge strips and fed one into the gun. The gunner set the sights and performed the necessary adjustments to the tripod for range and traverse. Within forty seconds, a skilled and well-drilled crew would have the Hotchkiss firing at the enemy. Because the ammunition would not last long, other men of the squad and any infantrymen they could find brought full boxes forward; everyone had to know where the gun had been placed.

"Our own machine guns, the Wisconsin lads manning them, had followed the advance," recalled Father Francis Duffy with the New York infantry, "the gunners fighting with desperate courage. The ammunition was carried up by their men and ours [165th] at a frightful cost. Five feet or so a man might run with it and then go down. Without a moment's hesitation, some other soldiers would grab it and run forward to go down in his turn. But the guns had to be fed and still another soldier would take the same dreadful chance. Finally the guns were put out of action by German shell fire . . . and there they stood useless, their gunners lying dead around them."[36]

Ammunition resupply remained a priority for the 150th. The cumbersome boxes of cartridges were hauled in the mule-drawn two-wheeled carts, which had finally caught up with the rest of the companies. The animals were essential, and men were assigned to care for and drive the indispensable ammo carts. The person in charge of the animals was the stable sergeant. His job was to watch over the company's forty mules to make sure they were healthy, fed, and shod.[37] These valuable soldiers seldom engaged directly in combat unless the situation was grave, for their knowledge and skills were far more valuable to the unit, and to the army, than their ability to shoot. The stable sergeant for Company C was Kurt Graf, a likeable twenty-four-year-old who grew up on a farm south of Oshkosh.

Typically the carts were only brought to within two kilometers (1.2 miles) of the action because it was too dangerous for the mules. When the cart reached that point, the men carried everything forward in sixty-pound loads. On the first day of battle, Graf had brought the vital carts as close to the line as he dared, but it was still in what was considered a rear area. But even these rear areas were subject to the searching reach of long-range German artillery. It was common practice for the enemy to periodically send heavy shells into these back areas, hoping to catch exposed soldiers and animals. Any part of the supply train was vulnerable. "A mule skinner learns to act quickly when he's driving and under fire," stated the postwar history of Ohio's National Guard. "He can't hunt a hole, he must stay on his seat. Consequently, almost as if pulled by one string the entire train turned from the road into the field as the first shells struck, and instantly were going at a run away from the danger zone. It was a chariot race. Men stood up and lashed at running mules."[38]

The unidentified chronicler of Company C described the last time he saw Graf. "When we hit the road, there was our gun cart and squad that had been left behind the day before and as we continued up the road. . . . I saw Stable Sgt. Kurt Graf standing beside a big tree and waved a farewell as we passed. It was the first time we saw him in two days but little did we think it was the last time any of us would see him. . . . At about 4:00 p.m. Lt. Wolf came out to us with a report that Sgt. Kurt Graf had been instantly killed along with one of the teamsters whose name was [Desire] DeGraves."[39] The unit's rolling kitchen was also destroyed.

Despite the scything fire, the infantry crossed the river in several places, including the bridge, and began to move up the long slope toward the Meurcy Farm and Sergy. Not every gun squad could use the bridge, and the men had no idea of how deep the slow-moving Ourcq was, only that it had to be crossed and their Hotchkiss set up on the other side. The river was swollen and muddy from the unending rain, and the banks were steep. Infantry crossed the river to the left of Graef and the New Yorkers, although with severe casualties. As well, 149th Field Artillery finally opened up on the Germans with coordinated, accurate fire. Between the American artillery and the diversion the Ohio Infantry assault caused, Graef's men were now across the river and put their guns into action. There was some shelter on the far side in a road cut, which allowed the men to rest and get organized.

But now Graef knew that his guns were too close to the infantry he was assigned to support and too close to the enemy. And because his guns were within view, including from enemy positions on the flanks, casualties continued to mount among his men. Graef made the decision to move his men back across of the river, where he had a better field of fire. "On the morning of the 29th we crossed the river we were in front of Villers-sur-Fere," he wrote to the mother of Edward Weinfurter after the war ended. "Edward and myself together with two or three others were in fox-holes when that locality was heavily shelled by heavy German artillery. Edward was wounded in the upper part of the legs. At the time I did not think it was serious and had him carried back to a dressing station. . . . I am afraid that his wound was more serious that I expected and that he died on his way to the hospital."[40] Splinter wounds often looked deceptively small, but the wickedly sharp shards cut in curving paths.

When an Oshkosh gun squad under the command of Sergeant Richard Procknow attacked the fortified Meurcy Farm, the fighting was so intense that Procknow, Eddie Steckbauer, Otto Spaedtke, Louis Suess, and Walter Thorne, the entire experienced crew, were killed. The comrades died together and were all buried together.[41] That day, July 29, Lieutenant Bahr noted in his diary that they had captured Seringes, but it had cost Oshkosh twenty-five casualties, including Lieutenant Art Wolf, who lost his left arm, and Lieutenants William Jung and Robert Proudfit. Since Bahr was the only unwounded officer, he was put in charge of Company C.[42]

The official history of the Ohio men in the Rainbow noted that an officer named Radcliffe had reported for duty with the Machine Gun Battalion only on July 20 and had had no previous experience with machine guns. He was thrown into the battle to support the infantry assault and the history reported that, "[T]he Machine Gun Company, under Lt. Radcliffe, supported the attack. . . . During the first twenty-four hours after the assault began, its casualties were severe, and among them were three lieutenants and six sergeants. . . . The platoons were commanded by sergeants, and the efficient work of the company and all its subsequent activity in this sector is proof of the qualities of initiative and leadership of these men. It is a record of which the company, and the entire regiment, many be well proud."[43]

Courage was commonplace. Men in all four companies somehow ignored the screaming metal and did the impossible through determination and leadership. Such was the bravery at the Ourcq that three men were awarded the Distinguished Service Cross. All were awarded for actions on July 28, 1918.

Tony Kramp, a thirty-seven-year-old private in Company B who had been born in West Prussia, was one such hero. Fond du Lac men in support of the Ohio infantry headed toward the village of Seringes-et-Nesles. His citation reads in part, "Private Cramp [*sic*] showed extraordinary courage and ability as a leader of men in the field of battle. When his section had been killed and his corporal wounded, he assumed command of his gun section and led them forward against the enemy, directing the fire with effect until killed."[44] Private Merlin Eaton, himself wounded in the face on July 28, served in the same platoon as Kramp and was his bunk mate. He told a reporter from the *Berlin Evening Journal*, and Tony's brother, August, that Tony "never complained and was ever willing to do any task asked of him."[45]

Fond du Lac's Corporal Elmer Grabinski, said to be one of the company's best men at handling a machine gun, was also singled out for his actions. His Distinguished Service Cross award states that "He directed the fire of his gun with excellent effect, shooting several enemy snipers. Showing always the greatest eagerness to press forward and always disregarding his own safety, he was killed after leading his men forward successfully to their objective." But there was far more to the story than what the award order stated. Grabinski saw a young German no more than fifteen years old lying wounded ahead of him. Taking pity on his bleeding enemy, he rushed forward and bound the boy's wounds, making him as comfortable as possible and giving the German precious water. He was killed while aiding the teenager. Dan Holterman witnessed this act of kindness and told the Grabinski family that they "can be well proud of their son, for he died the death of a hero, and was succoring a vanquished foe, utterly oblivious to the danger there was to his own life."[46]

The Fond du Lac men fought with amazing courage; a second man, Sergeant Anthony Halfmann, earned both the respect of his men and the Distinguished Service Cross. General Order No. 102, W.D., 1918, reads that he "displayed courage, coolness, and leadership . . . the machine gun crew which he was directing shot seven enemy snipers from their posts. He was killed while reconnoitering in advance of our lines for an advantageous position for his guns." Private John Laudolf, home in early 1919 to recover from serious splinter wounds, explained: "We were advancing to rout a German machine gun nest. On our left was a woods which we supposed had been cleared of Boche by the French, but it wasn't and bullets from it took their toll. Grabinski and Halfmann died on the banks of the Ourcq River."[47] One of the men in Company B, R. E. Kraemer, told his cousin, "A better sergeant than he [Halfmann] there never was. Always jolly and good natured. But it seemed his time was up."[48]

The frontal assault tactic of the first few days changed to small unit actions. Small groups of infantry worked forward to flank enemy machine-gun emplacements. "It was not a rush this time," said the postwar *Story of the Rainbow*

Elmer Grabinski of the Fond du Lac company was killed at Château-Thierry while giving aid to a German soldier. He was awarded the Distinguished Service Cross for his valor. Courtesy of the Fond du Lac County Historical Society.

Division, "it was a painfully slow crawl. German machine guns blazed from fields of tall, yellow wheat. . . . Then from the tall grass a brown streak would suddenly shoot ahead for a yard or two and disappear . . . then off to the left another brown streak . . . a little ring of olive drab would be around that machine-gun nest, and a "kill" would be on." Once they located a concealed Maxim, they concentrated several Hotchkiss guns on the German machine gun, keeping up an endless fire. One by one the German machine-gun nests grew silent.[49]

It was a slow, agonizing method of advance but proved less costly than outright assault. The 150th kept up a steady fire, often getting the guns into positions near hilltops to fire down into German gun positions. Still, casualties were high. Later, the official division history simply and factually reported, "The 150th Machine Gun Battalion did not have much opportunity to fire upon the enemy because they were so skillful in keeping from being much of a target even while inflicting considerable loss on our troops."[50] Writing from a hospital bed, Frank Coffers in Company C told his parents that as they advanced, they drove the enemy out of their positions, where they could at last fire on them. "I set up the gun [and] saw five Germans get up and run for a shell hole. I opened fire on them and they all dropped. . . . I tell you folks that war sure is hell."[51] But the official history did not reveal what the men experienced and endured. The periodic rain turned the shell-churned soil into sticky mud. Although the mud was terrible, it helped in one way. When some German shells impacted, they drove deep into the soft mud and failed to explode.[52]

Herbert Granger's diary entries plainly and bluntly told the story for Company B, the Fond du Lac men. "Sun. 7/28 Went over the top for the first time with the 2nd Section of the first platoon. . . . Drove the Germans for 1½ kilo. Our own artillery was falling short and killing our own men. German M.G. [machine gun] thicker than the devil. The first section was almost wiped out. . . . The German planes were shooting the wounded laying on stretchers. Believe me it was all the hell any body wanted." A day later he continued the narrative: "Mon. 7/29 They bombarded us all nite and all day. Serg. Drier and my self laid in a hole all day. Thot [thought] end was coming any minute. Every body about crazy. They sent over H.E. [high explosive] Gas. Shrapnel. . . . The way many was killed and wounded was something awfull."[53] Nathaniel Rouse, a soldier in the 165th Infantry, simply recorded in his diary, "I just can't tell what happened on each day. It was terrible. They just slaughtered us."[54]

It was vital to keep the combat troops supplied, and at times there was no manpower to devote to aiding and evacuating wounded soldiers. As a result, the wounded lay were they fell until stretcher bearers could come up. The men went into battle without much gear, often forgoing even their canteens. Graef mentioned his men traveled light, so they had probably dropped their haversacks and thus had no food to speak of. They suffered severely from their wounds, lack of medical aid, and dehydration, the latter made worse by the summer heat, adrenaline, and blood loss. Incredible thirst drove some of the men to drink from the Ourcq River, even though it was polluted by muddy run-off, German and American corpses, and the debris of battle. Men often became violently sick.[55] As Lloyd Kindness said, it was an awful place to be.

Combat is a harsh taskmaster with no second-place winners. The machine gunners quickly learned how to best use their weapons, moving often to give the infantry fire support. The Rainbows fought hard and skillfully. The men were being fired on from three sides, and they had to advance and take and re-take Meurcy Farm and the village of Sergy. The fighting was brutal, but that same day, July 30, both were in American hands for good. Despite the tenacious resistance, the infantry attack on Seringes-et-Nesles continued, and the town was initially taken on July 29, but German artillery was so fierce it drove the doughboys into open fields south of the village.[56] Once again the Pennsylvania company felt the strain. "Some of [the men] had gone insane," said the unit history. "It was deemed impossible to advance, as the heavy shells were falling continuously."[57]

The Jacob Washburn family in Fond du Lac had two sons in Company B, John C., and Arnold. Both had been badly gassed in March but were back with the unit at the Ourcq. John was reported missing on July 29, but the Washburn family had had no word or confirmation of his death until after the war. A year later, they learned that in the back-and-forth battle for the town, John's comrades had seen him run into a building to take shelter from the relentless artillery. A minute later, a heavy caliber shell totally demolished the building, and he was never found.[58] By July 31, the town of Seringes stayed American.

There was a lull in the fighting on July 30–31. The doughboys used the time to replenish and rest, and reserve gun squads were brought up; the Germans used the pause for a staged retreat. Fighting resumed on August 1. German artillery had the roads, villages, and woods under direct observation, and the men paid for it. From the edge of the Fôret de Nesle, platoons from C Company went forward with companies E, F, H and M from the 166th toward the village of Mareuil-en-Dole. "[E]nemy artillery poured out a devastating barrage. Perfect observation by the Germans as the Americans came over the hill, made the advance difficult, but never was there a pause."[59] Here, on August 2, twenty-eight-year-old Nicholas Mand, the man with one gray and one brown eye and an artistic skill at drawing, was mortally wounded by splinters to the legs and stomach.

The German Army was rapidly retreating toward a new defensive line on the Vesle River. By August 3, with most of their objectives taken but at an incredibly high cost, the 42nd Division was relieved by the fresh 4th Division at 4:00 a.m. The official history of the 166th Infantry gave the Machine Gun Company "much credit for the support it gave the 2nd Battalion in its advance from the Ourcq to Seringes-et-Nesles. Following the Battalion with covering fire and a well-directed barrage, it moved through a hail of German gun fire and the cool shooting of snipers from the village, and the enfilade fire from the exposed flanks. Yet the company completed its operation that day without serious casualty while the infantry companies suffered severely."[60]

When the 150th and infantry were pulled out of action, they were sent back to the miserable forest of death, the Fôret-de-Fère. Like the infantry, the machine gun battalion was in terrible shape. "We sure were a tough bunch," said a Pennsylvania soldier, "[and] many of us fell by the road," unable to continue. Everyone suffered from the lingering effects of dehydration; the men were filthy, caked with dirt, sweat, and probably dried blood and the detritus of combat. They had not eaten much for over a week and were forever hungry because there was little to eat anyway. The men were given fresh bread with molasses syrup, strong coffee, along with a few bottles of contraband wine and liquor. The army settled them in this "terrible place . . . flies and mosquitoes abounded, dirty pools of stagnant water gave forth terrible odors, and the stench from dead bodies of German and American alike, would have been unbearable under other circumstances." In this "filthy backyard of war with its sickening smells and sights," the soldiers fell into a deep sleep, a relief for their battered bodies and minds.[61]

Things looked up a bit the next day as salvage and burial parties went to work. Their caloric intake had been well below what was necessary to sustain an active combat soldier, and most had lost a great deal of weight. The priority was food, and the rolling field kitchens from the supply trains came up a day later. Supply companies brought up new clothing, soap, razors, towels, underwear, and socks. A portable cleaning unit arrived to steam filthy uniforms infested with body lice. Amid the gruesome aftermath that lay about, a miracle of sorts happened that helped the men temporarily forget about death. Whether by design or accident, a popular entertainer from Ohio, Elsie Janis, appeared on August 10 to amuse the weary doughboys. "Fluffy, beautiful, piquant—not at all unlike a goddess." Janis was put on a stage made from a wagon bed and sang and danced to the unwashed crowd. The tired troops "suddenly remembered that there was such a thing in the world as a pretty American girl."[62]

Awful as the Ourcq battle was for the 150th, the spirit of the Germans opposite them had been broken. The Ourcq River line was breeched, and the Germans retreated to the Vesle-Aisne line. The battle was a turning point: Ludwig Miller was a German soldier who fought against the Rainbows at

Château-Thierry. German morale, teetering on the edge for months, took a severe slump after the defeat, he told his American Army interviewers in December 1918. American soldiers were a "brave and worthy opponent."[63] Ernest Winger, an Oshkosh soldier, was wounded on July 29 by shrapnel in the left arm and left knee cap; he wrote home about the battle. His letter made it evident that he was proud of what his company and the army had accomplished. He summed it up and with: "The Americans went into the action with so much dash and spirit it took the wind out of the Germans."[64]

Lieutenant Bahr also wrote home about the big battle with obvious pride, revealing a bit of the bloodlust common in combat. "I have seen plenty of Huns at close range, and we played our machine guns on them in fine shape. You could see them fall, too, and oh, how the boys would cheer," he penned. Then perhaps thinking how his glee might be perceived by civilians, he changed his tone and explained, "It is a hard game, but we just set our teeth and go right to it." Because the men knew many of their comrade's families, Bahr solemnly stated, "I suppose by now you have heard about Kurt Graf. It sure will make it hard for his father."[65]

Soldiers became callous to the act of killing and, for self-preservation, grew almost numb to death. Perhaps it was their way of preserving sanity, or just the timeless understanding that it was kill or be killed. There was no time to mourn or grieve. In the hurricane of combat, with its fearsome sounds, smells, and sights, there was no time for introspection. Men had to constantly move and fight, and when a comrade fell, as shocking and heartrending as that was, there was no time to deal with it emotionally. When conditions allowed, a soldier was buried where he met death, and the company moved on. But in rest, the situation was much different. "When you are in the thickest of the fight you don't fear anything," Leo Uelmen told his mother and father. "It is after the fight when you are tired and worn out and think of the things that happened."[66] All the companies had suffered casualties, especially the Oshkosh company. Indeed, compared to the infantry, the units of the 150th certainly experienced far fewer casualties by number, but not by percent. However, the gun companies were smaller than an infantry company, and losses were keenly felt among the well-trained squads.

According to the official Casualty Report for Oshkosh's Company C, almost half the men became casualties during this last phase of the great battle. "I guess old F company has been just about shot to pieces," Walter Pochojka told a *Northwestern* reporter when he arrived home to recover from a severely wounded foot, "nearly every man in the company was either killed or wounded."[67] A few came through without any physical wound, but not many. "All the officers in the company were wounded except Lieutenant Bahr," said Private Everette

Lawrence. He then made it clear what he thought of Bahr: "[He] did wonderful work . . . the company owes lots for his careful handling of his men."[68] Among the Oshkosh dead were Elmer Bullis, Peter Daniel Johnson, Nicholas Mand, Frank Phillips, Richard Procknow, Louis Suess, Otto Spaedtke, Eddie Steckbauer, and Walter Thorne. Fifty-five men were wounded: eighteen by rifle or machine-gun fire, nine were gassed, four were shell shocked, and twenty-five by shrapnel; six men were missing.[69] The typed facts and figures in the after-action report did not reflect the suffering and grief that resulted.

A soldier's squad was his family, the center of his limited world. He was with his squad day and night and knew each person as well as it is possible to know someone. Men depended on their buddies, trusting them with their lives. When squad members became casualties, the impact could be tremendous. Buddies were no longer there to share a laugh and a cigarette, or talk about what was happening back home. Unexpressed grief and emotion held inside could not be released. They could not experience closure through a service and burial. Seeing the names of the fallen on kit bags must surely have been tough. In many cases, they had soldiered side by side for years, lived in the same community, and knew the next of kin. As they lay in their bedrolls, they thought of how the wives and parents of the deceased back in Appleton, Fond du Lac, and Oshkosh would bear the news that their soldier was dead. As in all wars, survivors no doubt felt guilt at being one of the lucky. "It is with deepest sorrow that we lost all those good men," Second Lieutenant Bahr wrote to his friend Frank Dubois in Oshkosh, "We speak of them often and their good deeds will remain fresh in the memory of all of us and our sympathy goes out to the loved ones at home. Surely it will be a sad day for them when this old company comes marching home and these brave men are not there to fill the ranks."[70]

The tight cohesion made it particularly hard for some men. In Company C, John Ruhl's best friend was twenty-two-year-old Walter Thorne, one of dead. Walter had been courting John's sister, Mary, and it was a serious relationship. "Now Mary cheer up," he wrote trying to comfort her. "It had to be that way. Try and cheer up his mother all you can." Ruhl told his sister that when he came home, he'd visit Walter's mother and tell her exactly what happened to her son.[71]

The fate of the unit's many wounded and gassed, carried off the battlefield by the overworked stretcher bearers and then eventually to a hospital, was unknown. Men who survived the battle did not know whether wounded comrades were alive or dead. Officers like Lothar Graef worked long hours to ascertain the fates of their men and let the company know what happened to others. Officers had to talk to the men about what they had seen in action, especially as it related to those missing, in order to file casualty reports. Brothers serving

together in a National Guard unit, and there were many in the 150th, could
be a wonderful thing stateside but a limitation in combat. It would have been
particularly difficult for those soldiers. A few days after the ordeal on the Ourcq,
Dan Holterman, with the Fond du Lac company, wrote to the C. J. Pinkerton
family. He closed his letter by noting he had not heard about the fate of his
brother, Robert. "Have not heard anything of Rob since July 28. I can only hope
for the best."[72] Carl Schneider, in Base Hospital No. 43, explained to Rose
Baier, "I haven't seen my brother [Anton] for some time. He got gassed. . . . I
don't know how he is getting along."[73]

Twenty-eight year old Otto Suess, in the Oshkosh company, lost his
brother Louis on July 30. He wrote home on September 1, complaining that
he was not himself and was still sick with diarrhea and headaches. While the
diarrhea may have been the result of drinking polluted water, no doubt some of
his illness was a consequence of the grief and depression he felt over the death
of his brother. He wrote to his sister Elanor, August 27:

> Dearest Sister,
>   . . . I am not feeling very good but I have to make the best of it . . . The
> weather over here is getting colder, the nights are awful cool and besides
> we have to sleep out side in the damp ground no straw to sleep on, morn-
> ings when you get up you have to twist every way to get your bones back in
> place. Well as long as we don't get it any worse I guess we can stand it all
> right . . . when you hear these Bock [Boche] planes drop these bombs you
> would think everything was going to pieces. Well, Ella I will have to close
> soon for my candle light is getting rather dim so give my heartiest regards
> and sincere wishes to all the family and neighbors.
>
>   With Love & Kisses,
>   From Bro, Otto[74]

It was the responsibility of Lieutenant Arthur Bahr to write to the families
of the fallen men in Oshkosh's Company C. Although each letter he wrote
home to the parents and wives of the fallen contained many of the same sentences, in clear, precise handwriting, Bahr carefully personalized each one. Bahr
had come through the ranks and was respected by his men. He was the type of
leader who would not ask his men to do something that he himself would not
do. He saw to it that his men were fed, received the supplies they needed, and
had whatever small comforts he could scrounge. Bahr knew many of the men
when they were civilians, had soldiered with them since 1908, and almost certainly knew some of the men's family members. It was evident that he put this
heart into those sentences and that his grief was real. Kate Mand had two sons

in Company C, Nicholas and Julius. Nicholas, the artist who had sent home well-done sketches of fashionable young women in New York City, had been killed. On August 24, Bahr wrote to her to tell her of the death of Nicholas.[75]

> Mrs. Kate Mand,
>   It is with deepest sorrow that I have to inform you that you have given to America—to Liberty and to the ideals of a free people—the supreme sacrifice—your son. Nick was seriously wounded about noon of August 2. He died peacefully a few hours later. I went to Nick shortly after he was wounded and gave him "first aid" and cheered him up a bit, he was brave to the last.
>   America grieves the loss of a soldier—you grieve the loss of a son. Though your grief be deep let it be a comfort to know that Nick was a true son and a brave soldier.
>   Expressing the sympathy of the Officers and men of Company C.
>   I remain yours truly,
>   Lieut. Arthur R. Bahr

"It was worse than terrible," Campbellsport's Alex Fleischmann said in a letter to his parent right after the battle. "By forced marches and night hikes and the last stretch in motor trucks we got to the scene about twelve hours before the show started. The boys went over the top at 4:30 a.m. and from then it was hell . . . that is where gruesome sights were seen. Dead (by far the greater majority were Huns) were lying scattered along side of the road, in the wheat fields and in the trenches. The bodies commenced to decompose immediately in the hot July sun and the stench was terrible. . . . The large majority of American casualties are leg wounds from machine gun bullets. . . . Folks, I thought I knew something about war."[76]

It took over a month for newspapers back in Wisconsin to report details about the human toll at the great battle around Château-Thierry. In bold, black headlines, Milwaukee's *Sunday Sentinel* reported on September 15, 1918: SIX MEMBERS OF OLD COMPANY F OF OSHKOSH, NOW WITH THE 150TH MACHINE GUN BATTERY IN FRANCE, DIE BENEATH THE STARS AND STRIPES ON FIELD OF HONOR. The article included photographs of Elmer Bullis, Kurt Graf, Frank Phillips, Richard Procknow, Eddie Steckbauer, and Louis Suess.[77]

The 150th was given the welcome orders that it would rest for six weeks at Villers-sur-Marne, for the campaigning was beginning to tell on the men. During this rest, Fond du Lac's Guy Gross, lightly wounded in the great battle and in the hospital recovering, had time for reflection in the aftermath of the fight. Sometimes small things take on great meaning during periods of stress, underscoring what is most significant. Gross had experienced much suffering, and he told his parents, "The pictures of the family that were taken last August . . . have been in my pocket ever since . . . carried across the ocean, into battle, hospitals and will continue to do so. I still hope to have them when this war is over and we come home again." Gross summed up the sense of loss more succinctly than any Badger soldier. He told his parents, "the company has changed somewhat since I left it and a few of the old familiar faces are not to be seen . . . [they were] greatly loved and now much missed."[78]

They had met the enemy in fierce combat and had overcome a determined, battle-hardened adversary, but also they had lost good friends. Their minds were seared with memories that would remain forever, to be replayed in dreams and quiet moments. The survivors understood what they had done, but how could dozens of personal tragedies be forgotten? These intense experiences could not be passed on to those who would never know the firestorm of combat. Many things remained unspoken and unrecalled in letters home. Instead, they wrote home about the big victory. Although they could not know it then, like all combat veterans, the memory of the seven days at the Ourcq would never leave them.

The little town of Fère-en-Tardenois is a quiet place today. The diminutive Ourcq River flows through the village, adding to the tranquility and charm. Nearby is the serene Oise-Aisne American Cemetery where some of the boys of 1918 sleep, as well as the Loupeigne French-German War Cemetery where the doughboys' French comrades, and their German foes, rest under carefully manicured stones and symbols. In the summer, the soft green fields and patches of woods in this agricultural area rise and fall in endless vistas. Here and there are beautiful and well-kept granite monuments, the chiseled features of the stone warriors a tribute to the sacrifices of a century ago. Grateful French citizens still lay wreaths of flowers on the graves of those who saved France. Lush beds of ferns grow in the woods where German artillery once smashed graceful, towering stands of beech and oak. Shattered guns and rusted artillery shells lay amid the moss and underbrush, but French law prevents the removal of artifacts from these sacred places.

This picturesque village was once the focal point for the Wisconsin boys in the 150th, and it was here that death found twenty-one-year-old Sergeant William B. Heiss on July 30. The son of immigrants from Germany and Poland, Heiss deeply believed in the war. A few months before, he had written to his brother, Thomas, in Appleton, "[The Germans will] wish they'd never started anything. They say the Americans want to attack too much. The Fr. [French] believe in waiting but we want to end it quickly and get back home again. It may seem hard to shoot the Germans but we could do almost anything to them after what we've seen and heard."

Heiss was the valedictorian of the Appleton High School Class of 1916 and was revered as "a mighty fellow with an excellent brain," and "one of the finest students Appleton High School has ever known." He was a good-looking man with blondish hair and a ready smile that brightened his whole face. Known as a gifted orator with a clear voice, Heiss had the unique ability to persuade others through rationale. He sent money home each payday because Heiss knew it was important to save his monthly pay for clothes and tuition, for he planned to continue his education when the war ended. But Heiss's dream, like the buildings in Fère-en-Tardenois and the beech trees in the nearby woods, was shattered by the relentless German artillery. The death of the handsome valedictorian Heiss, the man with the excellent brain, was a shock to people of Appleton. He was the only man from the Class of 1916 that the great European war claimed.

In August 1921, Thomas and Bertha Heiss asked that the body of their son be returned to Appleton, to be buried on American soil. Two veterans in full uniform stood as honor guards in the First Congregational Church. The coffin was festooned with colorful flowers and draped with the American flag. There had to be a way to remember this man so his death was not in vain. That year, the Class of 1916 "established what will henceforth be known as the William B. Heiss Memorial Contest." The purpose of the contest, the *Clarion Annual* said, was to "perpetuate the memory of William Heiss," promote a "deeper, keener interest in the world and national topics," and express a "loving appreciation for his great service to his country." At the first commemorative program at the school in 1921, Carl Damsheuser spoke to the assembled crowd on "International Folly." Each year thereafter, the Heiss silver cup was to be awarded in an annual oratorical contest. Today, however, he is forgotten, and there is no William B. Heiss Memorial Contest. In fact, it took time for school officials to even locate records on the man and the contest.

9

St. Mihiel

Drove them back 10 or 12 kilometers at Pannes they left their
loaded wagons and beat it.

Herbert Granger,
diary,
September 12, 1918

Lorraine's Plain of the Woerve has drawn people since ancient days, perhaps because of its fertile fields, undulating wooded hills and hidden lakes, a countryside laden with plum orchards, or the streams and rivers that lead to the mighty Rhine River. The countryside remains largely untouched by development. There are large areas designated by the French government as regional parks, protected for their natural beauty and history. Guidebooks send tourists to see Palace Stanislas in Nancy, a magnificent eighteenth-century citadel that once was home to King Louis XV's daughter and her Polish husband. Few tourists travel to the little town called Saint-Mihiel. The small community can hardly compare in splendor to Nancy. On the other hand, it gave its name to a great American victory that freed two hundred square miles of France after four years of German occupation.

Germany's momentous gamble had failed. They had thrown everything they had into the offensives. German forces were disconsolate and their spirit had

148

cracked; there was no faith that military victory was possible. Their men in the mud felt widespread dejection. Nonetheless, the struggle went on. The practiced German command sensed an enemy offensive was highly probable to follow up on the Allied victory at the Marne.

In the first year of the war, Germany had taken a large bite of France. This captured territory formed a huge bulge that pointed into Allied-held land. Because the small town of St. Mihiel was at the tip of that bulge, it became known by that name. Over the years, the Germans had reinforced defenses in depth in the bulge and created extensive supply and rest areas behind the front lines. Because they held the high ground, an imposing hill named Montsec [also spelled Mont Sec], spotters could easily call for artillery fire wherever it was needed, and their heaviest weapons could reach French rear areas. The Allies wanted to eliminate the bulge because it was so favorable to the enemy.

Despite their triumph at the Second Battle of the Marne, the Allies remained wary of their opponent. While they assumed Germany's offensive ability was gone, the St. Mihiel bulge was still perceived as a jumping-off point for new offensives. Regardless, it was critical that the Allies keep pressure on their enemy and not allow them to rest or begin work on fortifying new, deeper defensive positions. If the Germans were allowed to do that, then it was entirely possible that the static deadlock of the last four years would resume, with new lines farther east. An attack against the bulge was planned in secrecy, but at least one Swiss newspaper published details about the upcoming offensive. The Germans knew it was coming, but not *when*. Despite French doubts and attempts to prevent it, the upcoming battle was to be the first all-American effort, the initial battle of the new U.S. First Army. America's general, John Pershing, was determined that it would succeed. Around the salient, he arrayed a dozen divisions. Including those in reserve and a French colonial division, the force totaled 340,000 men. The First Army was composed of regular army divisions, divisions consisting of drafted men, and National Guard divisions, including the 42nd Division.

With almost no reserves left anywhere to stop attacks, German leaders understood that the St. Mihiel bulge was extremely vulnerable, the divisions there susceptible to encirclement and destruction. An attack from each side could pinch off and trap tens of thousands of troops. For that reason, the salient had to be abandoned as quickly as possible and defenses farther east consolidated and strengthened. A planned movement to pull back supplies, munitions, weapons, and men to the Hindenburg Line began.[1] German troops in the salient were under the command of General Max von Gallwitz, and he ordered his army to move into prepared positions in the Hindenburg Line; rear-guard detachments would resist as long as possible. Thus, the U.S. First Army faced about 23,000 enemy troops, most in the category of second-rate due to age, illness, previous injury, or because they were non-German divisions.

After the fierce struggle at Château-Thierry, the Rainbow Division moved south and east, back into Lorraine, on fine, firm roads. As they passed by the wheat fields that only a few days before was a horrific scene, the observed French farmers harvesting the grain. The convoy passed "charming hillsides" and clear streams. "In discolored uniforms, torn and out at the knees, the troops pushed by," the divisional history related. "Their transportation was scarred and marred by heavy usage. Its hard-driven animals were emaciated and worn." So were the men. The small villages and ancient churches in this area of France were not scarred and marked by the debris and destruction of battle. Aside from the absence of young men, life moved along here as it had for centuries, the landscape almost serene. The divisional history referred to the area as "pleasant and congenial," the weather unusually fine. The tranquility was much needed by men who had looked into the eyes of death and witnessed a type of apocalypse unfold before them. The pace was not demanding, and the division was strung out for miles as it moved through the countryside.[2]

The Machine Gun Battalion stopped on August 12 for rest and refit and was assigned a location near the village of Coupru. Some of the men in the Oshkosh Company immediately went to the Roman Catholic Church there for worship and prayer, an indication of how their faith sustained them. Otto Suess told his sister, Elanor, that the nights were cool and autumn was coming on, but that he could stand it for a while yet as long as things didn't get any worse. Suess was writing the letter by candlelight, and "it seems rather nice to have a candle burning around these places." He explained that prior to the rest, no form of light was allowed at night because any light attracted enemy bombers.[3]

Major General Charles T. Menoher of the 42nd Division issued a general order that allowed up to 10 percent of a company to have leave in Paris. Thirteen men in the Pennsylvania Company "spent two wild days in Paris," according to the history.[4] If the other companies were granted the coveted leave, it did not make it into their letters or diaries.

Replacements arrived to bring companies back to full strength, but none of the letters mention new men, perhaps because the new faces clashed with the old and familiar. Replacements faced a difficult test and seldom formed the same kinds of bonds that existed within the old National Guard soldiers. Officers requisitioned uniforms, animals, and spare and replacement parts for equipment and guns lost in the great battle; they also trained the new men. The Bucktails also went through the clothing of their fallen comrades and divided it among the survivors. Companies sent men to both machine-gun training and signal training, the importance of the latter clearly shown in the Ourcq battle.

Notwithstanding their losses at the Ourcq, at least a few soldiers expressed their commitment to the cause. After attending mass in a fourteenth-century church, Private Carl Nimmer wrote a long, impassioned letter to his mother. In a scolding tone, he told her that Americans did not "realize what an awful, awful thing war is and what an awful toll it exacts from the poor women of France." His emotion was evident as he praised France and said he was ashamed that Americans were not doing more. Perhaps recalling the sacrifices of comrades or responding to a letter or article he thought selfish, he wrote that "Americans fighting in France are not fighting for France alone, they are fighting for you, your kin, your liberty and freedom."[5]

The men themselves had changed as a result of their ordeal and so had the battalion, for they were all now truly battle hardened. But a major change had taken place on July 31, a much larger, more significant transformation. During the Second Battle of the Marne, the 42nd Division, as well as other American divisions, had been part of America's First Corps, which in turn was under command of the French Sixth Army. Since the United States had entered the war in 1917, the goal had been to create an American Army, under American command. It would fight alongside the French and British in coordinated strategy, but it would be independent of their command. The men in the 150th probably read this in the army newspaper, *Stars and Stripes*, but no one commented on it.

In typical army fashion, on the afternoon of August 28, the battalion was told to pack quickly, for they were to move out in only a half hour. This repositioning was to be in great secrecy, but the men scoffed at that idea because everyone seemed to know an attack was coming. The division had to move about one hundred kilometers at night, but as the long columns began to move the "unusually fine" weather came to an abrupt end. It started to pour and the rain was unceasing. The heavy overcast and rain made it a nightmare for the battalion and their mule carts. "Couldn't see more than 5 feet ahead," Bahr entered in his diary. They arrived in the Fôret de la Reine, "a dripping, soggy woods." It was full of tanks, trucks, supply columns, artillery, and men. The traffic churned the "rudimentary roads of this forest into deep grooves of sticky mud . . . [it] made the shortest distances the heaviest sort of burden for our transportation." And still the rain fell. "It became a division of mud-dwellers, lying quietly in the sticky black muck all day and wallowing about in it through the night, for by daylight no movement of men or transportation was permitted. Rain fell steadily and the roads became horrors."[6]

Although not recorded in men's letters, there was perhaps a sigh of relief when they learned that the battalion's guns would no longer move separately with the infantry companies as they had at the Ourcq. Machines guns already with the infantry regiments were divided up and given to the division's three Machine Gun Battalions to use however they saw fit to help the infantry. The Machine Gun Battalions were to remain independent and under the command and control of their major, and the guns were ordered to be used in the support role in which they had been trained and then follow behind the infantry. Each company was to improve liaison with the infantry, and the supply of food and ammunition was enhanced.

As they prepared for the attack, they could see Montsec in the distance, a gray mass looming over everything. French forces had tried since 1914 to take the hill from the enemy, and hundreds of thousands of men had died. The Germans held the heights above the Ourcq River, so the men obviously understood what they now faced.

On a night so dark it was impossible to see more than a few feet ahead, the companies "Went into the trenches to-night," Bahr put in his diary on September 11. But it was a lot more challenging for the machine gunner than Bahr's terse entry implied. The late summer storm front made for overcast days and black nights. "We had to carry our heavy equipment in the dark through thick lines of barbed wire, which we could not see," recalled Lieutenant Parkinson in the 151st. "It was pitch dark and raining. We had to cross several trenches, the bottom of which were deep in mud and water. With our heavy equipment we could not jump across the trenches."[7]

Finally arriving at their designated start point, Bahr noted in his diary that "[T]he trenches had 2 feet of water and mud in them." As they were setting up their Hotchkiss guns, the "Artillery barrage started at 1 a.m.," Herbert Granger jotted, "The guns were lined up hub to hub." Indeed it was an amazing display, and for four hours the shells flew. A few German guns replied, but not many. "At 5:00 a.m. we opened up the barrage with our Guns," Granger recorded, "this lasted till 5:30 a.m. and then we left the trenches and advanced on the Huns." Concentrated fire from dozens of guns created a lethal rain of fire. Well-planned and coordinated barrages like this were directed at assembly points, artillery batteries, and crossroads, and even though the gunners seldom actually saw the result of their work, they were powerful forces. The downside was that they used incredible amounts of ammunition. One company could go through sixty thousand rounds, or about three tons, in a short time.

At last the time came for American soldiers to "go over the top," the infantry leading along with four hundred light tanks under the command of Lieutenant Colonel George S. Patton. The machine gunners picked up their guns and followed behind the infantry." Oh! It was grand," wrote a soldier in Company D. "Thousands of our boys charged the Boche lines. I never could have believed there would be so much barbed wire . . . but nothing could stop us."[8] The idea was that the machine guns would be prepared to defend against German counterattack and guard the flanks, which were always vulnerable during attack. They could also be called on to reduce enemy strong points, using several guns firing from different angles, an extremely effective use of the guns.

"We found ourselves with part of the One Hundred and Sixty-Sixth Infantry and right in front of a number of tanks; a position of great danger," wrote Sergeant Jarrette in the Pennsylvania Company. "I sent runner forward and at last found our places. Big shells and machine gun bullets were flying around."[9] American forces moved forward against limited resistance, but it was by no means without casualties. Clarence Rhyner was hit in the stomach by a machine-gun bullet, and A. Boyd was wounded in the legs by shell splinters.[10] In one incident, a cook named Silvey serving with the Bucktails on Company D was eager to see action. He begged to be allowed to go forward with the guns, and finally the officer agreed. Cook Silvey was hit through the lungs by a bullet and died.[11]

The overwhelming superiority in infantry, artillery, and tanks, plus complete air superiority, was decisive. Montsec fell quickly, and the units continued toward assigned objectives. "The airplanes and tanks did some great work. . . . The Ger. Did not put up any fight at all they all give themselves up very gladly. Drove them back 10 or 12 kilometers at Pannes they left their loaded wagons and beat it."[12]

Private J. K. Bragg with the Fond du Lac men, wrote to some friends and enthusiastically explained that the artillery barrage was

> followed two hours later by a machine gun barrage by us and the rest of the divisional machine guns for about a half hour. Then while our artillery was still banging away at the Huns we went over the top and at the Germans, we never stopped for anything but our wind, of course, we had to duck a few shells but that is all in the fun. . . . In our catch we surrounded a big hill before the Huns could get out, making a whole Division of Dutch surrender—guns and all. I am going to send you a button that I took off a Dutchman that had the nerve to get in my way.

He closed with a bit of bragging by saying, "By this you can know that I am quite a fighter."[13]

Not every soldier was so bloodthirsty. Private Herbert Ambler, with the Pennsylvania Company, passed by many wounded Germans. "One of the

Germans was crawling toward us with his heel shot off when a doughboy rushed at him with a fixed bayonet. He was about to run him through when I yelled at the top of my voice, 'You damn fool, give him a chance, he's wounded'. . . he felt ashamed and walked away. I stopped and gave the Hun a drink of water and a few 'hard tacks.'"[14]

But now the problem that had plagued the adversaries since 1914 reared its head. A cold, driving, rain turned the artillery-churned ground into a sea of thick, gooey mud. Artillery, drawn by horses, could not move forward. Ambulances had the daunting task of navigating the sea of mud and oncoming traffic as they carried the wounded to the rear, each jolting slide an agony for their passengers. Supply trucks could not bring up ammunition, food, and other materials. Because their artillery could not easily travel through the mire and over the German trenches, the advancing infantry had to wait until the guns caught up. The machine-gunner's carts and kitchens labored in the mud and congestion to catch up with their companies, which they found two days later near St. Benoit.

The offensive ended on September 16, and it was a spectacular victory. Pershing had originally wanted to continue on to Metz, a railroad junction, but the French insisted his new army simply eliminate the bulge. "Took many thousands of prisoners, captured guns, ammunition and equipment of all kinds, among which were barrels of beer and sauerkraut. The Huns . . . gave themselves up gladly and said they were through with the war and also that they could see Germany's finish soon."[15]

"We only pushed them back twenty miles in one day. I think that is going some," bragged Simon Weiner to a friend back in Oshkosh. "We captured thousands of prisoners—this is the truth for I saw them myself. Many of the boys talked to some of them. They all seem to be sick of the war the way they talk. . . . I must tell you that our boys are doing great work . . . have done hard work in rain and sunshine, but we did it with a smile." He ended by signing "Your soldier pal."[16]

The 42nd Division alone captured 15,000 prisoners and 450 guns, which represented a severe blow to the already battered German Army. The National Guardsmen noted a distinct breakdown in German resolve, a major change from the confident enemy of summer. The doughboys captured numbers of old men and boys among the enemy ranks, some as young as twelve or thirteen. It was pathetic to look at these boys in uniforms far too large, without the physical strength to hold man-sized weapons. Amazed at the amount of food and material in the German trenches, they helped themselves to German beer, sausage, new leather boots, and other plunder.

Soldiers did not always wear their haversacks into combat and instead carried only what they absolutely needed. It was tough enough hauling the gun and boxes of ammunition through the mud after the infantry without extra weight. There was tradeoff for saving weight: when night fell and the temperatures dropped, they did not have their overcoats or blankets. As well, they might never see their haversacks again. Captured enemy gear was their answer. "Every body was wearing German shoes, overcoats, leggings and blankets. Slept in a shell hole with Lester. On the side of a hill. Colder than the devil," Granger recorded in his diary.[17]

Lothar Graef gave his dad a very fine account of the grand American attack in a long letter written while he was sitting in the second floor of a farmhouse on a hill, only seven miles from the German border. From the room he could see shells bursting in the distance on the enemy lines and said he hoped Fritz didn't send some his way. The letter merits repeating at length:

> Our attack was very fast and our company had no one killed and but seven wounded, though sometimes the wounds are more serious that we think. . . . A good bag of prisoners was taken, the exact number I do not know . . . [I] will relate one little incident: Our company was advancing when I saw a man off to one side waving a white flag—couldn't think for a second what he wanted, on looking closer however I saw he was a German and I called "Komm rueber" [come here] and he came on a run. He was delighted when I spoke to him in German and when I asked him what he wanted said, he and about fifteen others wanted to surrender. I called over four of my boys and went with him. When we came to where they were I told him to go and tell them to come out four or five at a time. Well they came out, instead of four or five at a time they climbed over each other to get out. They all came up smiling and saluted and when I got them lined up I found I had one Lieut., four non-coms and thirty-five privates. Put two men in charge and marched them to the rear. The Lieut. presented me with his field glasses when I remarked that I needed a pair, said he didn't think he would need them . . . the whole bunch said good-bye to me, evidently pleased to have someone who could talk German and not to be killed as they had been told they would be.[18]

"I thought that the whole German army gave up and a happier looking lot could not be found," Bill Techmann told his friend Joe Weishepl after the battle. "They all had a smile from ear to ear and a few made comical remarks about the Kaiser. One said: 'The war is over, but the Kaiser don't know it.'" A unit's morale, cohesiveness, and success depended in large part on how effective its officers were. Company C's enlisted men much admired Art Bahr, and Techmann told his friend, "Lt. Bahr is now promoted to first lieutenant and is wearing silver bars. The boys all think that he deserved them for he stuck with the boys in all scrapes and weather and kept cool on all hot days." He closed with, "Most of the boys now sing this: "Homeward Bound" or "Hello Broadway, Goodbye, France. We all have hopes, Joe."[19]

A few days after the big victory, Graef was in a German rest camp in the woods, a "comfortable cottage" with a stove and plenty of wood, and "quite artistic."[20] He wrote a letter to his father, "Dear Old Dad," he began, "It's been some little time since I've written you, but one can't be 'making history' and keep up with his letter writing at the same time. . . . [St. Mihiel] wasn't a battle, except for the four hours of bombardment by our artillery things went so fast we didn't have time to fight. Our company followed right on the heels of the assault battalion and we never had time to stop long enough to set up our guns to shoot." He explained they captured great stocks of German food and described it in some detail, but noted the German "war bread" was the size, shape, color and weight of a paving brick. "Soggy and sour." Soldiers were always thinking of food, for they never had enough to eat. With obvious relish, he told his dad that the battalion captured five hundred pounds of flour, which was "very dark but made excellent pancakes when mixed with US flour," sauerkraut, and three hundred pounds of cereal like cream of wheat, and two hundred pounds of dried vegetables like carrots. "All these things, added to what we got as our regular ration gave us a chance to last ten days and live like kings, which we did." Finally, he offered this assessment:

> It seems to me, the German soldier is beginning to become tired of the war. They are realizing how hopeless their case is. Then, too, they got their eyes open in regard to the United States soldier. In him they now see a soldier young, big and capable of fighting as they were told we never could. One German prisoner remarked your soldiers are like the ones we had at the beginning of the war, but we haven't got them any more. And there I think is the answer to the whole thing. Our young and big fellows are going to be too much for the older, weaker and tired German soldier.[21]

There was another assessment, too, and that was how the 150th Machine Gun Battalion performed in the offensive. On September 19, the brigade adjutant sent a memo to the company commanders of the 165th and 166th Infantry and the 150th Machine Gun Battalion. The subject line asked what could be learned and improved from the St. Mihiel operations. Major Newman Smith responded by stating that there could not be a hard-and-fast rule of whether the battalion's guns were most effective when operated assembled under one command, or detached and assigned to infantry. This was best determined by the tactical situation at hand. At the start of the attack, it was clear that the massed guns brought down "a very destructive fire." In spite of this, the offensive revealed two crucial weaknesses.[22]

During the battle on the Ourcq, the slower moving machine-gun squads were plainly unable to keep up with the light, fast-moving infantry. That dilemma was again apparent at St. Mihiel. The other problem was that it was almost impossible to maintain communication with the advancing infantry and with brigade headquarters. Machine guns were used little, if at all, after the initial jump off, even though there were times when massed machine-gun fire could have been used effectively on strong points. Major Smith explained that the gunners did not know when or where the infantry needed support, nor did they understand when the 83rd Brigade required the massed fire of the battalion's guns. The machine-gun companies depended on five or six runners to maintain communications. Yet, it was hard to spare the men; they wore out quickly from the constant back and forth of travel, or they became casualties. While headquarters kept fairly good liaison with companies as they moved forward, that was not the case with the gun squads and the infantry. Smith called the communication "slow and difficult." Runners did always know how to locate infantry, and by the time they did and an order was received, it was outdated. It was pointed out that the infantry needed *immediate* supporting fire in order to maintain momentum. It "would have been absolutely essential to the rendering of effective support had serious resistance been encountered," wrote Major Smith. In early November, the infantry and machine guns would work together much better as a result of the St. Mihiel lessons.

One solution was to assign more officers and men, or add a signal unit to establish and maintain telephone communication with headquarters. On the front end, the leading battalions of infantry should always have one company of machine guns for immediate use. To achieve that, the guns had to be kept on the carts so they could travel fast enough to maintain contact with the infantry. This would have the added benefit of keeping the men fresh and available as a reserve. The memo did not address the fact that the mules were sure to be wounded or killed.

One positive outcome of the offensive was that upon reaching an objective, quick consolidation was achieved by properly placing the guns in depth. However, infantry officers wanted to establish their defensive line first, then place the machine guns afterward. This was counter to best practices. The machine-gun officers, Smith pointed out, should first be allowed to establish the best defensive positions on the flanks *before* the infantry created their defenses. This dilemma was the result of infantry officers not understanding the power of machine guns, and therefore the machine-gun officer should always have the authority to place and control his guns as he saw fit.

The men most likely knew little about the headquarters critique, for they soon found themselves in a classic defensive routine. Some platoons would be in forward positions, while others were in support trenches and rear areas. The Germans opposite them had no intention of offensive actions, but neither were they ready to be submissive. As each day passed, the number of enemy aircraft increased as they reconnoitered over the American forces. German artillery became bolder and increased in accuracy. Both sides attempted raids to collect prisoners, but these were on the whole failures for the Germans. The machine gun battalions regularly sent barrages onto the Hindenburg Line, and infantry probed the defenses and captured prisoners. All this activity was for a purpose. The American intention was to keep the German Army on edge, to convince their enemy that the newly won St. Mihiel was the jumping-off spot for the next offensive.

The Rainbow Division was battle hardened, tested by combat, and they knew how to fight. "I don't suppose it will be long before they call on the "Rainbows" again and when they call we will be ready to go," Peter Sauver in the Fond du Lac company wrote to his family. "Some of our boys were talking with some German prisoners and they said that the 42nd Division was the only one they were afraid of and if it had not been for us they would not have been driven back as far as they were."[23]

On September 26, the division learned that General Pershing had launched a new attack north of St. Mihiel, in the Argonne Forest. Experienced divisions could not be spared at this crucial time, when it was crucial to keep pushing the Germans to inhibit their ability to form new lines of defense. At the end of September, the 42nd Division was relieved and sent north, toward the new battle in the forest. Long columns of trucks with their Indonesian drivers arrived, a sure sign that they were heading into battle once again. As the long columns started for the Argonne, they learned that Captain Graef had been promoted to major and put in charge of the 150th Machine Gun Battalion. As they were getting to move, Guy Gross sent a letter to his parents. "I wish I could save all your letters but we can only carry our equipment, though the letters you and dad wrote June 30 are in my pocket. I read and re-read those letters until there are only pieces left of them." He closed with, "With the best regards to everyone in dear old Fondy."[24]

10

Meuse-Argonne

Boys, she is hell.
Unknown soldier,
quoted in *Brief History*
of Old Company "F"

Within the Argonne Forest today are the skeletal remains of witches. Not the bodies of sorceresses in the sense of black-capped women of Halloween, but the hostile witches of the Giselher, Kriemhilde, and Freya lines. Moss and lichen cover old concrete blockhouses and gun emplacements, corroded iron protruding here and there. Walking paths with attractive interpretive signage guide visitors through sections of the Argonne because the woods are full of the rusted remains of unexploded shells and grenades, far too dangerous to handle or remove. And once in a while the adventurous hiker finds the pitiful remnant of some soldier who was lost to time.

Nature has the power to heal itself. When the Argonne battle ended, the crushed forest looked lifeless, as if it would forever be a land of raw earth and dead trees, not unlike the mythical evil place of Mordor in J. R. R. Tolkien's *Lord of the Rings*. Instead, one hundred years afterward, it is lush and beautiful in summer, soothingly green and quiet. And when summer slowly gives up to autumn and the days shorten, the rains come and valleys and hollows fill with mist.

◈

There is something about autumn rain that is different than rainfall in spring or summer. Maybe it is the short fall days and slanted light, or the low, gray cloud cover that seems to press down with such weight. It seems heavy, and it has the power to seek out every seam in one's clothing, to leak into your neck and pockets and down holes that you never realized were there. It sounds different, and it goes on hour after hour in steady, heavy downpours that have no limit, no reduction in volume. Dismal gray skies give the impression that they have unlimited capacity, and the glowering clouds never leave even if they are scudding across in a brisk wind. But above all, it is cold—far colder than a spring wetting.

In the clear air of a cool, crisp sunny day, trees look stately and grand, but under the somber deluge of a fall downpour everything takes on an aura of gloom. Wet tree trunks turn black, and the fallen leaves in the forest are soggy and flat. The mud seems deeper, clings ferociously to boots and clothing, and even has a different smell than summer mire. But maybe it is just that the green has long passed, and autumn rainfall signals that winter is waiting for its turn.

It is unlikely the Wisconsin and Pennsylvania men in the Argonne Forest had such thoughts. It was a wet cold that went through a man's body. Leather boots were waterlogged and covered with a thick pancake of mud that defied removal. They shivered and tried to find a little refuge in shell-damaged buildings or makeshift shelters. The incessant rain and the plodding of tens of thousands of men, horses, wagons, and trucks turned the shell-churned roads and trails into a mess that was almost hopeless to move through.

Many men in the 150th were hunters and had spent time pursuing game in fall, so they were familiar with the woods. But the Argonne was different. Hills were steep, cut by ravines and tough terrain, and small valleys and hollows ran one into another in mazelike fashion. Temperature inversions caused mists to fill these hollows, and with heavily overcast skies and no sun for orientation, each place looked like the last. Because poison gas was heavy, it lingered in every low spot. This forest was a sinister place.

German morale had declined acutely by October. Since the start of the spring offensives in March, the Germans had lost 40,000 officers and 1,181,577 other ranks.[1] Shortages and exhaustion were evident everywhere. The courage, fighting abilities, and sheer number of energetic and well-supplied Americans were all disheartening. Added to the German's sense of isolation and dismay was the fact that Austria-Hungary, Bulgaria, and Turkey had already accepted defeat and were now out of the war. At home, German civilians were suffering from lack of food, medicine, clothes, and long hours in factories. Influenza had also come to the Fatherland. The only course now for Germany was to inflict as many casualties as possible on their three enemies to slow the advance. German leaders hoped unacceptable cost in men would force the Allies to consider a peace that preserved the Fatherland.

The German high command thought the most logical axis of an allied advance was to continue the offensive from the St. Mihiel salient, toward Metz. The city was a central and therefore essential rail- and-road hub, and its loss would ensure that the German Army had no recourse but retreat. Differences within the Allied command required General Pershing to accept an offensive toward the city of Sedan, where railroad lines also radiated to serve the front. With Sedan in Allied hands, German defensive lines would have to be abandoned, eliminating the defensive advantage the Germans possessed. Sedan was a mere thirty-five miles away, but the route meant that an army had to pass through part of the Argonne Forest.

A section of the Hindenburg Line ran through the Argonne Forest. The grand plan was for the American forces to move to the right, or east of the forest, up the Aire River valley, as they attacked northward. The French would move west of the Argonne. The two armies would link and either trap the Germans between them or force them to retreat. But part of the way for the American Army was through that forest. The thick woods, steep hills, and narrow valleys were severe obstacles for infantry and artillery, and everything was fortified as only Germans could do.

The American Army's attack was part of a much larger grand strategy orchestrated by France's Marshall Foch. From the North Sea to the Swiss border, German lines would be attacked. The sheer scale of these combined offensives would force the enemy to defend the entire Western Front and prevent the Germans from weakening one part of their line to reinforce another. Without reserves, the enemy would either be forced out of France or forced to surrender. Nevertheless, when the plan for the American drive was reviewed, the French appreciated the magnitude of overcoming the forest defensive positions; they believed the American Meuse-Argonne offensive would fail.

Pershing's plan to convince the German command that he planned to continue an offensive from St. Mihiel. The Germans were only too willing to believe Pershing because it made military sense, and they were fatigued. While divisions like the 42nd aggressively raided and shelled that part of the Hindenburg Line, he had turned the rest of his massive army north in secrecy.

Since capturing Sedan from the French in 1914, the Germans had long understood that Sedan was a vital transportation hub. Sedan also had incredible symbolic meaning, the place of France's defeat in the Franco-Prussian war. The Germans recognized that the dense forest, steep hills, and limited road network offered extraordinary possibilities for defense in depth. The coordinates of these few roads were known to every artillery battery. Beginning in 1915, German engineers and construction battalions built three strong defensive rings, each named after three witches in the Wagnerian four-opera music drama *The Ring of the Nibelung*.[2] These places (*Stellungen*) were given the forbidding names of *Giselher Stellung*, *Kriemhilde Stellung* and finally, *Freya Stellung*, and they connected to other defensive lines, collectively known as the Hindenburg Line. Hundreds of miles of barbed-wire entanglements were established and maintained, and countless machine gun nests skillfully camouflaged and sited so that their fields of fire overlapped, positioned to ensure that flanking as well as direct fire would dominate any attacker. With typical thoroughness, they prepared well. Small tram systems ran throughout the region for easier, rapid resupply. Well-built, hidden trench systems and deep bunkers almost guaranteed that their soldiers would be protected as much as possible. Wounded soldiers would be cared for in nearby hospitals.

Some of General Pershing's most experienced divisions had suffered losses in the St. Michel battle, so he was compelled to start the Argonne offensive with inexperienced men. The American Army had 600,000 men, 2,700 artillery pieces, 189 tanks, and 821 aircraft, jammed in an area of operations about twenty-five miles wide. On Pershing's east flank was the Meuse River, too wide, deep, and swift to ford. On his west flank was the imposing forest and the Aisne River. Across the Meuse River were heights that dominated the lower western side. American divisions had to first reach the three witch defenses of the Hindenburg Line, which was fifteen miles deep and followed a sharp ridge that ran southeast-northwest from Montfaucon, Cunel, and Barricourt.

Because only a handful of roads led through the area, the transportation network was totally inadequate to support an army of this size and thus resulted in a logistics nightmare. Nonetheless, Pershing believed his forces would quickly shove their way through and outflank the high ground before the Germans could mobilize reinforcements. With French forces also moving swiftly forward, the Germans would be outflanked.

As the battle commenced on September 26, the 42nd Division was beginning its agonizingly slow move from St. Mihiel northward to join the battle. Few letters survive from the end of St. Mihiel to the start of the Argonne, perhaps indicative of the stress and constant movement over congested roads that allowed no rest periods. The initial American advance up the Aisne Valley by nine divisions, on a front almost twenty miles wide, attained eight miles; they breached the first line, *Giselher Stellung*. By the end of September, the army was poised to strike the far more forbidding main line of defense, the *Kriemhilde Stellung*.

Although the twelve German divisions were taken by surprise, they reacted swiftly. Despite low morale, the German's tremendous battlefield experience and discipline came into action to mount a cohesive defense that caught American forces ill-prepared to tackle such formidable resistance. The doughboys fought dense fog, tough terrain, rain, mud, and a battle-hardened foe. The *Kriemhilde Stellung* was dominated by the Romange Heights. From this commanding vantage point, German artillery fired from the heights across the Meuse River, out of reach of counterbattery fire; here the excellence of German artillery was apparent. The Americans now made little headway.

Pershing paused his attack in mid-October and brought up fresh divisions, including the veteran Rainbows. Dissatisfied with some commanders, Pershing put new leadership in place. The Americans reorganized, rested, refitted, and trained their infantry on infiltration tactics. The Germans did the same, and now the enemy had twenty-seven divisions facing the Americans. By this time, Germany had entered into negotiations to end the war. The frontline doughboys eventually heard about it, but their focus was what was facing them: *Kriemhilde Stellung.*

After spending about a week on slow, agonizing travel and a week camped around Montfaucon, the 150th began to move forward. The history of the 166th (Ohio) Infantry described it as "very difficult country, heavily wooded, far from level, and with few and bad roads and narrow valleys along which the progress of any considerable body of troops is extremely difficult."[3] Similar to the reaction of other units, the men of the 150th were amazed by the volume of American artillery, the endless columns of stalled traffic, and by what awaited them. "We went very slowly as the roads were jammed from fighting in this woods," said an unknown Pennsylvania soldier in Company D. "They were carpeted with Boche and American bodies."[4] The unknown scribe in the Oshkosh company recorded:

> This was a very hard hike as the country was exceedingly hilly. We were near the town of Avacourt which resembled one large mess of broken stone. The fields around were dotted with shell holes so thick that a man could not walk in any direction without walking on soil turned up by the shells. . . . It looked bad but we came over here to fight and fight we would to the last. The ground was all torn up, ammunition, guns, clothes, horse and dead men.

On a hike to look for their field kitchen, the writer "passed scores of returning wounded and as I passed several of them said to me, 'Boys, she is hell.'"[5]

The 42nd Division was to relieve the 1st Division and began doing so on the night of October 11 with the aid of guides. Weather conditions were terrible. It was cold, and rain fell constantly; roads and paths were a morass; wool uniforms became soaked with water and mud. The men were inadequately clothed, with no overcoats, only raincoats. The wet conditions caused a horrible problem as mustard gas became exceptionally effective when it came in contact with damp or wet skin. The Germans used a large number of these gas shells, and mustard gas lingered in the hollows and the brush-filled ravines long after the shelling ended. The miserable weather also made it hard for the men to get their bearings, for mists made it impossible to see what was ahead or beyond.

"As we climbed one ridge by a slippery path carrying our heavy loads, we suddenly came to a ridge almost perpendicular," wrote Lieutenant Parkinson in the 151st Machine Gun Battalion. "It was pitch dark. We could not see any way around, but we did see that the path led upward. The ground was so muddy and so slick one man could not go up alone. It was only by boosting one man after another that we formed a human chain that assisted the rest of the company forward. We passed through muddy ravine amid harassing shell fire and through a valley drenched with gas. At this point the guide informed us he was lost."[6]

In these conditions, supply wagons and carts and field kitchens could not meet the needs of their company. The postwar history noted that the machine-gun carts could not move forward, so everything had to be carried by hand for five excruciating kilometers (about three miles). The 150th soon suffered from a lack of food, clean drinking water, medical aid, and ammunition. Sleep was not possible, and it was necessary to sleep wearing a gas mask; fatigue led to poor decisions and costly mistakes. Wounded soldiers cried in agony for days, waiting for stretcher bearers who could not advance. The surviving soldiers listened to the wails and cries of friend and foe, and even though they tried to harden themselves it wore on them emotionally. Regrettably, commanders were far to the rear and had no idea of what combat was like for their men.

As dawn broke on the day following the relief of the 1st Division, the front-line platoons of the 150th realized that they faced hills and fields of rusting barbed wire that stretched for hundreds of yards. "These hills were covered with a dense forest filled with undergrowth and thickets," recalled Parkinson. In fact, over the years brambles and young trees had grown through the rolled tangle of barbed wire, creating an even worse obstruction than just wire. It was hard enough for an infantryman to cut through, and an almost insurmountable obstacle to a crew with a Hotchkiss. From their position on Hill 240, the men looked out on a landscape "particularly rugged, exceptionally arduous, and, during this particular season, peculiarly water-logged."[7]

Breaking *Kriemhilde Stellung* and the Romange Heights hinged on Côte de Châtillion. This fortified hill, the highest point, dominated the American lines. From there the Germans could see down into American lines with their powerful optics, directing artillery fire with unerring accuracy. The 84th Brigade was assigned to take Côte de Châtillion. At the same time the 83rd Brigade, with the 150th attached, was to attack toward the towns of St. Georges and Landres-et-St. Georges. The problems were many. The 84th Brigade first had to take Hill 288 and two fortified farms before they could even assault the main objective on the heights. Headquarters planners thought that it would take the infantry of the 84th Brigade six hours to secure Châtillon. In the meantime, the 83rd Brigade, with supporting platoons from the Machine Gun Battalion, was ordered to advance one mile across open fields in full view of Châtillon and its defenders.

The attack started in the early morning. Despite hours of intense American artillery fire and machine-gun barrages, the Germans were very much alive in their deep, solid bunkers since a direct hit was required to destroy their heavy fortification. As soon as the advance started, the enemy poured fire down onto the struggling American infantry and their supporting machine-gun units. Once the 83rd Brigade was committed, they were subject to relentless flanking fire from Maxim guns and artillery. Machine guns of the 150th were ordered forward to help overpower German gun emplacements by concentrated fire.

The Fond du Lac company, trying to find the 165th Infantry, bore the first brunt of the fury. The action and gruesome sights made it into Granger's diary on October 14: "[S]hells landing pretty thick. . . . Lost my helmet and had to wear a German one. . . . Germans got our range before we had fired eight clips."[8]

Sergeant Al Dreier was in charge of the first platoon and, to its right, was Sergeant Roy Kraemer of the second platoon. "On the night of the 14th [Al] took his Platoon and went on a raiding party with the infantry," Kraemer told Dreier's sister, Hazel, after the war. "On the morning of the 15th we . . . reached a hill and could not advance any further on account of machine gun fire. . . . The order came to send a section over to our left and hold the Dutch who were coming through on us [i.e., attacking their flank], and your brother was picked to do the job and I must say that all the men must thank him for his gallant work as he saved our lives and lost his own doing it."

The Germans launched localized counterattacks, and an attack on the flank could be especially devastating unless it was quickly stopped. From a flank position, enemy fire could run down the entire line and was more effective than frontal fire. "It was an awful sight and a day I will never forget. His gunners fought to the finish and died on the guns. Al was giving orders when he was killed and the one man that came back told me he died with the word 'fire' on his lips." But the sacrifice was worth it, for the German flank attack was stopped. He concluded his letter with "As much as you miss him at home his

loss is felt here in the company and I must say for the captain and the rest of the
company that we are proud to have had him in the company. Hoping that no
more sadness many enter your home."[9]

Another man in Company B, Lloyd Kindness, recalled the action this way:

> We entered the Argonne Forest. . . . What I saw I will never forget. There
> on the ground lay dead Germans and Americans . . . we advanced that
> morning. . . . Our platoon was assigned to throw a barrage over the in-
> fantry. . . . We were exposed to the enemy's fire and they got our range and
> started a creeping barrage on us. It was terrible as we looked in the valley
> below and saw the 166th Infantry walking right into that fire. . . . Finally it
> became too dangerous so someone yelled "out of action," so we scurried
> back of the hill to cover. . . . I didn't feel right lying there behind that hill
> under cover. So I just went ahead alone and helped carry in wounded
> soldiers, no matter who they were.[10]

The fire from the entrenched defenders was so fierce that two officers from
the Fond du Lac company, Captain Finn and Lieutenant Ames, were both
wounded within a short time, and there were growing casualties among the
gun crews. One Hotchkiss was served by two brothers, Albert and Otto Lange.
An artillery shell killed the older brother, Albert, and "[t]he sight broke the
younger's one's nerves," said Lloyd Kindness years later, "he shook like a leaf.
He pulled out his pistol. He started to go over alone and clean them up. He
yelled, 'They got my brother, I'll get them, I'll get them, let me at 'em.' It took
two or three to hold him." It took three men to get Otto to a dressing station
and from there to a hospital, a case of shell shock. Every man had his breaking
point.[11]

Pennsylvania Company D fared no better. Sergeant Smith's diary stated:
"October 14th. We dug in and Fritz pulverized the ground over which we had
advanced this morning. We paid dearly for our gains. Fritz bumped off four of
our boys with one shell. . . . Many of us were sick with disentery [dysentery].
October 16th Still raining. . . . Sure is hell to be lying in shell holes filled with
mud and water and practically no food. . . . October 17th . . . Boche artillery
combing the hill continuously." Even though the machine-gun squads were not
committed to direct attacks on enemy strong points and trenches, they were at
a distinct disadvantage under fire. "The men at the guns being unable to scatter
the way the infantry can offer a group target which enables one shell to do
much more damage."[12]

Traversing Maxim guns poured intense fire down on the advancing units
from both the front and flank. German infantrymen sniped at anything the
machine guns missed. "The Germans had the tops of these hills lined with

machine guns making us pay dearly for every foot we advanced."[13] The 83rd could advance no farther until the 84th Brigade wrestled the determined German defenders from Châtillon. In the meantime, they had no choice but to dig in and bear the German fire, the hail of bullets so thick and fast that Granger jotted, "a mosquito wasn't safe," and listed the company's dead and wounded.[14] Neither was there protection for platoons in support and reserve. They could shelter on the reverse slope of a hill, much safer than the top or forward side, but they were not out of reach of artillery and gas.

The enemy was hated with a deep, unfathomable passion, and combat took on an intensity and bitterness heretofore unequalled. By their third day in action, the men of the 150th were suffering severely from enemy action, dreadful weather, and lack of water and food. Granger recorded in his diary on October 15: "The Ger. using explosive bullets. We advanced a couple of hundred yards. . . . I laid in a shell hole for 12 hours . . . [the Germans] not a bit bashful about using up their big ammunition." The enemy used a large number of mustard gas shells because they knew it worked well when uniforms were wet, and Granger and many others were gassed as they lay there under cover. Granger was taken to a makeshift hospital located in a cellar. Once there, he found the conditions little better than at the front. Disgusted and eager to get back his comrades, he returned the next day. His diary reads: "When I got in they gave me two cups of hot chocolate and a package of cookies which was the best in one awful long time. Was sicker than the devil, rained hard. Every body was all in." Sergeant Smith in Company D recorded, "Many of our men are going back wounded. . . . The bombardment never stops."[15] Even the companies in support and reserve had no respite, as German artillery had a long reach. That day a German plane dropped leaflets that read in part, "isn't it better to live than to die no matter for how glorious a cause than to rot in the shell holes of France. You don't want to die til you have to." The leaflet angered the men and "the boys took [them] as an insult to our Army."[16]

The tough doughboys learned quickly that to succeed, to have a chance to live, they had to advance slowly. Small patrols would gradually flank and surround enemy strong points, then destroy them using rifle fire and grenades, and then finish the job with bayonet work. The battalion's machine guns working together from multiple angles would dominate enemy machine guns. No quarter was asked or given, and the combat was fierce. Arnold S. Hoke, an officer in the 168th Infantry, clearly did not want to relive the memory during his oral history. Instead, in a hesitant voice he said, "It was rough going and I didn't know if my brother and I were going to make it through that phase of it."[17]

At the height of the battle, sixty machine guns worked together under the direction of the 151st Machine Gun Battalion in order to create impenetrable zones of fire that prevented enemy movement. At the turning point of the battle, and using a group of fir trees as a reference point, every machine gun that could be spared was given a space fifty yards wide to cover, every gun had a specific target. Other Hotchkiss guns were assigned individual targets. "The firing data of each gun was carefully figured. The gun crews were given permission to fire as rapidly as possible without overheating the gun itself. . . . During the 45 minutes of this barrage nearly 1,000,000 rounds of ammunition were fired."[18]

The great hill of Châtillon was finally taken on October 16, and with its collapse the *Kriemhilde Stellung* broke. The excellent supporting fire from the massed Hotchkiss guns of the 150th and 151st Machine Gun Battalions were instrumental in helping achieve a breakthrough. Every gun had been put into action, including reserve guns, so that "every foot of the enemy trenches was covered so perfectly that the attacking troops were able to advance almost to their objective before receiving any of the enemy fire." They had laid down an incessant barrage of direct and plunging fire. A captured German officer stated that "the bullets had been so thick that they were unable to do anything."[19]

There was no relief, and there was another hill to take; combat continued. Lieutenant Bahr did not have the time or energy to write anything. But while he lay in a shell hole, Robert Holterman pulled out his small pocket diary and scribbled terse but telling entries: "rained"; "established line of resistance of machine guns"; "gas and H.E."; "Balthazor died of wounds gas & blew off both legs"; "Pollard buried alive dead when we dug him out."[20] One thing was clear to the men, and that was machine gun squads could not scatter like infantryman did. They were attached to their gun, so a single shell could kill the entire crew. "Our platoon was assigned to throw a barrage," Lloyd Kindness related in explicit detail. "We were exposed to the enemy's fire, and they got our range and started a creeping barrage on us. . . . Finally it became too dangerous so someone yelled 'out of action,' so we scurried back of the hill to cover." Later, the squad found the gun upset and large shell hole almost under it.[21]

Wounded soldiers could expect little assistance in the midst of the inferno. If they were lucky, their friends would pull them under cover and give rudimentary aid. An incident on October 17, related by Private Joseph B. Connolly with the Bucktails, illustrated the conditions.

> [T]welve of us were picked from the Machine Gun Company, 165th Infantry, to take a Machine Gun nest . . . under extremely heavy shell fire, large and small caliber. . . . Private Henderson carried the musette bag with the clips and extra barrel, I carried the tripod and other attachment. These things always weigh a ton . . . we cross a steep embankment which had a 60 degree angle drop . . . shells seemed to rain around us at this point . . . fallen [trees gave] us some protection and thus undoubtedly saved our lives.

Connolly's leg was severely broken from shrapnel during a bombardment. In incredible pain, he was trapped, unable to move. His comrade, James Billy, organized a rescue using men from B or D company, including Private James Meade, who later related what happened. Under fire, Meade explained, they took Connolly to a nearby aid station, although the rescuers had to drop him when a gas shell exploded so they could take cover and put on and adjust their gas masks. Once at the aid station, the medics could do nothing for Connolly since they were completely out of medical supplies. Eventually a Ford ambulance arrived, and he was loaded into the back with other wounded soldiers. After a grueling thirty-six-hour-long bouncing ride without treatment of any kind, and in dreadful agony, Connolly arrived at a hospital outside Paris. By then, he had contracted lockjaw (tetanus) in addition to his other injuries, but he survived. Connolly's squad did destroy the German machine gun nest.[22]

Lloyd Kindness, again in vivid description, was ordered to bring food up to the men from the company kitchen. Halfway back, shell fire drove them under cover, and a noncommissioned officer with them ordered Kindness to just stay under cover. But the warrior spirit in this courageous Native American, and his devotion to his comrades, would not accept that. Despite a wound to his hand, "I didn't feel right lying there behind that hill under cover. So I just went right ahead alone and helped carry in wounded soldiers, no matter who they were. . . . I done that till our company was relived from the front line, and the shelling was heavy, too."[23] Strange things happen in combat, and the fighting in the Argonne was no exception. Miraculously, in the midst of all that hell, mail reached the struggling front line companies on October 24; it gave everyone a morale boost.

German resistance was not as fierce as the AEF offensive continued toward the third, and weakest, of the witch rings, the *Freya Stellung.* "Things were quiet until the evening of the 22nd when the Germans began sending them [artillery shells] over faster than usual," recalled the unidentified Company C man. "About 7:00 p.m. while Lt. Ranney was holding a meeting of the noncommissioned officers a shell hit right in the circle they had formed, killing Sgt. F.[rank] Obersteiner and wounding Sgts. Peckman, Polier, Friday, Fauck, Cpl. Sphaat and Pvt. Coffers."[24] Arthur Bahr was part of the group. "Had a narrow escape to-day, when a shell a 105 landed 20 feet from me," he wrote in the diary. He listed the dead and wounded and ended the entry with, "I got only a scratch back of the right ear." Death, as usual, was a random thing.[25]

The Fond du Lac company truly was used up. "Capt. Finn is the only officer that we have and they wanted to send him to the hospital but he would not leave the company," Bugler Rudy Kraemer said in a letter to his friend James Farrell back in Campbellsport. "[He] grabbed a cane and led the company just the same walking through machine gun fire and shrapnel just as if he were made of iron, although his rain coat was full of machine gun holes." Kraemer simply described the Argonne battle in one word: "awful," and then recounted, "I don't believe we have 25 or 30 men left that we had when we left Fondy." Farrell had been sent home from training camp, and Kraemer told him he was glad for it. "I hate to hear that my old friends have to come over here and go through what we have had to."[26] About the same time that Kraemer was writing, in another part of the line, Corporal Horace Stever in Company C told his mother, "I was in hope that we would be home by Christmas, but it is doubtful as it will take some time to settle this thing . . . we are almost played out."[27]

Parents and family members wanted to know exactly what happened to their son or loved one, so it was not uncommon for comrades to offer an explanation. In a letter written after the Armistice, George Roble sent a letter to the parents of Waldo Balthazor, and Roble did not spare any details. "Waldo was struck by a high explosive shell and suffered the loss of both limbs." Roble went on to describe exactly what happened. "He was in a 'fox hole' at the time . . . after the debris had been cleared away they found [him] lying on the ground . . . some companions picked him up and carried him to a first aid dressing station. Waldo called for a glass of water and died in the arms of a companion."[28]

The division was relieved, but the fight continued for the machine gun battalions, as they were to help put over a monstrous barrage. A well-planned attack on November 1 was preceded by an immense artillery and barrage from two hundred machine guns from 3:30 to 5:55 a.m. This intense barrage, synchronized by the 151st Battalion's Major Winn, who had been promoted to Corps Machine Gun Officer, was the embodiment of perfected machine-gun fire. Every gun was given coordinates and ranges and when to adjust their fire as the infantry advanced, and they fired continuously. Corporal Holterman's gun alone went through 4,400 rounds. For the 150th, their target was the linchpin, Hill 272. The guns all fired until they reached extreme range, or about 4,800 meters (almost three miles). Lieutenant Ellis called the long, intense fire "a perfect hell" for the enemy. He continued, "the artillery drove the Huns out of their dugouts and the machine guns drive them back in. When the men passed the ground several days later, he said "every tree [was] marked with machine gun bullets." Lieutenant Parkinson said that every field had been "literally plowed and replowed" by artillery fire.[29] They did not know it at the time, but it was the last time there would be such an impressive coordination of machine guns.

The German lines bent and then broke, and the infantry poured forward "like dogs loosened from a leash."[30] With their lines in danger of being flanked, the enemy began a headlong retreat. Sedan was within reach, and American and French armies steadily converged on the city. On November 1, Granger noted in his diary, "The 6th marines went over the top and went thru Seen about 2,000 prisoners come in. Most of them seem very happy . . . we had some time."[31] (Holterman described it as "Boo-Coo prisoners," the doughboy version of the French "beaucoup," meaning "many.")

After forty-seven days and 120,000 casualties, the U.S. Army had done what French leaders thought impossible: They had broken through the fortified lines in the Argonne Forest. With the breakthrough and almost three weeks in the front lines, the 42nd was ordered into reserve. Lieutenant Parkinson in the 151st provided a vivid description of what the exhausted machine gunners faced as they moved miles to the rear along mud tracks hardly worth the name of trail. "There were many holes so deep that it was out of the question for a mule to pull a cart through. Some were so deep that even after the mules were unhitched there was a question whether they would not founder in a bog. . . . The mules had to be unhitched and the carts drawn through by men with long ropes, and with others at the wheels hip deep in mud."[32] Granger simply expressed it this way: "one hell of a mess."

Finally, the weary soldiers, gaunt from many days without food, reached their field kitchens, where the cooks had an abundance of hot food waiting. Their uniforms were filthy and in tatters, and new clothes were issued. The men were exhausted, but they were allowed only one day of rest before being ordered forward on November 4.

During their brief rest, Harvey Stich took time to write to his brother. "[Y]ou have waited for me to write, and you didn't hear from me for a long time . . . because we are after the Germans and we got them on the run all the time, and we are taking lots of German prisoners on all the fronts. . . . Well let's hope the war will end very soon and get back to the land of the free and the home of the brave." Nothing angered the men more than the folks back home who did not support the war, especially after what they just experienced. "Those guys that failed Uncle Sam in the Liberty Loans and other appeals will feel mighty small as will also those sneaks that are enjoying the fat of the land and preaching and whispering against the land that is giving them plenty," Stich angrily avowed. "They are traitors, each and everyone of them, and even the Hun would shun them."[33]

Sometime in late October, Rudy Kraemer told his cousin, "[B]y the way things look it won't be long before we are home, seeing that Germany is left all alone to fight it out. You can imagine how anxious we are at times to get home, but never the less we want to see the Huns beaten to stand still, and she will be beaten so she will never again be a powerful country. . . . When we come back we will never worry about Germany trying to start anything again."[34]

The last defensive line was breached, the forest was behind them, and the enemy was in retreat. Yet, it was a tough, demanding time. Many Rainbow soldiers would recall it as their worse period while in France. They were worn out from the recent battle, had been given no rest, food was totally inadequate so the men lacked energy and stamina, and the rain made life wretched. Nonetheless, the men knew now that Germany was on its knees.

The army was now in "a land of high ridges and deep valleys, heavily wooded throughout, containing clean fresh fields and undamaged towns. . . . Fine broad roads ran in all directions, and rapid deep brooks cut the fertile vales and cross under highways through stone culverts."[35] Small villages, occupied by the Germans since 1914, were finally liberated after four years; the white flag was raised, signifying the enemy was gone.

The doughboys had trouble keeping up with the enemy, yet pursued them night and day. The enemy had blown up bridges over the numerous streams, mined roads, and left well-sited machine guns, and they occasionally shelled the crowded roads with artillery in an attempt to slow the American pursuit. With machine guns kept in the carts, the men followed the infantry as best they could. "Nov. 4th we landed on a big farm 'all in' from the hike. We rested without breakfast. We had one meal in three days. The Germans were going so fast our kitchens could not keep [up] to us."[36] Food remained a problem, both for the men and their mules, and hunger sapped the strength of both. A mule needed twenty to thirty pounds of fodder a day, but there was none. The animals gnawed tree bark, and went lame because they could not be reshod or properly cared for. There was little food to scrounge because the Germans had taken everything of worth from the village. Lieutenant Parkinson in the 151st noted that they sometimes pulled up unharvested turnips, beets, and cabbages.

On the night of November 5, in the pitch blackness of a cold and rainy night, the 42nd relieved the 27th Division near the village of Sy, and the men were once more at the point as the AEF pursued the fleeing Germans. Although the German Army did not stop to fight, concealed machine gunners fought at their guns until they were killed, or they skedaddled before the advancing Americans. At one ambush, Lieutenant Arnold Hoke recalled, the enemy gunners had their sights set high and shot over the heads of his men. "Then they would take the machine gun apart real fast and then take off their army boots and retreat as fast as they could . . . there would be six or eight pair of those laying around the perimeter of the machine gun nest."[37] Using what they had learned from St. Mihiel, the gunners of the 150th kept closer liaison with the infantry. A machine-gun officer accompanied the advance units and could determine when the Hotchkiss guns could be put to good use.

The pursuit affected even the ever-cheerful Granger. "Every thing was blowed up along the road. One bridge there was not a stone left," he wrote on

November 5. Even as the end of the war seemed close, he had yet another close call with death. "A shell landed about 10 feet ahead of me killed 4 A Co. men. Slept on side of hill. Rained to beat hell. About 2 in. of water in my shoes from wading creeks where bridges were blowed out."[38] And a few days later, he wrote, "German M.G. fire held us a couple of hours. The hills were so steep that you would need a pair of pole climbers to hold on with."[39] The mud at least helped in one respect: shells sometimes failed to explode, instead burying themselves deeply in the ground. Duds, as they were called, were always worthy of mention, especially when they were close. "One place along the road the bridge was blown out," recalled Parkinson in the 151st. "The stream was not wide, but it was rather deep . . . the carts were pulled through by hand, and each mule skinner walked across a log and led his mule through the water. It was quite a scramble for the mules to ascend the opposite bank."[40]

The 150th were thoroughly hardened soldiers who realized that, despite their incredible weariness, the only way to get home was to kill the enemy. Once again in detail, Lloyd Kindness described bitter fighting in the cold mud on November 6:

> A shell would come and we'd drop down in the ditch. It went on like this until about midnight. I was the gunner then. I am small anyway. That Hotchkiss sure was heavy. We came to a steep hill with a road at the bottom. As we went down that hill, they started shelling again heavy. I fell head first, gun and all. . . . Some of our men stumbled into some wire that the Germans had placed there as a trap. When they did that, why, the Germans opened up with the machine guns and this was the closest call I'd had for some time. I dropped flat on the ground and could hear the bullets sing and whistles all around me. . . . Finally the Germans let up their fire after some of our men went down there and bayoneted them. I could hear some German shout, "Heinie, wasser, wasser." Some German wanted his partner to bring him water, but he never got water, as he died soon.[41]

Nor did Lieutenant Allan Ellis have qualms about killing Germans after the anguish of the Argonne. The same day as Lloyd Kindness related his experience, Ellis took evident delight in relating an incident on a less dramatic scale. The Germans had two hidden Maxim guns, and another group waved a white flag. When the American went forward to accept the surrender, the guns opened up. The doughboys unleashed hell on them, and Ellis recounted, "The best fun I had that day was snipping at two groups of Huns with a Springfield, range 1,200 yards, and making 'em hunt cover."[42]

The countryside leading to Sedan was a welcome relief from the Argonne. It was largely untouched by war, and at times they were able to sleep in barns and other buildings out of the rain. The Rainbows pursued as fast as they could move, often outstripped their long, winding, truck supply convoys. "We drove them thirty kilometers through rain and mud, and terrific machine gun fire," Edward Lutz in Company A told his mother in a November 24 letter.[43] In seven days, the men of the 150th had only five meals. Granger delighted in writing, "Had first warm meal in four days. . . . Most welcome thing in a long while was a pair of home knit socks."[44] Lieutenant Bahr's diary entries were short and to the point, clearly communicating his exhaustion. On November 6, he commented about the rain and mud, stating "we look like pigs."

When the French relived them on November 8, the men had to march twenty kilometers to the rear before being directed to a field. Lieutenant Bahr expressed his disgust by noting, "bivouacked in a mud field." The men in the Oshkosh company were "all in," having had but one meal in three days. The next morning the field kitchens were there and ready, and then they ate three meals a day. On November 10, they resumed the march and arrived at Fontaney, where they were ordered to billet inside. One of their wounded, Sergeant Elwin Ruppel, returned from the hospital that day and brought news that an armistice would be signed. Along that glad report, they also received news that they were to receive fresh uniforms and would be paid, which was three months overdue.[45]

The guns in Europe fell silent on November 11 at 11:00 a.m. "The French relieved us at four in the morning saying they wanted to be in the front line when peace was signed," Edward Lutz told his mother. "We didn't hesitate a minute as we only had four gun squads left out of twelve and we were nearly all exhausted mostly with rheumatism."[46] The Fondy boys had been on a hill overlooking Sedan when they were relieved by a French division and went into reserve, said Sergeant Leslie Timian, who in early 1919 had been sent home to recover from wounds. "At first we didn't believe it. We had been fooled before, but when we saw automobiles with lights lighted and fires burning in the open we knew it was true. And then we thought of home, home in great big capital letters." He told the reporter from the *Daily Commonwealth* that according to his calculation, the company lost nineteen men killed and had eighty-six wounded, but it was being brought back up to full strength for occupation duty. "They were as fine a bunch as ever went out in the war. They stick together through thick and thin."[47] The Oshkosh men didn't believe it at first, either, but when they saw "thousands of camp fires, each one surrounded by laughing and shouting boys . . . [and] the sounds of song and laughter drifted back and forth across the valley," their doubts vanished.[48] The Iowa officer with the 168th Infantry, Lieutenant Hoke, remembered, "we had the most gorgeous fire you ever seen . . . first open fire we'd had in countless months."[49]

There were celebrations, to be sure, but the men were too worn out to party. Herbert Granger merely wrote in his diary, "Never knew anything about the armistice until 10 o'clock that morning. Some celebration that nite. Nice out."[50]

11

Victory and Occupation

The sound of the joyful cries of *Vive L'Amerique* and *Vive les
Americains* still ring in my ears and how the bells pealed forth.

Allan B. Ellis,
A Brief History of Appleton's "Old Company G"

Suburban sprawl is not unique to the United States. As new construction
expands the limits of traditional Belgian and French communities, every now
and then work stops because excavators uncover skeletal remains. While archaeologists gently remove the claylike soil, curious onlookers text photos of
the discovery, amazed that it was once a battlefield. Maybe that is as it should
be, to forget war. On the other hand, the loss of memory demeans the tragedy
that once played out under the now-gentle fields. Other residents, with backs
bowed and skin no longer tight with youth but with eyes still bright, frail
bodies supported by the arms of grandchildren, know who the archaeologists
bring into the twenty-first-century sun. As children, these elderly observers
heard the fresh stories of the Great War from parents who witnessed war
firsthand. Today's well-paved roads, then muddy tracks, once held long columns of youthful doughboys marching east to the tearful cheers of the
war-weary.

The 42nd Division, one of the first divisions in France, had been in almost
continuous action since February. It was a year filled with boredom and ordeal,

tragedy, grief, excitement, and victory. The men had seen many of their best comrades fall. They rightfully assumed they would be among the first to be sent home. But the Allies elected to send combat experienced divisions to the Rhine River crossings as a safeguard in the event the German government rejected the terms of the Armistice.[1] The 42nd Division was one of the units chosen. No doubt choice words were spoken when they were told that they would become part of the Army of Occupation, and their area of activity would center on the city of Coblenz.

One thing that had not changed in the year they had been at war was that it was a soldier's destiny to "hike." On November 16, the 150th "made packs and was on our wearry way," the start of a long walk to Germany, but at least they were sporting fresh, new uniforms, and a band from the 166th Infantry played "snappy American pieces" as they hiked. "Marching in the winter under the best of circumstances is not particularly pleasant," explained the official history of the division. "Marching when physically exhausted from nearly three months spent in the face of the enemy . . . is a hard task. When it is accompanied with the mental and spiritual let down which the knowledge that the fighting is over inevitably brings, the task is still more difficult."[2] The men were soon in a portion of France that had been occupied by German forces since 1914. For months near the front it seemed that every French village and farmhouse the men had seen had been totally shattered by shells. Now it was very different. "There was absolutely no sign of war," Allan Ellis wrote to his mother on November 22, 1918, that the land had "no shell holes, no ruined buildings," and then went on to tell his mother that the Germans had used a fourteenth-century Gothic cathedral as a stable. Even more notable than the landscape was the 150th's reception by weary French civilians. Major Lothar Graef, in command of the battalion, was presented with a huge bouquet, school children sang "La Marseillaise," and numerous toasts were raised. "I can't describe the ceremony, so heartfelt and simple and so very moving," he wrote. "No young men, only grey beards, women, girls and children."[3]

The long column cut through the corner of Belgium, the small nation that had bravely delayed the German colossus in 1914 and had suffered grievously for their courage. Belgian citizens flew handmade American flags; some of the flags were inaccurate and had the stripes vertical or a few white circles instead of a field of stars. But the meaning of those scraps of multicolored cloth was not lost on the footsore, bone-tired, doughboys. "I can't describe how touching it was to me to see the pitiful attempts of these war torn people to manufacture that beautiful flag," Ellis expressed with heartfelt emotion.[4]

"We marched for nearly two days in Belgium and as long as I live I will never forget those two days," Leo Uelmen wrote to his father once they were in Germany.

Every town was decorated with green trees and the trees trimmed with red neckties, silver from tobacco wrappings, anything that was colored was hung on the trees, and flags, mostly hand made, hung everywhere. On entering the town . . . children would be singing and cheering for all they were worth, old men and women would cry out, "Vive les Americains," meaning "hurrah for the Americans" and then again there were old men and women that stood there heads bare and hands clasped as if they thought it must only be a dream that their suffering under Hun rule was over. Just think of coming out of battle and then see with your own eyes what you have been fighting for. If only the parents of the dead American soldiers could see the happy faces of the Belgium people.[5]

The pace of the march was punishing. The retreating German Army was only a day ahead of the Americans, and the objective was not to let the vanquished enemy get too far ahead. The roads were in poor condition from four years of war traffic and minimal upkeep, the weather once again awful, the men hungry, their boots worn out. The mules were also in tough shape, sometimes too weak to pull the cart, and fodder was scarce for the weakened animals.

The battalion stopped near Boevange, Luxembourg, on November 28, to celebrate Thanksgiving. "[T]he people all talked German so the boys of our company began to feel quite at home," explained Company C's chronicler, acknowledging the men's lineage. They all bathed and slept inside homes and barns. The field kitchens were somewhere well behind the company, so that meant eating their reserve rations. This was salty canned beef or salmon, canned vegetables, usually stewed tomatoes or beans, and hard bread (crackers) sealed in an eight-ounce can. Herbert Granger wrote, "Thanksgiving day. Every one thankfull that they were alive. Had corn willy in place of turkey. The lady [where they stayed] gave us apple pie. Rain."[6] The age-old difference between enlisted men and officers was obvious on the national day of thanks, a day especially enjoyable now that the guns were silent. While the enlisted men were eating corned willy, at least some of the officers of the 150th fared far better. Ellis, in the Headquarters Company, boasted to his mother that while they did not have the traditional turkey, "we have managed pretty well. . . . Roast Beef, Mashed Potatoes with Brown Gravy, Creamed Carrots, Bread and Butter, Coffee, Coffee Cake." He could not resist adding that, "The coffee cake is the piece de resistance. Our own cooks bake it to perfection—using Luxemburg yeast."[7]

The Thanksgiving pause was welcome, but the march was far from over. They covered twenty to thirty kilometers (twelve to eighteen miles) each day, although they rested every other day due to the men's profound exhaustion. The soldier's weariness was offset to some extent by the welcome they received as they marched through Belgium and Luxembourg. "Every town was lined with people and a mass of streamers, rows of evergreens trimmed with colored paper and ribbons," recalled Ellis. "The sound of the joyful cries of *Vive L'Amerique* and *Vive les Americains* still ring in my ears and how the bells pealed forth. I am repaid for my poor sacrifices."[8] During a rest stop in Luxembourg, Edward Lutz told his mother that "the Belgian people were glad to see us. They gave us coffee, bread, and jam and their best rooms to sleep in, a stove and a clock in each room." In the next sentence, he expressed his anger and frustration about how the Belgian people charge the doughboys exorbitant prices for food. "The people are highway robbers," he claimed. "Eggs are twenty-five cents a piece, chicken $10."[9]

They did not know what to expect once they crossed the border into their enemy's heartland, and the battalion was ordered to wear their pistols at all times. The army had impressed on the troops that while the shooting was officially over, a treaty had not yet been signed and it was possible hostilities would resume. Would the doughboys be reviled as hated conquerors, responsible for Germany's chaos? Would snipers and saboteurs harass the long columns and cause casualties? "We anticipate no trouble," wrote Ellis, "but are prepared for all eventualities."[10] But there was excitement, too. Germany was the land of the enemy, but for many it was also the land of their birth or their parent's birth. At the first village they billeted, the Germans greeted the battalion with smiles. The owner of the home where Company A's officers were billeted spread a white table cloth, set out fresh bread, butter, prune jam, and preserved apples, all served on the owner's best china plates. His men got coffee and bread.[11]

They walked the final few days in the rain and finally arrived at their place of occupation, a village named Bodendorf, on December 17. This area was to be their home for the next four months. "Every body all in even the mules were dragging their legs," Granger wrote in his diary.[12] With a bit of smugness, Bahr put in his diary that the battalion covered 288 kilometers, or 181 miles. "Out of the 30 days it took us to get here, we hiked 16 days and rested 14 days."[13] Upon arrival, Allan Ellis ordered his 1st Sergeant, Edward Lutz, to account for the men in Company A. "He found sixty-five men and three officers who were on the roll when we left Camp Douglas for Camp Mills," he wrote to his mother. "The rest not killed are scattered all over France and some are back home."[14]

Shortly thereafter, some of the wounded rejoined their unit. For wounded, there was always the very real possibility that once they were pronounced fit, they would not be sent back to their old company and the comrades they knew so well. Sadly, news also arrived that some of their comrades did not recover. Joseph Lorenz, an Ohio lad who enlisted in Company C while in Wisconsin looking for work, was wounded August 3 at Château-Thierry by both bullet and shrapnel. Seeming to recover well despite the amputation of his leg, he died November 21, 1918, probably from influenza.[15] The terrible influenza raging across the globe seemed to crown the tragedy of the last four years, putting an exclamation point on what had been a time of profound change, transition, destruction, exhilaration, and grief.

For the most part, the German population was friendly to the Americans and eager to billet them, as it meant extra food and money. Lothar Graef felt somewhat at home among the German people. "Am making very good use of my German," he explained to his father. "Have had many say that I must have lived in Germany as I speak it so well. . . . Knowing how I used to talk I know you will smile. . . . I sometimes get stalled on some words but they are generally some words we never used in the United States." He found the people quite willing to talk. "Everywhere we go or rather have gone, we find hatred for the Prussian and the military powers." He talked to German soldiers recently released from the army and they told him: "The Americans never retreat. The Americans are crazy. They fight as though it were sport. They were very brave and reckless and came right through the bullets."[16] The men were put in various homes, which one anonymous Appleton solider wrote were "small, low-ceilinged rooms, with but space enough for from two to six men (invariably furnished with a picture of the Kaiser and a great general or two) . . . some of us are fortunate in having a room with a bed in it. . . . Of course we are forbidden to fraternize with the people here and the order is being successfully carried out—even though half the battalion speaks 'German.' The relations between us that are necessary are of a friendly character." His letter also explained that food was extremely expensive, and that many ex-German soldiers were returning home.[17]

Not every interaction with the German population was cordial. When Sergeant Earl E. Young of Company D was assigned to a small house, the family gave him a tiny six-foot by twelve-foot room, hardly big enough for his section. He ordered the family to remove the furniture, but the man refused so the machine gunner piled the furnishings in the street. Young then ordered a large painting of the kaiser to be removed, and the family again refused, saying they would obey the kaiser and no one else. "So I drew my colt .45 automatic and smashed the glass. Then I took the picture down . . . and took from my pocket a photo of myself taken in France, and hung it on the wall in the same place, telling 'Hock, dat is der Kaiser.' They looked at the photo and at me. I made them salute the new photo, which they did after a little argument. . . . I told all that I would be the Kaiser of Bodendorf."[18]

The day after Christmas and ten days after the battalion arrived in Germany, the army sent one officer and one sergeant from each company back to France to attend a weapons school at Chatillon to learn about their new gun, the American-made Browning Model 1917. "We sure had some time on the train," Lieutenant Bahr entered in his diary. "Some soldier spied a wine barrel, he took out his pistol shot a few holes thru it, then they all rushed out and filled their canteens and cups. The next stop someone spied a carload of champagne and they unloaded [and] we had 41 bottles in our car for 6 men." The school concluded on January 17, 1919. The trip back to Germany, however, was a much different situation. "Officers & N.C.O's alike were back in Box Cars, without heat of any kind and not even a seat to sit on," he rightly complained to his journal. "55 men in a car. . . . It took 52 hours to make the trip to Coblenz we were shipped in Trucks to Bodendorf."[19] At least one of the men had reservations about the American Browning machine gun. The Hotchkiss "was a good gun and stood a lot of hard knocks," Rex Spencer wrote home. "It weighed fifty-four pounds [without tripod and traversing mechanism] while the Browning only weighs thirty seven full of water. The Browning is a good gun but it has too short a range." The latter comment referred to the fact that the Browning shot a lighter-weight bullet that did not carry as far as the heavier, streamlined Hotchkiss bullet.[20]

Time dragged for the soldiers, for they were anxious to leave Europe and return to Wisconsin. Moreover, there was no real sense of stability, as officers were reassigned to other companies while some of the men joined and others left the companies. The men also composed letters to the families of the dead. In a big, scrawling hand, Rex Spencer in Company A said to Tom Heiss, "The old company isn't the company that it used to be. We have quite a few of our old men back but there are a lot that can't come back to us. The Company is full of strange faces and they ain't the class of fellows that we started with."[21]

In the typical way of the Regular Army, one of the first things the Guardsmen did was drill. So now, even in the glow of victory over a skilled and fearsome adversary, they had to endure the tedium of parade-ground training. Ellis explained this to his mother: "The men were badly in need of disciplinary drill, owing to a large percentage of replacements who seemed fated to always arrive just before a push and who had never had close order drill since arriving."[22] It seemed petty to the old hands.

The 150th Machine Gun Battalion remained as part of the Army of Occupation for four long months. There were sporting competitions for the 83rd Brigade, and the machine gunners were in excellent physical condition from manhandling their heavy guns. Many of the Guardsmen excelled in baseball and football, and it showed on the playing field. The 150th came out the winner, being awarded a "banner and handsome cup." There was even a horse show. The 150th, which prided itself on its care and appearance of its horses and mules,

On the train heading to Camp Grant for discharge in May 1919 one man came down with measles. The entire car was quarantined for two weeks and the men spent their time playing ball. Peter Lamensky is in the middle row, second from the left. Courtesy of the Lamensky Family Collection.

took six of the seven prizes in the division, including three first-place awards. Officers and men were given leave to sightsee, General Pershing inspected the Rainbows in March, and of course the soldiers "fraternized" with German women despite orders to the contrary. Of note, the division held a "convention" on April 2, 1919, to organize the "Wisconsin Chapter Rainbow Division Veterans." Bahr proudly recorded, "Next Convention will be held in Oshk. June 17–18–19 1920." But there was also news that a beloved officer was leaving, Lieutenant Fred Finn in Company B, who had been wounded in October. A newspaper article said, "the boys had a 'very warm spot in their hearts' for him. . . . They want to be led home by the man who led them in battle."[23]

It was a year of euphoria for most Americans. The war was over—it had been a blazing victory, and it was easy to think that costly, bloody wars were now a thing of the past. The nation's heroes were coming home to parades and joyous crowds. So while the battalion was drilling, sightseeing, and fraternizing, plans were being made for stupendous welcome-home festivities in all the communities.

The 150th left Germany on a beautiful morning, April 8, 1919. "Many natives gathered along the Main St. (about the only street in town) to wave us a fond farewell. Many of the boys carried with them sandwiches . . . put up by some pretty fraulein,"[24] an indication that their stay in the country of their former enemy was not unpleasant. The American Expeditionary Forces had brought its own rolling stock to France, and the men were overjoyed to see that they would travel in big American boxcars, provided with plenty of clean straw for bed ticks for the three-day journey to the port city of Brest. And perhaps, as they started the final leg of their journey, the Wisconsin men recalled that back home the ice on Lake Winnebago and the Fox River had broken, and steamboat traffic was resuming.

Arriving in Brest on April 12, they waited for three days before boarding the ship that was to take them home. The 150th had left for France aboard a former German vessel, and now they learned that they would return to American on another ex-German liner, the USS *Pretoria*. "Our trip across was enjoyed by all, as the weather was fine. . . . We were treated to solos, piano, violin and singing and dancing."[25] Hans Rose, a former and highly successful U-boat captain who ended the war having sunk seventy-nine ships, was also onboard. Rose spent time talking to the officers. The *Pretoria* arrived in Boston in early May, where discharges were processed.

So eager were the folks back in Wisconsin to get information about their men that the *Appleton Crescent* sent a reporter named John Steele to visit the battalion in Camp Devens, outside of Boston. Steele and his wife arrived at night and found the boys in a big tent camp, where the men were being deloused and cleaned. "[I] saw the jolly sun-bronzed faces of the lads who went through hell and faced death again and again," he reported, "but who seemed to have forgotten the horrors of war and to be filled with only one desire, get home as soon as possible." On seeing Major Graef, he was surprised that he did not have white hair but looked in fine shape, since as Steele understood, "He carried the welfare of the boys on his soul at all times." There was much levity, and Steele learned something of the close and abiding feelings the men had for one another when he found out that the company had given Elmer Reider, who was the company comedian and a man who loved to eat, a special "war cross" "for his prowess at the mess table." He also learned that the Appleton Company did not want to participate in a parade in Milwaukee, but instead wanted "to cut out fuss and feathers and get home at the earliest possible moment." The Oshkosh and Fond du Lac companies preferred the Milwaukee parade.[26] The battalion left Boston by train on May 12, and two days later arrived at Camp Grant, Illinois, where they turned in their equipment and prepared for the final leg of their long journey home.

Anticipation must have been high, the men anxious to see their families and to be home at last. But maybe they also felt pangs of guilt that many combat veterans experience. Why did I survive and my friends did not? What will I say to the family and friends of those who did not return? Each man knew others with a familiarity known only to those who together had endured the unimaginable. The men had lived together side by side for two years, depended on each other for everything, shared everything from memories to their last cigarette. At times they must have thought, "How can I return to being a civilian again after this?"

The following day, "we received our pay and discharges and boarded a streetcar for E. Rockford where we took a special train for dear old Oshkosh, reaching there at 6:00 p.m. amid the din of bells and whistles," wrote the unknown soldier in Company C, "and such a rousing welcome that the boys never thought of and now, dear reader, that we are back again in dear old Oshkosh, I will bid you adieu."[27]

At home, families waited with eagerness, relief, and anxiety, and in some cases a profound sense of loss and grief. All three communities were alive with anticipation at the return of their beloved National Guardsmen. Committees organized a rousing and proper welcome for the war heroes, and newspapers printed special supplements when the *Pretoria* docked in Boston in late April. The May 3 *Appleton Evening Crescent* supplement included photographs of the ship with the men of the 150th cheering at the rails. At the bottom were photos of some of the Appleton men as they came off the ship, with heroic Major Lothar Graef in the center. "Welcome Home" bulletins and programs were printed and newspapers ran special editions and sections devoted to the unit and its men.

The communities knew within minutes of when the trains left Camp Grant and were kept abreast of the train's northward progress. Everything had been meticulously arranged in all three cities. In Appleton, citizens and schools were assigned by block to sections along the parade route according to their ward. Special police were detailed to keep crowds in check, and whistles and bells throughout Appleton would announce when it was time to close all businesses so that citizens could reach their assigned parade locations. Oshkosh and Fond du Lac constructed temporary victory arches as physical symbols to show their gratitude and respect for what their companies had achieved. The massive steel, wood, and plaster arch vaguely resembled France's Arc de Triomphe. Later that year, after the soldiers had time to reconnect with their families, Appleton and Fond du Lac had more welcome-home ceremonies.

The return of the Guardsmen to the hometowns was an amazing event. When the train pulled into Fond du Lac at 5:15 p.m., for example, the fifty-four returning men of Company B were greeted with cheering crowds, pealing church bells, and the blaring steam whistles of factories as well as a band playing patriotic music. The entire city was festooned with flags, banners, flowers, and other decorations, which the newspapers claimed exceeded anything ever done before.

For Wisconsinites, the 150th Machine Gun Battalion was clearly a star, for it was part of the celebrated Rainbow Division. Every American knew about the division, for it had been a grand experiment that pulled Guardsmen from twenty-six states and formed them into one homogenous, hard-fighting unit. "One of the most glorious pages in the history of the world war," said Ivan Spear, the state editor of the highly regarded *Milwaukee Sentinel*, "has been written by Wisconsin soldiers, three crack badger companies, who had the honor and distinction of being chosen to represent the state in that all-American organization." Accompanied by photographs of the Wisconsin machine gunners, the article ran in many other newspapers across the state.[28]

12

Aftermath

I don't want to see any more young men lose their lives and I don't want to see any more mothers mourn the loss of their sons.

Lothar Graef,
quoted in *Appleton Post-Crescent*,
July 18, 1923

The war was never over for most of these ex-soldiers. It is true of all wars and all generations: the war lived on inside them. Hugh S. Thompson, the officer who served with the 168th Infantry, the Iowa boys, wrote in the years after the war, "but some of me, much of me, was buried in France, I knew. I knew, too, that things could never be the same again, for war, like Frankenstein, vivisected a man, as if to see what made him tick and then failed to put all of the pieces back. War stripped a man of protective illusions and left only a terrible wisdom, which he neither wanted nor consciously sought."[1]

War could kill a man quickly with the snap of a bullet, a sudden death that shocked comrades and family. But war could kill slowly, too. Year after year, the battles ate away at some. Family and friends witnessed the ex-soldiers fight memories and demons, unable to help, failing to comprehend, not wanting to know or share the pain. Most veterans were able to bury it, to contain their visions of Hell and their witness of death. For others, the war was never far from the surface.

In the euphoria and zeal of welcoming and honoring returning soldiers, there was also a solemn element that called for venerating the dead of the world's most awful war. The Fond du Lac employees of the Soo Line Railroad raised money to erect a bronze plaque that listed the veterans, those who lost their lives indicated by a star behind the name. The railroad donated a large rock, and the area was handsomely landscaped. The memorial eventually became neglected and fell into disrepair. In 1965, Soo Line employees again rallied, raised money, and restored the monument.

Oshkosh decided the best way to remember the fallen was to dedicate a state highway bridge in memory of one of the fallen, Kurt Graf, who died at the Ourcq. A notable artist created a superb bronze bas-relief of Graf, which was embedded into a concrete pillar. It was dedicated in 1920 amid tremendous ceremony and with the widespread belief that the bridge and its beautiful memorial would be "an inspiration, as long as time shall last." Ten years after the Kurt Graf Bridge was dedicated, the highway was widened and a new bridge constructed. The old bridge and its memorial were sold to the Oshkosh Country Club. The memorial was not kept up, and in due course was forgotten by the public. Forty years later, the remaining veterans of the Oshkosh company succeeded in having a new park named "Rainbow Memorial Park." The name was eventually shortened to just "Rainbow Park," a word of diverse meaning.

The veterans created new organizations to help ex-soldiers and thus enable the men to gather to rekindle and share the sense of camaraderie that existed during the war. Within a year, they formed the Rainbow Division Veterans Association with the purpose of keeping their friendships and memories alive. The first local meeting was in the Elks Hall in Appleton on June 19, 1920.[2] The ex-commander of the 150th, Lothar Graef, was a leading figure and instrumental in its creation and growth. Doughboys, including Wisconsin's ex-machine gunners, were the foundation of organizations that endure today as the Veterans of Foreign Wars and the American Legion. New American Legion posts were named in memory of the dead: Pearson Brown Post in Campbellsport and Eoney Johnston Post in Appleton.

In 1920, the French government awarded memorial certificates to the families of those who had lost loved ones in the great World War. "The memorials are an expression of appreciation of the French people for the soldiers who made the supreme sacrifice," Fond du Lac's *Daily Commonwealth* explained. In a solemn ceremony held at the armory in late February 1920, Bishop Reginald H. Weller of the Episcopal Diocese of Fond du Lac spoke to a full hall. "Our brave boys died for human liberty; that you and I might have it. . . . [The French people] want the families to keep them forever to show the great esteem and respect in which they are held by the French people."[3] The two-foot by eighteen-inch certificate, on heavy paper, was full of artistic symbolism, including a mother holding a baby to her breast.

Five years after Company A won fame for helping stop the last German offensive at Champagne, the one-armed French General Henri Gouraud visited the United States. There would be only one stop in Wisconsin; Lothar Graef chaired the committee whose charge was to make sure that the stop would be in Appleton. Through great effort and by offering $500 to the former general, Graef and the committee made that happen. On July 17, 1923, the general's train arrived in the nearby city of Neenah, and he was driven to Appleton. He was greeted by representatives from Appleton, Neenah, and Menasha; Oshkosh and Fond du Lac were not represented. Hundreds of cheering residents lined streets that were splendid with French and American flags, and the local band played "La Marseillaise" and "The Star-Spangled Banner." That evening at a reception and banquet held at the Elk's Club, Gouraud spoke to a packed hall. Through an interpreter, Gouraud praised the 150th Machine Gun Battalion and said, "It was soldiers like Graef, who told his men to hold out to the last cartridge and to the last man — that there would be no retreat — that made the victory at Champagne possible." But it was Lothar Graef's words of introduction that had the most impact on the audience. Among those attentive listeners must surely have been those who had lost a son, husband, or brother. Almost overcome with emotion, Graef told them, "I don't want to see any more young men lose their lives and I don't want to see any more mothers mourn the loss of their sons."[4]

Appleton built a new high-level bridge over the Fox River in 1924, and twelve thousand citizens watched as it was dedicated as the "Soldiers and Sailors Memorial Bridge" to honor the veterans. Ten years later, the Eoney Johnston American Legion Post raised $700 to purchase a sculpture called "The Spirit of the American Doughboy."[5] It was installed on the bridge's south end and dedicated to comrades who gave their lives. The artist, E. M. Viquesney, said that his doughboy sculpture helped people "realize the suffering, sorrow and loss to individuals and nations that wars cost." The American Legion Post planted fifty-seven elm trees on Memorial Drive, one tree for each man from Outagamie County who fell during the Great War. When vandals cut all the trees down, the Eoney Johnston Post quickly raised money and replanted the trees within a month. And finally, the Post purchased a twenty-five-foot-long captured German artillery piece and placed it on the other end of the new bridge, a symbol of victory over the enemy.[6]

The bodies of the fallen had been buried in France, usually where they fell. Graves were marked as carefully as possible given combat conditions, and company officers had followed the army's procedures for setting in motion notifications of next of kin. But the bodies could not remain in their temporary graves, which were often quite shallow. The Graves Registration Service began methodically surveying and walking the old battlefields, using the landmarks and notes that officers provided that indicated where the dead were supposed to be buried. When found, the dead were carefully and respectfully removed, and the deceased's belongings meticulously cataloged for return to the family. This was a slow, gruesome process that was often done by African American units. American military cemeteries were created in France, but families also had the option of having their loved one returned for burial in the United States.

The U.S. Army was appalled at the idea of disinterring and sending tens of thousands of bodies home, and so were leaders in Britain and France. But public feeling was strong that the nation not leave its sons buried in a foreign land. The War Department surveyed eighty thousand families who had lost a soldier and asked if they wanted the body returned or whether the remains should stay in France. About 60 percent of those responding asked for the body to be returned home. In 1920–21, the United States spent approximately $30 million on this course of action, with the remaining 40 percent buried in cemeteries under the management of the American Battle Monuments Commission.

Some of the Badger boys who died in France remain there, interred in beautiful, well-maintained cemeteries. "We feel it more honor that he lie where he fell with his comrades," said Mr. and Mrs. John Koehne about their son, Otto, who was with the Appleton Company. "[He is] in that beautiful spot which is given constant and loving care by the French people."[7] Many other families, however, wanted the body of their loved one buried at home. Anthony Halfmann, Nicholas Mand, William Heiss, John Pierre, and many others were brought home for reburial, and they began arriving in 1920. They were buried with not just a sense of closure for the families but also with a display of profound respect by community members. Comrades dressed in their uniforms were pall bearers, attendants, and helped and comforted mourning family members. When the bodies of Herman Jahnke and William Lang returned to Appleton in 1921, in a sign of deep reverence, fully five thousand residents turned out for the procession, and businesses closed for several hours to allow employees to attend.[8]

At the same time the three Wisconsin communities were burying their boys, the nation symbolically laid to rest one of the soldiers whose identity had been lost. In November 1921, President Warren G. Harding unveiled the Tomb of the Unknown Soldier in Arlington National Cemetery in Washington, DC. Every state was asked to send a veteran of the World War to the unveiling and thus demonstrate the esteem Americans had for the dead. One-legged John Hantschel was selected to represent the Badger State. In an eloquent, moving

The remains of William Heiss and Eoney Johnston were brought home in the early 1920s. Two uniformed comrades ceremonially guard their coffins at Appleton's Congregational Church. Joe Gaerthofner Personal Collection.

address, Harding told the nation, "Ours are lofty resolutions today, as with tribute to the dead we consecrate ourselves to a better order for the living, to mothers who sorrow, to widows and children who mourn, that no such sacrifice shall be asked again." Indeed, many believed that the nation would never again enter a war on that magnitude. Within a few years of the Armistice, the overseas battlefields became tourist attractions, and popular Michelin maps directed sightseers to key points. Souvenir hunters wandered the scarred fields and forests seeking both understanding and mementos.

The Gold Star Mothers Association lobbied Congress to sponsor a trip to France for the families who had a boy or husband buried in France. The organization emphasized the bond that existed between not only a mother and her son but widows as well. Congress finally agreed and passed legislation in 1929 to allow mothers and widows to visit graves. Other family members were not permitted. The government paid for travel, food, and lodging. These "pilgrimages" were carefully organized and supervised. Eventually, 6,693 women made the trip before the program ended in 1933.[9]

As the decade continued, the 1920s became a time to forget the trenches. The Jazz Age was also a time of growing disillusionment over the war itself, the role of the United States, and what had been taking place in Europe. No one could agree on who was to blame for the war. Eventually, Congress convened hearings on America's entry into the war, and many blamed bankers and munitions manufacturers for their influence in bringing the nation into the European war. Some peace advocates believed that America had invested so much money with England and France that the real reason for the war was to prevent their defeat by Germany and thus prevent defaulting on debt. They thought that the ghastly war was just not worth it. By the 1930s, the doughboys were no longer heroes. Instead, they were increasingly seen as victims. As America retreated into isolationism, the war was left behind and forgotten as citizens faced the nightmare of the Great Depression. America and the world forgot the First World War, the Great War, the "war to end all wars," to the bitterness of the veterans who in 1919 heard "We will never forget."

The ex-soldiers did not forget the soldiers who slept under French soil or the men who came home with broken bodies and minds or those unable to take a deep breath because their lungs were scarred by poison gas. They were true comrades: they had endured the worst conditions any American combatant had been asked to do up to that point. In an ironic way, the harsh conditions they endured in France helped prepare them for the bleakness of the Great Depression. Joyce Kilmer, a poet-soldier in the 165th Infantry, tried to explain what this meant in a letter to his wife, Aline: "Dangers shared together and hardships mutually borne develops in us a sport of friendship I never knew in civilian life, a friendship clean of jealousy and gossip and envy and suspicion— a fine hearty roaring mirthful sort of thing, like an open fire of whole pine-trees in a giant's castle, or a truly timed bombardment with eight-inch guns. I don't know that this last figure will strike you as particularly happy, but it would if you'd had the delight of going to war."[10]

Many former doughboys became bitter. They left Europe knowing they had done what they came to do, but they also saw that Germany was not defeated. They became cynical when it became apparent that their young sons faced a rebuilt Germany eager for revenge: the victorious and vengeful Allies had disarmed Germany, and the entire German Empire was taken away; areas were carved from Germany and given to Belgium; France took Alsace-Lorraine; South Tyrol was taken from Austria and given to Italy. Then, a new country called Czechoslovakia was created, a nation where 3.25 million Sudeten Germans lived. The new Poland was awarded the great German port city of Danzig, long a proud and important part of the Fatherland, and an eighty-mile strip of Germany from Silesia to the North Sea was taken away. Germans were forbidden to create or maintain any form of union with their longtime friend and trading partner, Austria. Germany had an enormous pride in its military, but according to the treaty they could not have an army of more than 100,000 men nor could they send troops west of the Rhine River, a part of their own country. Germany was in chaos in the aftermath of the war, until a charismatic leader arose, one who had spent time in the trenches as a common soldier. That was Adolf Hitler. He promised to restore pride, prosperity, and territory to the war-torn country. He told a population hungry to understand what had happened to them that Germany's soldiers did not die in vain. Instead, he advocated that it was time to visit vengeance on those who had so dishonored the once-great Germany. The actions of the vengeful Allies ensured that an angry, humiliated Germany would seek to erase its dishonor.

Epilogue

Greatness of a nation or state does not depend on fertile fields or great factories. Its greatest glory is its citizenship and Kurt Graf was one of the highest types. . . . [His friends] have been inspired to establish this monument to his memory on this public highway, that it might be an inspiration, as long as time shall last, to the men and women and children who shall view it.

Governor Emanuel I. Phillips,
quoted in *Oshkosh Daily Northwestern*,
August 2, 1920

Their voices are now silent. No one is left to tell the tales of Heiss and Spaedtke and a hundred other comrades. Carefully written words sent home on cheap paper, once cherished, lie unread. Ghost soldiers in shades of gray stare out of crinkled snapshots, a smile forever frozen. If the image had a story, its secret has been lost. But the dog-eared photos and the faded letters still whisper stories, a connection to the past. Memories are what we make them. They will either endure or grow dim like stars in the morning.

The old battlefields are quiet, reclaimed by nature. Scars on the earth have been slowly absorbed by time. Waving fields of grain and rich pastures, nourished by blood, have replaced trenches. Urban sprawl, the nemesis of all historic battlefields, eats into the fields where history was made. Bulldozers digging foundations for new homes unearth subterranean bunkers that a century ago hid men from artillery. In places, debris still clings to the land a century later—the annual "Iron Harvest" in Belgium and France still gives up countless lethal mementoes

193

of the Great War. Bones, rusted barbed wire, and corroded artillery shells poke through the earth in fields and forests.

People hurriedly buy a red paper poppy in front of the grocery store from a smiling member of the American Legion. They toss it onto the seat of the car, seldom taking time to think of what the crimson flower represents. We have lost our memory.

Youth is a fleeting thing, not really valued until it is beyond recall. Dreams of adventure and love are its hallmark. Only a few live out their dreams but for the rest, time slowly dims the vision. War steals youth and its promises. In its place, it leaves scars and nightmares.

Almost every city and town has its war monuments, those weathered bronze faces that impassively gaze through blistering heat and mind-numbing cold. Lichen covers chiseled words, seldom read, that list the names and places but do not reflect that these, too, were men with dreams.

Life is to be cherished and enjoyed, not spent dwelling on the sobering facts of a forgotten war. But perhaps life can be more fully appreciated when we accept that enjoyment is made possible by the gift that some were asked to give. To pause every now and then in front of the silent warriors of another age is a good thing. Squeeze the hand of those we love and whisper, "Remember them."

In Remembrance

Arthur Bahr survived the war without physical injury, but the experience of war alters a person. He returned to Oshkosh in May 1919 to find his wife, Nina, changed. They divorced a month later, and Bahr moved to Milwaukee, where he eventually remarried. He became vice president of the Checker Cab Company. He died at the Wisconsin Veterans Home in King, Wisconsin, in 1966, at age seventy-seven. His meticulously kept diary, photos, uniforms, and mementos of his military experience were sold. They eventually came into the hands of Andrew J. DeCusati, who recognized and appreciated what they represented and willingly and graciously shared everything he had with the author of this book.

Elmer "Dad" Bullis, who at age forty-five could easily have stayed home, died of shrapnel wounds along the banks of the Ourcq River on August 3, 1918. He left his wife, Maude, children, and the baby son he never saw or held. He is buried in the Aisne-Marne American Cemetery in Belleau, France, in Plot B, Row 6, one of 2,300 graves. The Bullis family wanted a headstone, a marker that signified he was not forgotten. So they saved enough money to erect a granite stone in the small cemetery in Eureka, Wisconsin, as a remembrance to the tough sergeant who soldiered on in France with his comrades. Maud Bullis named her new son Elmer Jr., to honor her husband fighting so far away in a foreign land. He was the living embodiment of her husband, the reminder of their marriage and their love. When little Elmer was just over two years old, he contracted scarlet fever, a dangerous illness. His rash, fever, and sore throat worsened as the weeks went along. There were no antibiotics in 1920, so there was nothing to be done for the toddler other than wait it out and hope the little boy took after his father and had a tough constitution. On August 31, 1920, the fever won the battle.[1] It must not have been easy carrying on as a war widow, but Maud did. She died in July 1951, at age seventy-three, six years before the men of Company C were commemorated in Oshkosh's new Rainbow Memorial Park.

Company C's Harvey Christensen was severely shell shocked and hospitalized during the Ourcq River offensive. He returned to Oshkosh after the war and married Esther Traugott on June 23, 1920. Harvey worked for the Buckstaff Furniture Company for forty-two years until his retirement. Harvey fought his internal battles until his death in October 1951 at age fifty-five. During the 1920s or 1930s, Esther commissioned a local artist, Flora M. Smith, to paint a battle scene depicting the 150th, perhaps to help Harvey exorcize the memories that haunted him.

Allan Ellis returned to Appleton and in 1920 married Mildred E. Pynn. He went into the toy-making business with Lothar Graef. Despite a promising start to the Toy Company of America and its innovative Rocker Plane, the Great Depression ended the business. Ellis decided to make his career in the National Guard and reenlisted. He died August 17, 1943, at age fifty-five, while the United States was again at war with Germany.

Lothar Graef, the commander of Company A and later the battalion, and who was cited for bravery, was instrumental in creating the Rainbow Division Association and served as its president for twenty years. He returned to Appleton and leased fourteen thousand square feet in an old warehouse and started a toy business called the Toy Company of America with Allan Ellis, the former battalion adjutant. When the toy company failed in the Great Depression, Lothar ran the Graef Lumber Company in Appleton. He died in Oshkosh on September 22, 1957, and is buried in Appleton's Riverside Cemetery.

Smiling, good-natured Kurt Graf, the farmer's son who was in charge of Company C's mules, was a casualty of the battle along the Ourcq River. A bridge over State Highway 45 was named after him in 1920, dedicated with great fanfare and a speech by the governor of Wisconsin. George Buckstaff, owner of Oshkosh's Buckstaff Furniture Company, commissioned Oshkosh artist L. Merton Grenhagen to create a striking bas-relief bronze plaque of Graf, which was set into a concrete column near the bridge. The bridge, it was proclaimed, would "be an inspiration, as long as time shall last, to the men and women and children who shall view it." A new highway bridge was built, and the Graf memorial became part of a Country Club and eventually was forgotten by the public. Graf rests with his dead comrades from the 150th in Plot A, Row 8, Grave 18 in the Oise-Aisne American Cemetery at Fère-en-Tardenois, France.

Herbert Ralph Granger survived the war, returned to Fond du Lac in May 1919, and married Adeline Olson on August 3. He left for Minnesota with his bride in 1920 and soon had two sons. Herbert worked as a carpenter in the Duluth shipyard until 1930, when he moved to Oshkosh to work as a mail clerk for the railroad. After retirement from the railroad in 1956, he started a trailer sales business. He died of a heart attack on April 23, 1960, at the age of sixty-five while putting out a grass fire. One of his sons, Lester, recognized the diary's historical value and donated it to the Oshkosh Public Museum in 1997.

Corporal Guy Gross, who wrote so eloquently about aspects of the war, inhaled deadly phosgene gas in the Argonne Forest on October 15, 1918. His comrades took him to an aid station, but he died a short time later. He is buried in the Meuse-Argonne American Cemetery in Plot H, Row 25, Grave 26. His mother, Jennie, journeyed to France in June 1930 on a Gold Star Mother pilgrimage. When she returned to Fond du Lac on July 17, she told a reporter from the *Daily Commonwealth* that she was "pleased with the manner in which the graves are kept up."

John Hantschel was selected by E. J. Barrett, the State Commander of the American Legion, to represent Wisconsin at the unveiling of the Tomb of the Unknown Soldier in 1921, a tremendous honor. A year later, he was elected clerk of Outagamie County and served in that role until ill health forced him into retirement at age sixty-two. He was known for passing out witty cards of "homespun philosophy" to couples applying for a marriage license, as well as telling tall tales about hunting and fishing. He was active in veterans' organizations his entire life. He died in 1956. Of note, his son, Ensign John H. Hantschel Jr., was a fighter pilot in Squadron 16 on the USS *Randolph* in the Pacific during World War II. His Hellcat fighter was shot down off the coast of Japan. While everyone was celebrating the end of that war, the Hantschels received word that their son was missing. It was later learned that John Jr. had been taken to the city of Hiroshima for interrogation and was there on August 6 when the atomic bomb was dropped. He was posthumously awarded the Navy Cross.

William Heiss, the good-natured Company A soldier once called "a mighty fellow with an excellent brain" and who was saving his money to return to school after the war, was killed during the battle on the Ourcq River. His body was returned to Appleton in August 1921; after a service in his parents' home he was buried in Appleton's Riverside Cemetery in Lot 4, Block 11. The Appleton High School class was so moved by Heiss's death that they created an annual oratorical contest in his memory, with a silver cup to be awarded to the winning speaker. Today, both the cup and the man have been forgotten.

Robert K. Holterman resumed farming after the war. He married Luella L. Clepham in 1921 and farmed near Taycheedah in Fond du Lac County. He died September 8, 1952, at age sixty-three and was buried in Rienzi Cemetery in Fond du Lac under a flat granite government headstone. Robert and Luella had four children; one son, Ralph, followed his father's footsteps and joined the Wisconsin National Guard. Robert's son rose to the rank of colonel and was cited many times for bravery in combat.

Everett "Eoney" Johnston, a sergeant in Appleton's Company A, was killed in the Fère-en-Tardenois as part of the Ourcq River battle. Appleton named their American Legion Post 38 in honor of Johnston and a World War II sailor.

Lloyd F. Kindness, the Brothertown Native American, returned to Fond du Lac. He took a job at the Reupling Tannery but moved to Milwaukee a few years later to work in a paint factory, then later moved to Red Springs, Wisconsin. He married and had a daughter, Madeline, in 1938, and son, Douglas, in 1944. He died in Sturgeon Bay, Wisconsin, on December 21, 1971, at age seventy-three. His brief, three-line obituary in the *Door County Advocate* mentioned he was a veteran of World War I.

Returning to Appleton, Edward Lutz held a variety of jobs before becoming the undersheriff of Outagamie County in 1930. He was deeply committed in a variety of veterans' organizations, including Appleton's American Legion Eoney Johnston-Blessman Post 38, and he eventually became the county Veterans Service Officer. Lutz passed away at age seventy-four on September 20, 1964.

The body of Nicholas Mand, who died of shrapnel wounds on August 3, 1918, was returned to Oshkosh in October 1920. He was reinterred at Riverside Cemetery in Lot 10, Block 7, with a military funeral attended by his former comrades in Company C.

Julius Mand, Nicholas's brother, returned to Oshkosh in May 1919 and marched in the welcome-home parade. He married Esther Hughes in 1924. Later, he donated materials related to his brother, Nicholas, to the new Oshkosh Public Museum. Julius found employment with the City of Oshkosh as a firefighter in 1920, rising to the rank of assistant chief before he retired in 1968. He died in 1977 at the age of seventy-nine.

Company's C mess sergeant, John Matschi, born in Austria as Johann, returned to Oshkosh with the rest of his company in 1919. He married Mary Youngwirth and worked for the Paine Lumber Company until his retirement.

Photographs, uniforms, and other objects representing his experiences in the
World War were donated to the Oshkosh Public Museum in 1935. He died in
September 1972.

Appleton's Walter Melchior, awarded the Silver Star and the French Croix
de Guerre for his courage, returned to school after the war. He graduated from
the University of Wisconsin Law School and was admitted to the bar in 1925.
He was the city attorney for New London, Wisconsin, and was involved in
politics, becoming a member of the State Assembly in 1950. When Melchior
was a candidate for U.S. Congress in 1940, he was strongly opposed to the
United States' entry into the European War, stating "the welfare of the country
requires that the United States stay out." Nonetheless, when the Japanese attacked Pearl Harbor in 1941, he reentered the National Guard and served for
the duration. He died October 22, 1976.

The battle in the depths of the Argonne Forest claimed Frank Frederick
Obersteiner on October 22, 1918. Born in the Tyrol region of Austria in 1894,
he came to the United States in 1914 with his mother and siblings. His family
elected to keep his remains in France. He is buried in Plot C, Row 17, Grave 38
in the Meuse-Argonne American Cemetery, Romagne-sous-Montfoucon,
France.

Handsome, dark-eyed Harvey Pierre of Company A was the first soldier
from Appleton killed in World War I. He was killed in the fierce fighting in
Champagne on July 15, 1918, but his body could not be found after the battle.
His remains were finally located and identified in December 1920. His body
was returned to Appleton in August 1921, and a funeral was held in the parents'
home, 784 Superior Street. He was reburied with full military honors in Appleton's Riverside Cemetery. To honor Harvey, the Appleton veterans named the
Veterans of Foreign Wars Post 2778 in his memory.

John Pierre Jr., Harvey's brother, survived the war and married Louise
Becker. He was plagued by shell wounds to his upper thighs that he received on
July 15, 1918, at the Champagne battle that took his brother's life. The wounds
required him to undergo many painful surgeries over a ten-year period. John
took a job as Appleton's city assessor and was known for his innovation, developing new ways of conducting assessments. John was energetic and proud of
his life. He died while at work in 1969 at age seventy-four. His widow donated
her husband's photographs to Appleton's local museum in 1977.

Elmer J. Reider, known in the Appleton Company as "The Original Elmer"
and whose exploits on July 15 won him the French Croix de Guerre, moved to
Chicago in 1919. Before the war he was known as an outstanding halfback, and
many thought he might play professional football after the war. His days as an
athlete were ended two days before the Armistice when shrapnel ripped open
his knee. He became active in veterans' organizations and affairs in Chicago in

the 1920s and was a contender for the National Commander of the American Legion. Reider returned to Appleton sometime after the Second World War. He passed away on January 8, 1952, at age fifty-nine. He is buried in St. Joseph's Cemetery in Appleton under a flat granite government headstone.

Oshkosh's happy-go-lucky Otto Spaedtke was killed on July 30, 1918, during the great Château-Thierry offensive. His mother, Augusta, donated a dog-eared photograph of her son, standing with a group of his comrades, to the Oshkosh Public Museum in 1935. No other image of him survives. Otto's body was disinterred from French soil and reburied at Oshkosh's Riverside Cemetery in Lot 4, Block 159.

Edward C. Steckbauer, son of Herman Steckbauer, a prominent Oshkosh politician and leader, and his wife, Mary, was killed by shrapnel on July 30, 1918. He was the battalion's clown, the man who made everyone laugh despite their misery. Eddie's body was removed from its temporary resting place in France and returned to Oshkosh's Riverside Cemetery, where he was buried with full military honors on July 25, 1921. The newspaper reported that a "large contingent" of ex-Rainbows attended.[2]

Edward's brother, Jacob Steckbauer, also served in Company C. Returning to Oshkosh after the war, he was active in veterans' organizations and local politics his entire life. Jake, as he was known, ran a tavern and corner store that was the center of the neighborhood. He kept a large, framed, oval portrait of his brother, Eddie, in the bar as a remembrance. Jake died in 1979 at age eighty-eight.

Harold L. Smith died of shrapnel wounds on July 29, 1918. His body was returned to Oshkosh after the war, and his parents, Henry and Minna, had his remains reburied in Oshkosh's Riverside Cemetery, Lot 4, Block 110.

Harvey Stich, a press-room operator at Oshkosh's Diamond Match Company before the war, survived combat in France and marched toward Germany as part of the Army of Occupation. In what may have been one of his last letters home, he wrote on December 12, 1918, "I am well and happy. . . . We have been on a long hike, but we soon got there to the place where we can stay for a while. And I hope they will send us home very soon. . . . As always your Soldier boy, Harvey." Stich fell ill, no doubt from influenza, although it was not recorded as such, which, in the second wave of the epidemic rapidly turned to pneumonia. His condition steadily worsened, and he died two days after Christmas 1918 at the age of twenty-two. Stich was buried in France, but his body was returned to his father, Charles, in September 1920 and reburied in Doty Lutheran Cemetery in Oshkosh.[3]

Otto Suess survived the war and returned to Oshkosh with the rest of Company C. It is unknown whether he returned to his job as a shipping clerk at the Giant Grip Horseshoe Company. He later taught in a trade school in

Racine and Milwaukee. Suess returned to Oshkosh and became a stagehand at
the Grand Opera House and Strand Theater. He was found dead in his car in
Oshkosh's Menominee Park on April 10, 1974, near a granite Veterans Memorial that had been erected in 1963. The base of that memorial includes part of
the famous World War I poem "For the Fallen" by Robert Laurence Binyon:
"They shall grow not old, as we that are left grow old." He was eighty-four.
Suess is buried in Riverside Cemetery.

Ewald Treichel was severely shell-shocked during the battle at Champagne.
He returned to Oshkosh in January 1919 as a convalescent but never recovered
from the trauma of war, as he was constantly in a state of depression. Ewald
ended his life in 1936, just as much a casualty of war as those who died in
France or at sea. He is buried in Oshkosh's Riverside Cemetery.

Leo J. Uelmen returned to Campbellsport and married Daisy Ferber; they
had a son named Donald. Leo returned to high school and graduated, then
went on to college and dental school. He ran a successful dental practice in
Campbellsport and was also the president of the First State Bank in that village. Leo died on January 11, 1967, and is buried in Saint Matthews Catholic
Cemetery in Campbellsport. Leo's grandson, Dean Uelmen, followed his grandfather's footsteps and also became a dentist and graciously shared images from
Leo's photo album.

Notes

Prologue

1. The forty-foot-long Kurt Graf Bridge over Weyerhorst Creek south of Oshkosh was formally dedicated on August 1, 1920. The address was delivered by the governor of Wisconsin, E. I. Philipp. The "beautiful and impressive" ceremony was attended by thousands of citizens. The bronze bas-relief plaque of Graf, placed on a concrete pillar, was created by well-known artist L. Merton Grenhagen. Today the bridge is no longer part of the highway and instead leads into the former Oshkosh Country Club. The crumbling pillar still bears the bas-relief of Graf's profile.

2. The bronze monument, *The Hiker* by Theo Alice Ruggles Kitson, was dedicated October 21, 1939, forty years after Oshkosh's Spanish-American War veterans returned home.

3. George Holland Collection, World War I Small Collections, Oshkosh Public Museum Archives, Oshkosh, Wisconsin.

Chapter 1. The War to End All Wars

1. It is estimated that about 1.5 billion artillery shells were fired by all sides from 1914 to 1918. By some estimates, as many as one-third failed to explode. This was due mainly to defective fuses.

2. "Military Casualties of World War One," http://www.firstworldwar.com/features /casualties/, accessed June 2, 2018. The term "casualty," as used throughout this work, refers to both wounded and dead.

3. "Military Casualties of World War One." About half died from influenza. In comparison, in World War II the United States suffered 1,078,162 casualties, including 292,131 dead.

4. Princip went on trial in October 1914. He was found guilty but was spared the death penalty because he was a minor. He died of tuberculosis in prison on April 18, 1918. In Serbia Princip is now revered as a hero, and there is an official Gavrilo Princip Day.

5. "The European War," *Oshkosh Daily Northwestern,* July 29, 1914, 6.

6. "Worst War in the History of World," *Appleton Evening Crescent,* August 1, 1914.

7. Russia had another reason for reacting so vehemently to Austria's invasion: she wanted a buffer zone in the Balkans to help shield it from powerful European enemies. For France, war would not only erase the humiliation of her sound defeat in 1870–71 by a newly unified Germany but also regain French border territory lost by the treaty. Britain had historically pledged to defend Belgium, although no agreement existed.

8. "England Fears for Men in Battle in Belgium While No News Is Obtained," *Oshkosh Daily Northwestern,* August 26, 1914, 1.

9. "Appleton Germans Enlist," *Oshkosh Daily Northwestern,* August 26, 1914; "Germans to Leave Tomorrow to Join Army," *Appleton Evening Crescent,* August 4, 1914. Newspapers occasionally reported on the whereabouts of the ex-residents. In Fond du Lac, for example, on May 8, 1917, the *Daily Reporter* noted on its front page that Oswald Sapper of Mayville, a small town nearby, had been awarded the Iron Cross. Sapper had returned to Germany in 1914.

10. "Substitute Was Killed," *Oshkosh Daily Northwestern,* October 15, 1914, 1.

11. "Cannot Fight World," *Oshkosh Daily Northwestern,* August 26, 1914, 10.

12. "The War and Fashions," *Oshkosh Daily Northwestern,* August 26, 1914, 6.

13. "May Help Servant Problem," *Oshkosh Daily Northwestern,* August 26, 1914, 6; "Does Talc Powder Rise with War," *Appleton Evening Crescent,* August 5, 1914, 1.

14. In secret negotiations, Italy signed the Treaty of London in 1915. In return for joining on the side of France and England, Italy was offered large sections of Austrian territory adjoining the Adriatic Sea—Tyrol, Dalmatia, and Istria.

15. Archaeological evidence confirmed that the *Lusitania* was carrying munitions in her hold, although it remains unclear whether that would have caused such an explosion. Passenger liners were not made to withstand combat, and their longitudinal coal bunkers filled quickly with water. As a ship carrying war materials and contraband, the German U-boat, the SM U-20, was justified in sinking *Lusitania,* but in 1915 it was considered a cold-hearted act to torpedo a ship filled with passengers. By World War II, combatants thought little of sinking a liner. The U.S. Collector of Customs, Dudley Field Malone, a friend of President Wilson, turned a blind eye to the practice of shipping munitions on British liners.

16. "German American View of Situation," *Appleton Crescent,* May 15, 1915.

17. In Belgium in 1914, the Germans deliberately burned three hundred thousand rare medieval manuscripts and books at the University at Leuven and murdered or caused the death of 248 civilians.

18. When Wilson's political opponents criticized his one-side approach, he dealt with them harshly and accused them of "pouring poison" into national life. The German press published a caricature of Wilson as a fork-tongued snake.

19. Douglas Botting, ed., *The U-Boats: Seafarers Series* (Alexandria, VA: Time-Life Books, 1979), 50.

20. U.S. industrial output had by this time become essential to the Allied war effort. Almost half of their war budget was spent on American material. The British Munitions Ministry had agents working in American factories, on munitions trains, and with shipping firms to ensure American munitions flowed to the Allies.

Chapter 2. Men of the Guard

1. "New Armory Plans Are Announced," *Daily Commonwealth*, January 16, 1911, 5.

2. "Boundless Immigration History," https://boundless.com/u-s-history/textbooks /boundless-u-s-history-textbook/world-war-i-1914-1919-23/american-neutraility -177/the-debate-over, accessed June 2, 2018.

3. "Does Stunts with Auto," *Oshkosh Daily Northwestern*, August 3, 1916, 2. In general, the men were excited and eager to learn about trucks and autos.

4. "Food Is Improving," *Oshkosh Daily Northwestern*, August 10, 1916, 8.

5. "On the Rifle Range. Good Marks Expected," *Oshkosh Daily Northwestern*, August 12, 1916, 11. The army has three levels of proficiency: marksman, sharpshooter, and expert. There were shooting societies and clubs in the three communities of Appleton, Oshkosh, and Fond du Lac.

6. Charles Horne, ed., "Belgium's Martyrdom," in *The Great Events of the Great War*, vol. 4, *1916* (National Alumni, 1923), 4–5.

7. *Oshkosh Daily Northwestern*, July 1, 1916, 10.

8. "All Germany Believes War with American Is Certainty" and "Nothing Gained as Yet by U-Boats," *Oshkosh Daily Northwestern*, February 28, 1917, 1.

Chapter 3. War Comes to America

1. "The Supreme Test of Patriotism," *Oshkosh Daily Northwestern*, April 6, 1917, 4.

2. Botting, *U-Boats*, 50.

3. *Appleton Post*, April 10, 1917, quoted in "Company G Back; City's Finest Hour," by Lillian Mackesy, *Appleton Post-Crescent*, November 5, 1967.

4. Quoted in "Company G Back; City's Finest Hour."

5. "Co. E Ranks Good in Regiment," *Daily Reporter*, May 1, 1917, 5.

6. "Trier Receives Gift of Horse," *Daily Reporter*, April 19, 1917, 5.

7. Pearson Brown, Dewey Keno, Rudy Kraemer, and Leo Uelmen.

8. *Appleton Evening Crescent*, April 7, 1917. Pierre barely made the enlistment requirements. His friends came up with creative ways to bring him up to minimum weight and height.

9. This was commonly acknowledged as a reason why men joined. The additional money was important, too. The Otto Suess pay book shows that a private first class gunner in federal service received $36.60 per month, a corporal $40.20.

10. Arthur Bahr to the ex-Members of Company F, April 7, 1918, "Hiking in France," *Oshkosh Daily Northwestern*, May 1, 1918, 4.

11. *Appleton Evening Crescent*, February 28, 1917, 1.

12. "It's Major Trier Now; Lieut. Brunet to Lead," *Daily Commonwealth*, July 17, 1917, 5.

13. Raymond Sidney Tompkins, *The Story of the Rainbow Division* (New York: Boni and Liveright, 1919), 11.

14. Botting, *U-Boats*, 57.

15. James J. Cooke, *The Rainbow Division in the Great War, 1917–1919* (Westport, CT: Praeger Publishing, 1994), 3.

16. The patch was modified to a quarter-circle after the Armistice in November 1918 in honor of the fallen.

17. Tompkins, *Story of the Rainbow Division*, 11.

18. *Oshkosh Daily Northwestern*, August 2, 1917, 3.

19. "Nearly $700 Cleared at Dance," *Daily Commonwealth*, June 6, 1917, 5.

20. "Nearly $700 Cleared at Dance," 6.

21. "Co. E's Off Amid Cheers and Tears," *Daily Commonwealth*, August 6, 1917, 1.

22. George T. Raach, *A Withering Fire: American Machine Gun Battalions in World War I* (Bradenton, FL: BookLocker.com), 371.

23. Arthur Bahr to the ex-Members of Company F, April 7, 1918, "Hiking in France," *Oshkosh Daily Northwestern*, May 1, 1918, 4.

24. "No More Company E in a Short Time; Being Made Over," *Daily Commonwealth*, August 18, 1917, 5.

25. "Men Are Anxious to Start Eastward," *Daily Commonwealth*, August 30, 1917, 5. Puttees protected the lower leg and kept sand and grit out of boots. Once in France, they were issued regulation wool wrap puttees.

26. Harold Stanley Johnson, foreword to *Roster of the Rainbow Division (Forty-Second)* (New York: Eaton & Gettinger, 1917).

27. *A Brief History of Old Company "F" 2nd Wisconsin Infantry, Now Company C 150th Machinegun Battalion, 42nd Division, Better Known as "Rainbow Division,"* World War I Small Collections, Oshkosh Public Museum, 3. The author believes that the mess sergeant John T. Matschi created the narrative, most likely in 1919.

28. Diary of Arthur R. Bahr, transcribed, September 3, 1917. Private Collection of Andrew J. DeCusati, Fairfield, Pennsylvania.

29. "E Boys Grin on Way to War," *Daily Commonwealth*, September 5, 1917, 5.

30. William Heiss Collection, Wisconsin Veterans Museum, Madison, Wisconsin.

31. Bahr diary, September 5, 1917.

32. The article ran in the *Sheboygan Press* on September 24, 1917, under "Tells of Visit to the Rainbow Division." The article profiles some of the personalities. It was reported that Eddie Steckbauer (mistakenly written "Steckmeyer") was Company C's clown, making everyone laugh.

33. Otto Spaedtke to friend, October 13, 1917, World War I Small Collections, Oshkosh Public Museum.

34. William Heiss to Tim Heiss, September 30, 1917, Heiss Collection.

35. The Oshkosh Public Museum collection holds sketches of stylish women by Mand. While there is no conclusive proof that Mand did these sketches while on leave in New York City, they are all dated 1917. The author believes that most were sent back to his family in Oshkosh before the unit left for France.

36. "Melchior with the Rainbows," *Crivitz Advocate*, October 12, 1917, 1. Ford trucks had mechanical problems, especially with the transmissions, but they were faster than a mule-drawn cart.

37. Tompkins, *Story of the Rainbow Division*, 14.

38. Tompkins, *Story of the Rainbow Division*, 14.

Chapter 4. Hello France

1. 42RDVF, "WWI," accessed June 2, 2018, http://www.rainbowvets.org/wwi .#rainbow-patch/.

2. Walter Thorne to Emma Thorne, n.d., World War I Small Collections, Oshkosh Public Museum.

3. "Baggage Marked A.E.F. France," *Daily Commonwealth*, October 18, 1917, 5.

4. "Member of Co. E Writes of Trip," *Daily Commonwealth*, December 3, 1917, 5.

5. Bahr diary, September 19, 1917.

6. Bahr diary, September 20, 1917.

7. Ben Golz to Mr. and Mrs. Louis Golz, March 1918, *Oshkosh Daily Northwestern*.

8. *Brief History of Old Company "F."* Few U.S. troop ships were in fact sunk during the war. However, the *Covington* did become one of the victims, torpedoed by U-86 on July 1, 1918. Lake Poygan is northwest of Oshkosh and was a popular place to hunt ducks.

9. Nolan, *The Reading Militia in the Great War* (Reading, PA: Historical Society of Berks County, 1921), 24.

10. Bahr diary, October 31, 1917.

11. Frank Freidel, *Over There: The American Experience in World War I* (Short Hills, NJ: Burford Books, 1964), 50–51.

12. Freidel, *Over There*, 50–51.

13. Pearson Brown to father, January 8, 1918, "Letter from Local Boy," *Campbellsport News*, February 14, 1918, 1.

14. Edward E. Lutz to mother, November 2, 1917, "A Letter from Appleton Boy," *Berlin Evening Journal*, December 29, 1917, 1.

15. Walter Melchior to friends, December 2, 1917, "Getting Near the Trenches," *Crivitz Advocate*, January 4, 1918, 4.

16. Attributed to Lieutenant Colonel Charles E. Stanton at the Paris grave of Marquis de Lafayette on July 4, 1917.

17. The 42nd Division fought alongside French units, but other American divisions fought beside the British.

18. The United States was not formally allied to France and England. Rather, America was considered an "Associated Power."

19. Meaning they could hold forty men or eight horses. French railroads were a common topic of letters.

20. *Brief History of Old Company "F."*

21. Tompkins, *Story of the Rainbow Division*, 20.

22. Allan B. Ellis, *A Brief History of Appleton's "Old Company G," with the Rainbow Division in the Great War* (n.p., 1919), 7. Ellis compiled this after the war from letters he sent to his mother. It was self-published, and the pages are not numbered.

23. Diary of Robert K. Holterman, November 6, 1917, Fond du Lac County Historical Society, Fond du Lac, Wisconsin.

24. Bahr diary, November 10, 1917.

25. Lloyd Ray to Alva Ray, n.d., "Co. E Billeted in French Village," *Daily Commonwealth*, December 19, 1917, 5. Wisconsin's lumbering era had just ended, and life in a lumber camp would have been common knowledge.

26. Walton B. Cooper to mother, November 17, 1017, *Appleton Evening Crescent*, n.d., World War I Small Collections, History Museum at the Castle, Appleton, Wisconsin.

27. Peter Taylor, *The Smoke Ring: Tobacco, Money and Multinational Politics* (New York: Zonderzan, 1984), 1.

28. Nicholas K. Johnson, June 27, 2014, "World War I, Part 5: Tobacco in the Trenches," https://pointsadhsblog.wordpress.com/2014/06/27/wwi-part-5-tobacco -in-the-trenches/, accessed June 2, 2018.

29. Walter Ludwig to parents, March 15, 1918, *Oshkosh Daily Northwestern*, April 20, 1918, 6.

30. Stephen L. Harris, *Duffy's War: Fr. Francis Duffy, Wild Bill Donovan, and the Irish Fighting 69th in World War I* (Washington, DC: Potomac Books, 2006), 117.

31. Frank Ruechel to Edward Haslam, January 5, 1918, *Oshkosh Daily Northwestern*, February 6, 1918, 6.

32. Bahr diary, November 12, 1917.

33. "The French People and How They Impress the Boys from Oshkosh Now in France," *Oshkosh Daily Northwestern*, May 6, 1918, 6.

34. Harris, *Duffy's War*, 120.

35. Lorenzo Reed to Jack Rouse, May 26, 1918, World War I Nevitt Scrapbook, Oshkosh Public Museum. Not all pages in the scrapbook are numbered.

36. Tompkins, *Story of the Rainbow Division*, 27.

37. Arthur Bahr to John Mulva, February 28, 1918, "The Oshkosh Boys. Letters Show That Those in France Are in the Best of Health," *Oshkosh Daily Northwestern*, April 1, 1918, 4.

38. Guy Gross to Mrs. Frank Shaurette, n.d., "Guy Gross Writes from Over There," *Daily Commonwealth*, June 11, 1918, 5.

39. Leo Uelmen to parents, n.d., *Campbellsport News*, January 24, 1918, 1.

40. Bahr diary, November 28, 1917.

41. British losses at the Third Battle of Ypres and at Cambrai were not made up by replacements because new men were kept in Britain to prevent their use, and loss.

42. Bill Heiss to Tim Heiss, December 10, 1917, Heiss Collection.

43. Lloyd Ray to Alva Ray, n.d., "Co. E Billeted in French Village," *Daily Commonwealth*, December 19, 1917, 5.

44. Arthur Bahr to John Mulva, February 28, 1918, "The Oshkosh Boys," *Oshkosh Daily Northwestern*, April 1, 1918.

45. Justice B. Detwiler, *Soldiers' French Course* (New York: Foreign Trade Press, 1917), 113.

46. George Luther to parents, January 26, 1918, *Oshkosh Daily Northwestern*, April 18, 1918.

47. Bahr diary, November 28, 1917.

48. Art Bahr to mother, March 27, 1918, World War I Small Collections, Oshkosh Public Museum.

49. Arthur Kroll to his father, Herman Kroll, May 25, 1918, *Oshkosh Daily Northwestern*, June 24, 1918, 4.

50. *Brief History of Old Company "F."*

51. *Field Service Pocket Book, United States Army, 1917*, War Department Document No. 605 (Washington: Government Printing Office, 1917), 32.

52. Tompkins, *Story of the Rainbow Division*, 24.

53. Holterman diary, December 28, 1917.

54. *Brief History of Old Company "F."*

55. Walter Thorne to Emma W. Thorne, January 9, 1918, World War I Small Collections, Oshkosh Public Museum.

56. "Somewhere in France," *Oshkosh Daily Northwestern*, February 13, 1918, 5.

57. Bahr diary, January 8, 1918.

58. Bahr diary, December 3, 1917.

59. August Arens to friend, February 10, 1918, "Soldier's Letters," *Appleton Evening Crescent*, n.d., private collection of Joseph Gaerthofner, Appleton, Wisconsin.

60. Most divisions arriving after the 42nd were issued either Colt Vickers Model 1915 or, late in the war, the American-made Browning Model 1917.

61. Walter Thorne to Emma Thorne, March 1918, Walter Thorne Collection, Oshkosh Public Museum.

62. Harvey Stich to Hilda [Schenk] Stich, May 26, 1918, World War I Small Collections, Oshkosh Public Museum.

63. Elmer Grabinski to mother, n.d., "Corp. Grabinski Downs a German Airman in Fight," *Daily Commonwealth,* June 4, 1918, 5.

64. "Direct Fire of Machine Guns," Bahr papers, Andrew J. DeCusati Collection.

65. "Direct Fire of Machine Guns."

66. Albert Lange to Otto Zoellner, n.d., "Home Boys Suffer Gas and Shrapnel Wounds in Night Boche Assaults," *Daily Commonwealth*, April 25, 1918, 5.

67. "Direct Fire of a Machine Gun."

68. "Automatic Weapons Schools, Characteristics of the Machine Gun," Bahr papers.

69. "Night Firing," Bahr papers.

70. Freidel, *Over There*, 86.

71. *Brief History of Old Company "F."*

72. Bahr diary, January 8, 1918.

73. Leo Uelmen to Mr. and Mrs. Peter Uelmen, n.d., *Campbellsport News,* January 24, 1918, 1.

74. Bahr diary, February 22, 1918.

Chapter 5.   Into the Trenches!

1. Tompkins, *Story of the Rainbow Division,* 28.

2. William Heiss to Tim Heiss, January 24, 1918, Heiss Collection.

3. Tompkins, *Story of the Rainbow Division,* 31.

4. Shrapnel shells burst in the air and sent a shower of one-centimeter lead balls down on anything below. Shrapnel was sometimes used interchangeably with the word "splinters": splinters of steel from exploding shells.

5. This was probably the volatile French F1 grenade with a percussion fuse.

6. Herman Sawall to his wife, March 7, 1918, *Oshkosh Daily Northwestern*, April 8, 1918, 6.

7. Diary of Herbert Ralph Granger, Transcript, World War I Small Collections, Oshkosh Public Museum.

8. Holterman diary, May 7, 1918.

9. Arthur Guy Empey, *Over the Top* (New York: G. P. Putnam's Sons, 1917), 30–31.

10. Granger diary, May 7, 1918; and Cooke, *Rainbow Division,* 61.

11. Hugh S. Thompson and Robert H. Ferrell, eds., *Trench Knives and Mustard Gas: With the 42nd Rainbow Division in France* (College Station: Texas A&M University

Press, 2004), 48. Thompson's experiences were first published serially in the *Chattanooga Times* in 1934. His columns were later edited into a book. He provides a vivid, well-written account of what combat was like, as well as general observations about service in France and the bonds of camaraderie that develop between soldiers.

12. Frank Coffer to Henrietta Kuehn, April 1, 1918, *Oshkosh Daily Northwestern*, May 28, 1918, 6.

13. Henry Witt to Mr. and Mrs. Herman Gomoll, March 31, 1918, *Oshkosh Daily Northwestern*, May 18, 1918, 6.

14. Arthur Bahr to Frank Kellerman, May 22, 1918, World War I Small Collections, Oshkosh Public Museum.

15. Harvey Stich to Hilda [Schenk] Stich, May 16, 1918, Harvey Stich Collection, Oshkosh Public Museum.

16. "A Letter from Appleton Boys," *Berlin Evening Journal*, December 29, 1917.

17. Tompkins, *Story of the Rainbow Division*, 31.

18. Walter B. Wolf, *A Brief Story of the Rainbow Division* (New York: Rand, McNally, 1919), 12.

19. Granger diary, March 13 and 15, 1918. This would have been the Rouge Bouquet. A powerful large-caliber German shell destroyed an old French bunker that held sleeping men of Company E of the 165th (New York) Infantry.

20. *Brief History of Old Company "F."*

21. Arthur Davis to Carl Okerberg, March 30, 1918, *Oshkosh Daily Northwestern*, n.d.

22. Isaac G. Walker, reel 30/0466 in Dale R. Grinder, ed., *The World War I Survey: Papers Compiled from the United States Army Military History Institute Collection Carlisle Barracks*; cited in Raach, *Withering Fire*, 33–55.

23. Leo Moguin to Cousin Loretta, May 10, 1918, "Sergt. Moquin Wants Revenge," *Daily Commonwealth*, June 4, 1918, 6.

24. Ernst Junger, *Storm of Steel* (New York: Penguin Books, 2004), 240.

25. Much of the advance and ground taken had little value to the Germans because the offensive had no strategic goals. Susanne Everett, *World War I: An Illustrated History* (London: Bison Books, 1980), 199–200; H. P. Willmott, *World War I* (New York: Dorling Kindersley, 2003), 252–53; and Ian Passingham, *The German Offensives of 1918* (South Yorkshire, UK: Pen and Sword Books, 2008), 40–61.

26. Albert Lange to Otto Zoeller, n.d., "Home Boys Suffer Gas and Shrapnel Wounds in Night Boche Assault," *Daily Commonwealth*, April 25, 1918, 5.

27. "Home Boys Suffer Gas and Shrapnel Wounds."

28. Holterman diary, March 17 and 20, 1918.

29. Holterman diary, March 22, 1918.

30. Frank Wheeler to Charles F. Wheeler, n.d., "More Details of the Gas Assault," *Daily Commonwealth*, April 26, 1918, 6.

31. Leo Moquin to Loretta Moquin, May 10, 1918, *Daily Commonwealth*, n.d.

32. "Lieut. John Smith Arrives in City; in France a Year," *Daily Commonwealth*, October 18, 1918, 5.

33. Leo Moquin to Cousin Loretta, July 14, 1918, "Confessions Are Heard in Y.M.C.A.," *Daily Commonwealth*, August 8, 1918, 4.

34. Guy Gross to Mrs. Frank Shaurette, n.d., "Guy Gross Writes from Over There," *Daily Commonwealth*, June 11, 1918, 5.

35. Tompkins, *Story of the Rainbow Division*, 36.

36. Earl E. Zoch to Martha Bohlman, n.d., "Alvin Bohlman Died as a Hero; Shrapnel Wound," *Daily Commonwealth*, April 25, 1918, 5.

37. Leo Uelmen to Herman Pass, n.d., "Pearson L. Brown Was Killed in Active Service," *Daily Commonwealth*, June 8, 1918, 5.

38. "Our Hero," *Campbellsport News*, April 4, 1918, 4.

Chapter 6. Baccarat

1. Wolf, *Brief Story of the Rainbow Division*, 15.

2. Walter Billborg to Iver Billborg, March 26, 1918, *Oshkosh Daily Northwestern*, May 10, 1918, 6.

3. Summary of Intelligence #236, 42nd Division, February 2, 1919, in *Candid Comment on the American Soldiers of 1917–1918 and Kindred Topics by the Germans, Soldiers, Priests, Women, Village Notables, Politicians and Statesmen* (Prepared by the Intelligence Section, the General Staff, General Headquarters, American Expeditionary Forces, Chaumont, France, 1919, https://fas.org/irp/agency/army/wwi-soldiers.pdf, accessed June 1, 2018), 9.

4. Bahr diary, April 4, 1918.

5. Joel R. Parkinson, *Commanding Fire: An Officer's Life in the 151st Machine Gun Battalion, 42nd Rainbow Division during World War I* (Atglen, PA: Schiffer Publishing, 2013), 57–58.

6. Corporal Walter Pochojka to Mr. and Mrs. Frank Pochojka, n.d., "Company F Hit Hard Beating Back Huns," *Oshkosh Daily Northwestern*, n.d., World War I Scrapbook, 146.

7. Raymond Smith to mother, April 18, 1918, *Oshkosh Daily Northwestern*, May 18, 1918, 6.

8. Parkinson, *Commanding Fire*, 50.

9. Summary of Intelligence #236, 42nd Div., February 2, 1919, in *Candid Comment on the American Soldiers*, 9.

10. World War I Small Collections, Frank Obersteiner Collection, Oshkosh Public Museum.

11. William Heiss to Tim Heiss, May 7, 1918, Heiss Collection.

12. Parkinson, *Commanding Fire*, 48.

13. Called Operation Georgette, it also failed to break the British line.

14. *Brief History of Old Company "F."*

15. Gust Schroeder to wife, April 2, 1918, *Oshkosh Daily Northwestern*, May 10, 1918, 6.

16. Leo Moquin to Loretta Moquin, May 10, 1918, "Sergt. Moquin Wants Revenge," *Daily Commonwealth*, June 4, 1918, 6.

17. James H. Hallas, ed., *Doughboy War: The American Expeditionary Force in World War I* (Boulder, CO: Lynne Rienner Publishers, 2000), 68.

18. Junger, *Storm of Steel*, 45.

19. *Brief History of Old Company "F."*

20. "As Y.M.C.A. Worker He Made Visits in Time to Witness and Share Dangers at St. Michel," *Appleton Evening Crescent*, November 9, 1918.

21. Private Henry Witt to Mr. and Mrs. Herman Gomol, March 31, 1918, *Oshkosh Daily Northwestern*, May 18, 1918, 6.

22. Empey, *Over the Top*, 188.

23. "Boche Mustard Gas Hurts Eyes," *Daily Commonwealth*, April 29, 1918, 7.

24. Wolf, *Brief Story of the Rainbow Division*, 18.

25. Elmer Bullis to Bert Washburn, June 9, 1918, World War I Small Collections, Oshkosh Public Museum. The archivist of the Oshkosh Public Museum was told by a descendant that the explanation the family was given is that Paul Faulk was twirling his Colt M1911 pistol around his finger and it went off. The museum holds a photo compilation of all the men in Company C, and in the compilation Fauck's photo is turned upside down.

26. "Rainbow Troops in Hard Fighting on West Front/ Fond du Lac Men in Fight," *New York Times*, April 12, 1918.

27. William Heiss to Tim Heiss, May 7, 1918, Heiss Collection.

28. George Luther to Mr. and Mrs. A. H. Luther, June 16, 1918, "Furloughs & Figs," *Oshkosh Daily Northwestern*, n.d., World War I Nevitt Scrapbook, 18.

29. Ben Golz to Louis Lothman, May 17, 1918, "To Former Comrades," *Oshkosh Daily Northwestern*, n.d., World War I Nevitt Scrapbook, 7.

30. "Furloughs & Figs."

31. Wolf, *Brief Story of the Rainbow Division*, 20.

32. Elmer Bullis to Bert Washburn, June 9, 1918.

33. Harold Smith to parents, June 6, 1918, Transcript, World War I Small Collections, Oshkosh Public Museum.

34. Harold Smith to parents, June 2, 1918, "It Was Sunday," *Oshkosh Daily Northwestern*, n.d., World War I Nevitt Scrapbook, 53.

35. Granger diary, June 25, 1918.

36. Ralph H. Granger to Addie Olson, n.d., "Has Letters from Private R. Granger," *Daily Commonwealth,* June 27, 1918, 5. Art Bahr wrote to a friend, "I would like to meet the guy that called this sunny France. [It] rained four or five days out of every week since we came here." Arthur Bahr to Frank Kellerman, "Sunny France," May 22, 1918, World War I Nevitt Scrapbook, 10.

37. George Luther to Mr. and Mrs. A. H. Luther, June 16, 1918, "Furloughs & Figs." Luther's comments are not unusual. The Y.M.C.A. raised money in the United States for its mission to serve the troops in France, yet they charged the doughboys for goods. Doughboys saw young, healthy Y.M.C.A. men in easy positions selling goods to combat soldiers. This did not sit well with many troops.

38. Charles Horne, ed., *Great Events of the Great War* (National Alumni, 1923), vol. 6, *The Year of Victory,* 206.

39. Guy Gross to Mrs. Frank Shaurette, n.d., "Guy Gross Writes from 'Over There,'" *Daily Commonwealth,* June 11, 1918, 5.

40. Harvey Stich to Hilda [Schenk] Stich, May 26, 1918, World War I Small Collections, Oshkosh Public Museum.

41. Harold L. Smith to parents, July 6, 1918, World War I Small Collections, Oshkosh Public Museum.

42. *Brief History of Old Company "F."*

Chapter 7. The Lousy Champagne

1. Elmer Bullis to Bert Washburn, June 9, 1918, World War I Small Collections, Oshkosh Public Museum.

2. William Heiss to Tim Heiss, May 7, 1918, Heiss Collection.

3. Harold Smith to parents, July 6, 1918, World War I Small Collections, Oshkosh Public Museum.

4. Elmer Bullis to Bert Washburn, June 9, 1918, World War I Small Collections, Oshkosh Public Museum.

5. Wolf, *Brief Story of the Rainbow Division,* 22.

6. R. M. Cheseldine, *Ohio in the Rainbow: The Official Story of the 166th Infantry, 42nd Division in the World War* (Columbus, OH: F. J. Heer Printing, 1924), 154.

7. Lice plagued the men of all armies and they referred to this as being "lousy."

8. Wolf, *Brief Story of the Rainbow Division,* 21.

9. Granger diary, July 7, 1918.

10. Rudy Kraemer to friend Jim, July 10, 1918, "Letters from France," *Campbellsport News,* August 8, 1918, 1.

11. Henry J. Reilly, *Americans All: The Rainbows at War, Official History of the 42nd Rainbow Division in the World War* (Columbus, OH: F. J. Heer Printing, 1936), 300–301.

12. Harvey Pierre to Dr. D. S. Runnels, *Appleton Crescent*, July 2, 1918.

13. John Pierre to parents, July 12, 1918, *Appleton Evening Crescent*, August 20, 1918.

14. Cheseldine, *Ohio in the Rainbow*, 160.

15. Thompson and Ferrell, *Trench Knives and Mustard Gas*, 119.

16. Cheseldine, *Ohio in the Rainbow*, 163.

17. Don Anderson, "Rainbow Vets Look Back to Battles of 1918," *Appleton Post-Crescent*, July 13, 1943.

18. Cheseldine, *Ohio in the Rainbow*, 165.

19. "Letters, Diaries and Biographies," Diary of Nathaniel Rouse, July 14–17, 1918, Doughboy Center, http://www.worldwar1.com/dbc/biograph.htm, accessed June 2, 2018.

20. Granger diary, July 15, 1918.

21. *Brief History of Old Company "F."*

22. Bahr diary, July 16, 1918.

23. Private Art Davis to Frieda, July 31, 1918, *Oshkosh Daily Northwestern*, September 14, 1918, 1.

24. Thompson and Ferrell, *Trench Knives and Mustard Gas*, 123–25.

25. Anderson, "Rainbow Veterans Look Back."

26. Harold L. Smith to parents, July 21, 1918, *Oshkosh Daily Northwestern*, September 14, 1918, 6.

27. Nolan, *Reading Militia in the Great War*, 64, 67.

28. Horne, *Great Events of the Great War*, 6:256–57.

29. Anderson, "Rainbow Veterans Look Back."

30. Francis Patrick Duffy, *Father Duffy's Story: A Tale of Humor and Heroism, of Life and Death with the Fighting Sixty-Ninth* (New York: George H. Doran, 1919), 133.

31. Casper L. Schommer to John Schommer, n.d., "Freedom News, Casper L. Schommer Tells of Heroic Work at Front," *Appleton Evening Crescent*, October 16, 1918.

32. Martin J. Hogan, *The Shamrock Battalion of the Rainbow: A Story of the Fighting 69th* (New York: D. Appleton, 1919), 127–28; quoted in Cooke, *Rainbow Division*, 198.

33. Tompkins, *Story of the Rainbow Division*, 66.

34. "Distinguished Service Cross Recipients from the 150th Machine Gun Battalion during World War I," http://www.b-1-105.us/history/ww1/DSC-150mgbn.html, accessed September 30, 2018.

35. Roy Watson to Mrs. Jeannie Edgell, July 21, 1918, "Last Letter from Sergt. Roy Watson," *Daily Commonwealth*, September 9, 1918, 5.

36. Elmer Grabinski to parents, July 19, 1918, "Fondy Soldier Says Appleton Boys Did Trick," *Daily Commonwealth*, August 17, 1918, 8.

37. E. J. Stark to Mrs. Carrie Stark, July 18, 1918, "Wagoner Stark Wounded at Front," *Daily Commonwealth*, August 17, 1918, 1.

38. Art Davis to Theresa Davis, July 21, 1918, "How the Boys Feel," *Oshkosh Daily Northwestern*, August 14, 1918, 6.

39. Edward C. Steckbauer to parents, July 21, 1918, World War I Small Collections, Oshkosh Public Museum.

40. Harold L. Smith to parents, July 21, 1918, World War I Small Collections, Oshkosh Public Museum.

41. *Brief History of Old Company "F."*

42. John Pierre to mother, July 28, 1918, *Appleton Evening Crescent*, August 20, 1918.

43. "Three More Fell on Battle Field from County," *Appleton Evening Crescent*, August 5, 1918.

44. "Bodies of 3 War Heroes on Way Home," *Appleton Post-Crescent*, July 20, 1921, 1.

45. *Brief History of Old Company "F."* The storyteller made it a point to note that Private Treichel was shell shocked. The men did not dismiss or demean shell shock in any way and saw it as a very real consequence of battle.

46. Roy Watson to Mrs. Jeannie Edgell, July 21, 1918, "Last Letter from Sergt. Roy Watson," *Daily Commonwealth*, September 9, 1918, 5; Nolan, *Reading Militia in the Great War*, 69.

47. Arthur Bahr to Mayor A. C. McHenry, July 21, 1918, *Oshkosh Daily Northwestern*, September 14, 1918, 6.

48. Bill Heiss to Tim Heiss, July 20, 1918, Heiss Collection.

49. *Brief History of Old Company "F."*

50. A. J. Kraemer to Cousin Alex, August 8, 1918, *Campbellsport News*, September 12, 1918, 5.

51. Granger diary, July 22, 1918; Ellis, *Brief History of Appleton's "Old Company G."*

52. "Cook William Lang Killed by Airbomb Dropped by German," *Appleton Post*, December 13, 1918.

Chapter 8. Château-Thierry

1. Tompkins, *Story of the Rainbow Division*, 77.

2. Douglas MacArthur, *Reminiscences* (New York: McGraw-Hill, 1964), 59.

3. *Brief History of Old Company "F."*

4. Cheseldine, *Ohio in the Rainbow*, 191. German forces systematically ruined or removed anything of value in their retreat.

5. Parkinson, *Commanding Fire*, 85.

6. Parkinson, *Commanding Fire*, 85.

7. Cheseldine, *Ohio in the Rainbow*, 191.

8. Nolan, *Reading Militia in the Great War*, 72–73.

9. Casper Schommer to John Schommer, n.d., "Freedom News. Casper L. Schommer Tells of the Heroic Work at Front," *Appleton Evening Crescent,* October 16, 1918.

10. Tompkins, *Story of the Rainbow Division,* 79.

11. Runners were essential, for there was no other way to communicate with units and with headquarters. Radio was not available, and stringing telephone line was impractical in an advance and under fire. Units had flares, signal flags, bugles, and whistles, but they were useless in the midst of battle. Typically, two runners were sent with the same message because casualties were great for men given this dangerous assignment. Runners traveled light, with just a pistol, gas mask, canteen, and first-aid pack. Raach's *Withering Fire* has a good explanation of runners.

12. Anderson, "Rainbow Veterans Look Back."

13. *Brief History of Old Company "F."*

14. Each company kept platoons in reserve so that there were fresh sections available to replace those in action.

15. "Appleton Soldier Gives Graphic Description of Life at the Front," *Appleton Crescent,* n.d.

16. Company A's Patrick Sullivan was badly wounded in the leg by shrapnel. Years later, Sam Crouch told Patrick's son, Thomas, that he helped carry Patrick to the aid station. However, he explained that he received quite a tongue-lashing from a company officer because they had left most of their equipment with the gun, except for one pistol, when they took Patrick. Tom Sullivan to author, September 2017.

17. "Hantschel Will Represent State at Soldier Memorial," *Appleton Post-Crescent,* October 4, 1921, 1. Lieutenant Parkinson in the 151st might have seen Hantschel. He recalled a badly wounded sergeant.

18. "Hantschel Will Represent State at Soldier Memorial."

19. "Medicine in the First World War," Kansas University Medical Center, http:// www.kumc.edu/wwi.html, accessed June 2, 2018; and Col. Charles Lynch et al., *The Medical Department of the United States Army in the World War,* vol. 3, *Field Operations* (Washington, DC: Government Printing Office, 1925) http://history.amedd.army.mil /booksdocs/wwi/fieldoperations/default.htm, accessed May 15, 2018.

20. Conrad Paffenroth to sister, August 20, 1918, *Oshkosh Daily Northwestern,* September 14, 1918, 11.

21. Carl Schneider to Rose Baier, August 10, 1918, "Stands Up for States," *Oshkosh Daily Northwestern,* n.d., World War I Nevitt Scrapbook, 67.

22. Earl Day to Mrs. Frank R. Day, August 4, 1918, "Oshkosh Boy Surprised and Delighted to Meet Two Nurses from Home in France," *Oshkosh Daily Northwestern,* August 26, 1918, 4.

23. Mary Nigl to Minnie Prautch, July 16, 1918, "Appeals to Nurses," *Oshkosh Daily Northwestern,* n.d., World War I Nevitt Scrapbook, 21.

24. Reilly, *Americans All*, 445.

25. Anderson, "Rainbow Veterans Look Back."

26. Reilly, *Americans All*, 433.

27. Arnold Stephen Hoke, oral history with Patricia Munson-Siter, April 12, 1971, Veterans History Project, American Folklife Center, Library of Congress.

28. Ellis, *Brief History of Appleton's "Old Company G,"* 16.

29. Isaac G. Walker Reel 30/04666 in Grinder, *World War I Survey*, cited in Raach, *Withering Fire*, 2735.

30. Reilly, *Americans All*, 448–50.

31. Cheseldine, *Ohio in the Rainbow*, 197.

32. Reilly, *Americans All*, 450. Narratives commonly mention the large numbers of dead horses and mules.

33. These deadly weapons fired a huge shell for short distances that could clearly be seen in its approaching arc.

34. Casper Schommer to John Schommer, n.d., "Casper L. Schommer Tells of the Heroic Work at Front," *Appleton Evening Crescent*, October 16, 1918. The machine gunners had only a pistol for defense and it was not uncommon to pick up a rifle for more firepower if attacked.

35. Reilly, *Americans All*, 447. Major Winn in command of the 151st Machine Gun Battalion said the same thing.

36. Duffy, *Father Duffy's Story*, 172.

37. Animals were so essential that the army operated veterinary hospitals. Horses and mules were treated for wounds, shell shock, gas, diseases, and worms. Animals suffered despite the efforts of men like Graf. Poor or inconsistent feed, exposure, and exhaustion took their toll. Of note, horse trailers were first developed on the Western Front as a way to extend an animal's useful life.

38. Cheseldine, *Ohio in the Rainbow*, 275.

39. *Brief History of Old Company "F."* Teamster Desire DeGraves was from Oconto and was part of the Headquarters Company.

40. "Fourth Ward Boy Buried in France," *Appleton Evening Crescent*, April 22, 1919.

41. "Graves of Heroes," *Oshkosh Daily Northwestern*, n.d., World War I Nevitt Scrapbook, 134.

42. Jung was hit in the stomach by a machine-gun bullet on July 29, and Proudfit by shrapnel on July 31. Both recovered.

43. Cheseldine, *Ohio in the Rainbow*, 197–98.

44. "War Medal Given to Fallen Berlin Hero," *Berlin Evening Journal*, February 1, 1919, 1.

45. "Soldier in Same Platoon with Late Tony Kramp," *Berlin Evening Journal*, March 6, 1919, 3.

46. "Was Shot Through the Heart Says New Holterman Letter," *Daily Commonwealth*, August 20, 1918, 1.

47. "Tells of Plight at St. Hilaire on Night of July 23," *Daily Commonwealth*, February 11, 1919, 10.

48. R. E. Kraemer to A. J. Kraemer, August 8, 1918, "Letters from France," *Campbellsport News*, September 12, 1918, 5.

49. Tompkins, *Story of the Rainbow Division*, 86–87.

50. Reilly, *Americans All*, 447.

51. Frank Coffers to parents, July 31, 1918, "Shrapnel Hits Arm," *Oshkosh Daily Northwestern*, n.d., World War I Nevitt Scrapbook. The Germans put their machine guns in flanking positions when possible. Because they were often mounted on a special sled, the crew was able to crawl and pull the gun back to new positions with minimal exposure.

52. Cheseldine, *Ohio in the Rainbow*, 212.

53. Granger diary, July 28–29, 1918.

54. "Letters, Diaries and Biographies," Diary of Nathaniel Rouse, July 14–17, 1918, Doughboy Center, http://www.worldwar1.com/dbc/biograph.htm, accessed June 2, 2018.

55. Wolf, *Brief Story of the Rainbow Division*, 33.

56. Cheseldine, *Ohio in the Rainbow*, 202.

57. Nolan, *Reading Militia in the Great War*, 75.

58. "Corp. Washburn Died in Action," *Daily Commonwealth*, July 19, 1919, 5.

59. Cheseldine, *Ohio in the Rainbow*, 210. This was probably Company C.

60. Cheseldine, *Ohio in the Rainbow*, 212–13.

61. Cheseldine, *Ohio in the Rainbow*, 211; Nolan, *Reading Militia in the Great War*, 76.

62. Tompkins, *Story of the Rainbow Division*, 95.

63. 42nd Div. Summary of Intelligence, #150, December 15, 1918, in *Candid Comment on the American Soldiers*, 57.

64. "Was in Big Drive," Sullivan Scrapbook, World War I Small Collections, Oshkosh Public Museum, 25.

65. Arthur Bahr to dad, mother, and all, "A Great Deal of War Has Been Seen by the Men of Oshkosh on the French Front," *Oshkosh Daily Northwestern*, August 27, 1918.

66. Leo Uelmen to Mr. and Mrs. Peter Uelmen, August 16, 1918, "Speaks Highly of Red Cross," *Campbellsport News*, September 19, 1918, 1.

67. "Company F Hit Hard in Beating Back Huns," *Oshkosh Daily Northwestern*, n.d., World War I Nevitt Scrapbook, 146. The article used both excerpts from a letter Pochojka wrote as well as an interview.

68. Private Everette Lawrence to Mr. and Mrs. H. J. Lawrence, August 18, 1918, "Have Been Real Busy," *Oshkosh Daily Northwestern*, n.d., World War I Nevitt Scrapbook.

69. Official Casualty Report, World War I Small Collections, Oshkosh Public Museum.

70. Arthur Bahr to Frank A. Dubois, "Rumor Mongers That Are Denounced by an Oshkosh Officers in Active Service at the Front," September 23, 1918, *Oshkosh Daily Northwestern.*

71. "Death Toll Grows," *Oshkosh Daily Northwestern*, n.d., World War I Nevitt Scrapbook, 45. Part of Ruhl's letter was used in an article the newspaper published on the battle at Château-Thierry.

72. Daniel Holterman to C. J. Pinkerton Family, August 9, 1918, "Fighting with Rainbow Division," *Waupun Leader*, September 12, 1918, 1. Robert and Dan Holterman survived the war.

73. Carl Schneider to Rose Baier, August 10, 1918, "Stands Up for State," *Oshkosh Daily Northwestern*, n.d., World War I Nevitt Scrapbook, 67. Both brothers survived the war.

74. Otto Suess to Elanor Suess, August 27, 1918, World War I Small Collections, Oshkosh Public Museum.

75. Lieutenant Arthur R. Bahr to Mrs. Kate Mand, August 24, 1918, World War I Small Collections, Oshkosh Public Museum.

76. Alex Fleischmann to parents, n.d., "A Letter from the Front," *Campbellsport News*, August 22, 1918, 8. Fleischman served in the regular army and was not with the 150th Machine Gun Battalion. However, he saw Company B men often and was on the same battlefield.

77. World War I Nevitt Scrapbook, 25.

78. Private Guy Gross to parents, August 19–20, 1918, "Letter from Guy Gross," *Daily Commonwealth*, September 14, 1918, 7.

Chapter 9. St. Mihiel

1. The Hindenburg Line was constructed in 1917. It was not a single trench system but a defense in great depth that consisted of fortified lines, bunkers, and other strong points.

2. Wolf, *Brief Story of the Rainbow Division*, 36.

3. Otto Suess to Elanor Suess, August 27, 1918, World War I Small Collections, Oshkosh Public Museum.

4. Nolan, *Reading Militia in the Great War*, 78. The surviving letters of companies A, B, and C are silent on the desirable trip.

5. Carl Nimmer to Mrs. W. Nichols, August 24, 1918, "America's Task," *Oshkosh Daily Northwestern*, September 15, 1918, 6.

6. Wolf, *Brief Story of the Rainbow Division*, 37; Tompkins, *Story of the Rainbow Division*, 109; Bahr diary, September 7, 1918.

7. Parkinson, *Commanding Fire*, 118.

8. Nolan, *Reading Militia in the Great War*, 85.

9. Nolan, *Reading Militia in the Great War*, 86. Soldiers in front of tanks were liable to be run over.

10. Bahr diary, September 11 and 17, 1918. Rhyner told his mother in Oshkosh, "The doctor said that I was lucky . . . [the bullet] entered on the left side just below the ribs and stopped over the right side just below the liver. It is still open and has to be sewn up. I dread the time to come." "Two Boys Wounded," World War I Nevitt Scrapbook, 88.

11. Nolan, *Reading Militia in the Great War*, 87.

12. Granger diary, September 12, 1918.

13. Private J. K. Bragg to Mr. and Mrs. Carl Lund in Oakfield, September 17, 1918, "Letters from the Yanks," *Daily Commonwealth*, October 22, 1918, 6.

14. Reilly, *Americans All*, 571.

15. Arthur Bahr to Frank A. Dubois, "Rumor Mongers That Are Denounced by an Oshkosh Officer in Active Service at Front," September 23, 1918, *Oshkosh Daily Northwestern*. American casualties were seven thousand killed and wounded; and two thousand dead for the Germans.

16. Simon Weiner to Ira Parker, September 21, 1918, *Oshkosh Daily Northwestern*, November 2, 1918. "Soldier Pal" Parker was the owner of Parker & Sons Company, a maker of paint and window-glazing putty.

17. Granger diary, September 12, 1918. Parkinson in the 151st said the men had no overcoats, only lightweight raincoats.

18. "Forty Germans Surrendered to Captain Graef in St. Mihiel Fight," *Appleton Evening Crescent*, October 17, 1918, 1.

19. Corporal William Techmann to Joe Weishepl, n.d., *Oshkosh Daily Northwestern*, November 2, 1918.

20. This sector was designated as an area for divisions to rest and recover. The Germans had built comfortable, rustic cottages and barracks, bath houses, recreational facilities, and had planted large gardens; they kept all of this well-supplied.

21. Lothar Graef to father, September 22, 1918, "Capt. Graef Tells What Appleton Boys Are Doing," *Appleton Evening Crescent*, October 22, 1918, 4.

22. Memo, September 21, 1918, Herbert W. Rowse Papers, U.S. Army Heritage and Education Center, War College Library, Carlisle, Pennsylvania.

23. "Germans Are Afraid of Rainbows," *Appleton Evening Crescent*, September 18, 1918. It was not common for local newspapers to print letters from men from other communities. However, this letter reflected on the entire machine gun battalion and the division, so it was an exception.

24. Guy Gross to Mr. and Mrs. Mathew Gross, September 24, 1918, "Letters from the Yanks," *Daily Commonwealth*, October 22, 1918, 6.

Chapter 10. Meuse-Argonne

1. Peter Hart, *The Last Battle: Victory, Defeat, and the End of World War I* (Oxford, UK: Oxford University Press, 2018), 243.

2. Richard Wagner was a nineteenth-century German composer, primarily known for his operas set in pagan times and featuring romanticized Nordic characters. An excellent description of Pershing's Army and what they faced is found in Mitchell Yockelson, *Forty-Seven Days: How Pershing's Warriors Came of Age to Defeat the German Army in World War I* (New York: New American Library, 2016).

3. Cheseldine, *Ohio in the Rainbow*, 247.

4. Nolan, *Reading Militia in the Great War*, 93.

5. *Brief History of Old Company "F."*

6. Parkinson, *Commanding Fire*, 149.

7. Cheseldine, *Ohio in the Rainbow*, 249.

8. Granger diary, October 14, 1918.

9. Sgt. Roy Kraemer to Hazel Dreier, December 17, 1918, "Sergt. Dreier Met His Death Bravely—Fought to Last," *Daily Commonwealth*, January 29, 1919, 10.

10. Reilly, *Americans All*, 713–15.

11. Reilly, *Americans All*, 715.

12. Nolan, *Reading Militia in the Great War*, 94–95; Reilly, *Americans All*, 715–18.

13. *Brief History of Old Company "F."*

14. Granger diary, October 15–16, 1918.

15. Nolan, *Reading Militia in the Great War*, 95.

16. *Brief History of Old Company "F."*

17. Arnold Stephen Hoke, oral history with Patricia Munson-Siter, April 12, 1971, Veterans History Project, American Folklife Center, Library of Congress.

18. Reilly, *Americans All*, 712–13.

19. Reilly, *Americans All*, 717–18.

20. Holterman diary, October 16–27, 1918.

21. Reilly, *Americans All*, 713–14.

22. Reilly, *Americans All*, 702–4. Connolly's experience was not unusual. The medical service was simply overwhelmed with the volume of casualties and did the best they could. Approximately one in every three wounded men died.

23. Reilly, *Americans All*, 714–15.

24. *Brief History of Old Company "F."*

25. Bahr diary, October 11, 1918. He noted it was October 11 but the record show it was October 22.

26. Rudy Kraemer to James Farrell, n.d., "Letters from France," *Campbellsport News*, December 12, 1918, 5. Finn was wounded in the ankle.

27. Corporal Horace Stever to mother, October 23, 1918, "Chocolate Bars," *Oshkosh Daily Northwestern*, n.d., World War I Nevitt Scrapbook.

28. George Roble to Mr. and Mrs. Julius Balthazor, n.d., "Describes Death of Battle Hero," *Daily Commonwealth*, January 18, 1919, 5.

29. Ellis, *Brief History of Appleton's "Old Company G"*; Parkinson, *Commanding Fire*, 173.

30. Nolan, *Reading Militia in the Great War*, 97.

31. Granger diary, November 1, 1918; Holterman diary, November 1, 1918.

32. Parkinson, *Commanding Fire*, 162. Sadly, after making their way back, the men of the 151st were told a mistake had been made, and they had to retrace their route.

33. Harvey Stich to brother, November 3, 1918, World War I Small Collections, Oshkosh Public Museum.

34. Rudy Kraemer to Alex J. Kraemer, n.d., "Letters from France," *Campbellsport News*, November 14, 1918, 1.

35. Wolf, *Brief Story of the Rainbow Division*, 50.

36. *Brief History of Old Company "F."*

37. Hoke, oral history, Veterans History Project.

38. Granger diary, November 5, 1918.

39. Granger diary, November 7, 1918.

40. Parkinson, *Commanding Fire*, 189.

41. Reilly, *Americans All*, 838–39.

42. Ellis, *Brief History of Appleton's "Old Company G."*

43. Edward Lutz to mother, "Their Letters Home," November 24, 1918, *Appleton Crescent*, n.d., Gaerthofner Collection.

44. Granger diary, November 8, 1918. Women and girls on "the home front" knitted socks, sweaters, and scarves for soldiers following published patterns.

45. *Brief History of Old Company "F."*

46. Edward Lutz to mother, "Their Letters Home," November 24, 1918, *Appleton Crescent*, n.d., Gaerthofner Collection.

47. "Sergt. Timian Brings Latest News of Co. B," *Daily Commonwealth*, January 25, 1919, 5.

48. *Brief History of Old Company "F."*

49. Hoke, oral history, Veterans History Project.

50. Granger diary, November 11, 1918.

Chapter 11. Victory and Occupation

1. The Armistice was a truce until a formal peace treaty was signed. There was concern that if peace negotiations broke down, Germany might resume hostilities. The

army's best and most experienced divisions were selected to occupy the areas along the Rhine River—the border of Germany—in case that happened.

2. Reilly, *Americans All*, 853.

3. Ellis, "The Last Days of the War," November 22, 1918, *Brief History of Appleton's "Old Company G."*

4. Ellis, "The Last Days of the War."

5. Leo Uelmen to his father, Peter Uelmen, n.d., "Letters from France," *Campbellsport News*, December 26, 1018, 1.

6. Granger diary, November 28, 1918.

7. Ellis, *Brief History of Appleton's "Old Company G."*

8. Ellis, *Brief History of Appleton's "Old Company G."*

9. Edward Lutz to Mother, "Their Letters Home," November 24, 1918, *Appleton Crescent*, n.d., Gaerthofner Collection. Food was in short supply for civilians. During the occupation, the Germans took most of the food for themselves and gave limited amounts to civilians.

10. Ellis, "Through Belgium and Luxemburg," November 28, 1918, *Brief History of Appleton's "Old Company G."*

11. Ellis, "In Germany at Last," December 3, 1918, *Brief History of Appleton's "Old Company G."*

12. Granger diary, December 6, 1918.

13. Bahr diary, December 15, 1918.

14. Ellis, *Brief History of Appleton's "Old Company G."*

15. A letter to Lorenz's mother, written by Mrs. Agatha Wexler, a Red Cross worker in France, was published in the Dayton, Ohio, newspaper under the headline "Writes Letter to Mother of Soldier Buried in France."

16. Lothar Graef to father, December 10, 1918; "German People Very Friendly to the Yankee Troops Says Captain Lothar Graef," *Appleton Evening Crescent*, n.d., World War I Small Collections, History Museum at the Castle.

17. "Their Letters Home," January 16, 1919, *Appleton Evening Crescent*, n.d., Gaerthofner Collection. No writer was listed, only the statement that the author was "too modest to have his name published." The letter was signed "M. P." It might have been Philip Merkes Jr.

18. Reilly, *Americans All*, 874–75.

19. Bahr diary, December 26 and 29, 1918; February 1, 1919; Rowse Papers.

20. Rex Spencer to Tom Heiss, February 2, 1919, Heiss Collection.

21. Spencer to Heiss, February 2, 1919.

22. Ellis, *Brief History of Appleton's "Old Company G."*

23. Bahr diary, April 2, 1919; "The 150th Wins Field Meet, Has a New Officer," *Daily Commonwealth*, February 4, 1919, 5.

24. *Brief History of Old Company "F."*
25. *Brief History of Old Company "F."*
26. "Steele: Tells of Visit to Local Soldiers in Camp," *Appleton Crescent*, n.d. (May 1919), Gaerthofner Collection.
27. "Steele: Tells of Visit."
28. "Wisconsin in the Rainbow Division," *Daily Commonwealth*, May 17, 1919, 12.

Chapter 12. Aftermath

1. Thompson and Ferrell, *Trench Knives and Mustard Gas*, 188.
2. "175 Are Expected at Rainbow Vets'Convention Sunday," *Appleton Post-Crescent*, June 19, 1920, 5.
3. "French Memorial Awarded at Armory," *Daily Commonwealth*, February 23, 1920, 1.
4. "Big Reception Awaits French Argonne Hero," *Appleton Post-Crescent*, July 6, 1923, 1; "Appleton Greets French War Hero," *Appleton Post-Crescent*, July 17, 1923, 1; "Valley Pays Homage to 'Lion of Argonne' at Rousing Reception," *Appleton Post-Crescent*, July 18, 1923, 1; "Gouraud Says France Right in Ruhr Stand," *Appleton Post-Crescent*, July 18, 1923, 1, 10.
5. The *Spirit of the American Doughboy* statues can be found in thirty-eight states, with six in Wisconsin: Appleton, Fort Atkinson, Janesville, Markesan, Peshtigo, and West Bend. The Appleton sculpture was severely damaged by a vehicle in 1986. The legs were broken from the pedestal, as well as the soldier's backpack and right arm. The landmark symbol of remembrance and respect was repaired and reset within a year. The legs were filled with cement for stability, but that caused more problems. The people of Appleton responded again, and the sculpture was restored and rededicated in 2006. However, Viquesney's gallant soldier continued to deteriorate, and a newly cast bronze *Doughboy* was dedicated on Veterans Day 2017.
6. Myrna Collins, "Memorial Drive's 57 Elms Are a Monument to Appleton War Dead," *Appleton Post-Crescent*, November 10, 1964, B-1.
7. "Decline Government's Offer to Bring Son's Body Home," *Kaukauna Times*, June 16, 1921.
8. "Expect 5,000 in Line to Honor War Heroes," *Appleton Post-Crescent*, June 13, 1921.
9. Constance Potter, "World War I Gold Star Mothers Pilgrimages," *Prologue Magazine*, summer 1999, http://www.archives.giv/publications/prologue/1999/summer/gold-star-mothers-1.html.
10. Harris, *Duffy's War*, 272.

Epilogue

1. *Oshkosh Daily Northwestern*, August 31, 1920, 4.

2. "To Bury with Honors. Funeral of Oshkosh Soldier Who Fell in France Will Be of Military Character," World War I Nevitt Scrapbook, 16.

3. Harvey Stich to parents, December 12, 1918, World War I Nevitt Scrapbook.

Bibliography

Archival Sources

Andrew DeCusati private collection.
    Diary of Arthur Bahr and Arthur Bahr papers.
Fond du Lac County Historical Society. Fond du Lac, Wisconsin.
    Corporal D. V. Holterman Diary.
History Museum at the Castle. Appleton, Wisconsin.
    World War I Small Collections.
Joseph Gaerthofner private collection.
    Collection of scrapbook letters.
Oshkosh Public Museum Archives. Oshkosh, Wisconsin.
    Frank Obersteiner Collection.
    George Holland Collection.
    Herbert Granger Collection.
    Nevitt Scrapbook.
    Walter Thorne Collection.
    World War I Small Collections.
U.S. Army Heritage and Education Center, War College Library. Carlisle, Pennsylvania.
    Herbert Rowse Papers.
Wisconsin Veterans Museum. Madison, Wisconsin.
    William Heiss Collection.

Newspapers

Appleton Crescent (1914–19)
Appleton Evening Crescent (1914–19)
Appleton Post (1917)
Appleton Post-Crescent (1920–23; 1967)
Oshkosh Daily Northwestern (1914–20)
Daily Commonwealth (1914–19)

Selected Bibliography

Bleyer, Willard G., et al. *War Book of the University of Wisconsin: Papers on the Causes and Issues of the War.* Madison: University of Wisconsin, 1918.

Botting, Douglas, et al. *The U-Boats.* Alexandria, VA: Time-Life Books, 1979.

Candid Comment on the American Soldiers of 1917–1918 and Kindred Topics by the Germans, Soldiers, Priests, Women, Village Notables, Politicians and Statesmen. Prepared by the Intelligence Section, the General Staff, General Headquarters, American Expeditionary Forces, Chaumont, France, 1919. https://fas.org/irp/agency/army/wwi-soldiers.pdf.

Cheseldine, R. M. *Ohio in the Rainbow: Official Story of the 166th Infantry, 42nd Division in the World War.* Columbus, OH: F. J. Heer Printing, 1924.

Coffman, Edward J. *The War to End All Wars: The American Military Experience in World War I.* Lexington: University Press of Kentucky, 1998.

Cooke, James J. *The Rainbow Division in the Great War, 1917–1919.* Westport, CT: Praeger Publishers, 1994.

Duffy, Francis P. *Father Duffy's Story: A Tale of Humor and Heroism, of Life and Death with the Fighting Sixty-Ninth.* New York: George H. Doran Co., 1919.

Ellis, Allan B. *A Brief History of Appleton's "Old Company G," with the Rainbow Division in the Great War.* Np, 1919.

Ellis, John. *Eye Deep in Hell: Trench Warfare in World War I.* Baltimore, MD: Johns Hopkins University Press, 1989.

Empey, Arthur Guy. *Over the Top.* New York: G. P. Putnam's Sons, 1917.

Everett, Susanne. *World War I: An Illustrated History.* London: Bison Books Limited, 1980.

Faulkner, Richard S. *Pershing's Crusaders: The American Soldier in World War I.* Lawrence: University Press of Kansas, 2017.

Field Service Pocket Book, United States Army, 1917. War Department Document No. 605. Washington, DC: Government Printing Office, 1917.

Frazer, Nimrod T. *Send the Alabamians: World War I Fighters of the Rainbow Division.* Tuscaloosa: University of Alabama Press, 2014.

Freidel, Frank B. *Over There: The American Experience in World War I.* Short Hills, NJ: Burford Books, 1964.

Gregory, John G. *Wisconsin's Gold Star List: Soldiers, Sailors, Marines and Nurses from the Badger State Who Died in the Federal Service during the World War.* Madison: Wisconsin Historical Publications, 1925.

Hallas, James H., ed. *Doughboy War: The American Expeditionary Force in World War I.* Boulder, CO: Lynne Rienner Publishers, 2000.

Harris, Stephen L. *Duffy's War: Fr. Francis Duffy, Wild Bill Donovan, and the Irish Fighting 69th in World War I.* Washington, DC: Potomac Books, 2006.

Hart, Peter. *The Last Battle: Victory, Defeat, and the End of World War I*. Oxford, UK: Oxford University Press, 2018.

Historical and Pictorial Review of the National Guard and Naval Militia State of Wisconsin. Baton Rouge, LA: Army and Navy Publishing Co., 1939.

Horne, Charles F., ed. *The Great Events of the Great War*. Vol. 4, *1916*. National Alumni, 1923.

Horne, Charles F., ed. *The Great Events of the Great War*. Vol. 6, *The Year of Victory*. National Alumni, 1923.

Jackowe, David J. "Poison Gas Comes to America." *American History* 49, no. 5 (December 2014): 58–63.

Johnson, Lt. Harold Stanley, ed. *Roster of the Rainbow Division (Forty-Second). Major De. Wm. A. Mann Commanding*. New York: Eaton & Gettinger, 1917.

Junger, Ernst. *Storm of Steel*. New York: Penguin Books, 2004.

Keene, Jennifer. *World War I: The American Soldier Experience*. Lincoln: University of Nebraska Press, 2011.

Lengel, Edward G. *To Conquer Hell: The Meuse-Argonne, 1918*. New York: Henry Holt, 2008.

MacArthur, Douglas. *Reminiscences*. New York: McGraw-Hill, 1964.

March, Francis A. *History of the World War: An Authentic Narrative of the World's Greatest War*. Philadelphia: United Publishers of the United States and Canada, 1919.

Mead, Gary. *The Doughboys: America and the First World War*. Woodstock, NY: Overlook Press, 2000.

Neiberg, Mitchell S. *The Second Battle of the Marne*. Bloomington: Indiana University Press, 2008.

Nolan, J. Bennett. *The Reading Militia in the Great War*. Reading, PA: Historical Society of Berks County, 1921.

Parkinson, Joel R., ed. *Commanding Fire: An Officer's Life in the 151st Machine Gun Battalion, 42nd Rainbow Division during World War I*. Atglen, PA: Schiffer Publishing, 2013.

Passingham, Ian. *The German Offensives of 1918: The Last Desperate Gambles*. South Yorkshire: Pen and Sword Books, 2008.

Preston, Diane. *Lusitania: An Epic Disaster*. New York: Walker & Co., 2002.

Raach, George T. *A Withering Fire: American Machine Gun Battalions in World War I*. Bradenton, FL: BookLocker.com, 2015.

Reilly, Brig. Gen. Henry J. *Americans All: The Rainbow at War, Official History of the 42nd Rainbow Division in the World War*. Columbus, OH: F. J. Heer Printing, 1936.

Stallings, Laurence. *The Doughboys: The Story of the AEF, 1917–1918*. New York: Harper & Row, 1963.

Taber, John H. *A Rainbow Division Lieutenant in France: The World War I Diary of John H. Taber*. Jefferson, NC: McFarland, 2015.

Thompson, Hugh S., and Robert H. Ferrell, eds. *Trench Knives and Mustard Gas: With the 42nd Rainbow Division in France.* College Station: Texas A & M University Press, 2004.

Tompkins, Raymond Sidney. *The Story of the Rainbow Division.* New York: Boni and Liveright, 1919.

Willmott, H. P. *World War I.* New York: Dorling Kindersley, 2003.

Wolf, Walter B. *A Brief Story of the Rainbow Division.* New York: Rand, McNally, 1919.

Wroe, Ann. "The Great War." *Economist,* November 18, 2013, 83–85.

Yockelson, Mitchell. *Forty-Seven Days: How Pershing's Warriors Came of Age to Defeat the German Army in World War I.* New York: New American Library, 2016.

Index

Printed in the United States
By Bookmasters